Golfing
in Ireland

Golfing in Ireland

The Most Complete Guide for Adventurous Golfers

ROB ARMSTRONG

PELICAN PUBLISHING COMPANY
Gretna 2000

First edition, September 1997
Second edition, March 2000

*The word "Pelican" and the depiction of a pelican are trademarks
of Pelican Publishing Company, Inc., and are registered
in the U.S. Patent and Trademark Office.*

Library of Congress Cataloging-in-Publication Data

Armstrong, Rob, 1949-
    Golfing in Ireland : the most complete guide for adventurous
golfers / Rob Armstrong.— 2nd ed.
       p. cm.
    Includes index.
    ISBN 1-56554-726-8 (pbk.)
       1. Golf—Ireland—Guidebooks. 2. Golf courses—Ireland
Directories. 3. Ireland—Guidebooks. I. Title.

GV985.I7 A76 2000
796.352'06'8417—dc21

                                           99-054587

Printed in Korea

Published by Pelican Publishing Company, Inc.
1000 Burmaster Street, Gretna, Louisiana 70053

To my mother and father,
Freda and Murray Armstrong,
for all their love and for teaching me the game

Contents

Acknowledgments

No undertaking of this nature can be accomplished in a vacuum, and it turned out that this second edition took almost as much work as the original. So once again I needed a little help from countless friends and colleagues on whom I leaned for their kindness, wisdom, generosity, and assistance in putting this book together.

I am profoundly grateful to my wife, Barbara, who played most of these golf courses with me, replayed several, helped me haul my photo gear around, and gave me the benefit of her keen insight and perspective. She applied her considerable editing skills to the rough manuscript of the original book and prevented me from making too big a fool out of myself in print. And she painstakingly waded through the second edition as well.

I am grateful to publisher Milburn Calhoun, my patient and marvelous editor Nina Kooij, and the fine people at Pelican Publishing Company for having enough faith to take a chance on the first edition and enough skill to turn it into a real book. I remain indebted to them for their efforts in making the second edition a reality as well, and for helping me pursue other book projects.

For their ideas, suggestions, insights, and useful information I offer special thanks to Johnny McGuire in Killarney, William Power in Wicklow, Brian and Lindy O'Hara in Sligo, Morris Switzer in Killarney, Sean Browne in Navan, Gerry and Marion Cunningham in Killarney, Michael Delany in Baltray, Noel Moore in Killarney, Richard Wilson in Bushmills, Seamus O'Doherty along with Con, Christy, and Liz at the Laurels in Killarney, Ruth Moran at Bord Failte—The Irish Tourist Board in New York, Louise McKeown at the Northern Ireland Tourist Board in New York, and travel expert Beth Payne in Ponte Vedra Beach, Florida. Sadly, Michael Shanahan, longtime manager at Dooks Golf Club, lost his battle with heart disease in 1999, just as I was starting the research on this second edition.

This project would have been far less enjoyable without the constructive suggestions, interest, and friendship of Tom and Marjorie Taylor, Sheila Vidamour, Jamie Dupree, and Alex and Mea Gillies, along with my colleagues Caroline Dow and Doug Covert at Flagler College in St. Augustine.

I am especially grateful to my former boss, producer, editor, and friend at CBS News, Larry McCoy, for making it possible for me to get away when I needed to complete the research on the first edition and, now that he is retired, for his intelligent and insightful questions while I was working on the second. And I am grateful to all of my erstwhile colleagues at CBS and in the House and Senate Radio and TV galleries for their encouragement and support.

Introduction

I simply love to play golf. Over the years, I have sampled golf courses from Banff to the Bahamas, from New York to New Mexico, and I have found something to savor in each. But for all the golf that I have played and—apologies to Julio Iglesias—all the courses I have loved before, I have a special passion for golfing in Ireland. That statement is clearly enough to cause my Scottish ancestors to twirl in their graves, but there you have it.

Some of those dour old Scots were the same people who invented golf.

Scotland is a nation whose favorite color is plaid. The national dish is haggis (a sheep's innards cooked with oatmeal in the poor beast's own stomach). Scotch whisky, curling, and tossing the caber (a highland sport in which the object is to hurl a telephone pole through the air as far as possible without getting a hernia or losing your kilt) are all inventions of the Scots. Haggis notwithstanding, the Scots—throughout history—have contributed mightily to world culture. Robert Burns, the poet, was a Scot. So was Sir Walter Scott.

But without doubt, the greatest Scottish contribution to the civilized world is golf. The Scots originally called it "goff," which was later transmuted into "gawf." The *l* was chucked in there somewhere along the etymological line and ultimately it evolved into its present form.

The uninitiated and unenlightened believe that golf is an easy and simpleminded game, in which the object is to propel a small, usually white, dimpled ball across an expanse of grass into a four-and-one-quarter-inch hole with no more than fourteen implements that are totally unsuited for the purpose.

For the serious player—which is not necessarily to be confused with being a good or championship-level player—golf is more than a mere sport. It is an art, a quest, and an obsession. It approaches the level of religion. It is cerebral, spiritual, emotional, challenging, energizing, frustrating, cosmic, and all consuming. It requires physical agility and coordination combined with mental strength. It rewards success with a deep feeling of pride and accomplishment.

It's like a fine wine—it gets better with age. Perhaps one of golf's most endearing attributes is that you can play it from cradle to grave.

There is no precise date for the invention of golf, but history tells us that a golflike game was banned in England around the time Columbus set sail because it was keeping those who played it from attending church on Sundays. The word itself is traced to Middle English of the fifteenth century. It is assumed that golf began with Scottish shepherds amusing themselves by striking stones with sticks. Over time, it became an organized game in which the stones were propelled over a specific stretch of pasture and into holes dug in the ground. Variations of the modern game were widely played in the mid-1700s.

Golf migrated across the Irish Sea in the middle of the nineteenth century. One of the earliest records of an organized golf game in Ireland dates to the early 1850s on the plains of Kildare (now renowned for its horse racing and thoroughbreds) not far from today's Curragh Golf Club.

Scores of Irish golf courses had their roots in the late 1800s. In addition to The Curragh, Dooks, Waterville, Royal County Down, the Old Course at Ballybunion, Lahinch, Royal Portrush, and County Sligo Golf Club are only a few of the golf clubs that predate the dawn of the twentieth century. Most started as nine-hole layouts and were subsequently expanded to eighteen holes.

The first Irish Amateur Open was played in 1892 at the formidable Royal Portrush links on the Antrim coast. The first Irish Ladies

Amateur Championship followed two years later, in 1894 at Carnlea. The first professional championship was not played in Ireland until 1907.

Every few years somebody or other writes an article or even a book about the "best" golf courses in Ireland or the British Isles or the world or the universe. (Alan Shepard, you'll remember, pioneered golf on the moon.) These various writers usually try to come up with some scientific or empirical method for calculating which courses are "the best." They'll survey pros, golf writers, or other golfers, calculate yardage or average scores, or invent some other yardstick.

In this book, I have eschewed any such measurements. This is a book by a passionate golfer for other passionate golfers. I have attempted to present a biased, sometimes irreverent, and iconoclastic review of the Irish golf courses I have enjoyed playing the most. I have taken the same approach to the best hotels, restaurants, and other diversions in close proximity to the golf courses.

I have attempted to offer a variety of price ranges and naturally I can't promise that the prices quoted or the quality will remain exactly the same everywhere. After all, Ireland is a hot golfing venue, and that kind of success invariably means prices go up or quality suffers, especially for those of us who remember the days before Irish golf was "discovered," when hotels and meals were genuine bargains and green fees were dirt cheap.

Naturally, if you get there and don't happen to agree with my analysis, that's the stuff of which lengthy and animated nineteenth-hole discussions are made!

CHAPTER 1

Do's, Don'ts, and Local Knowledge

Since the first edition of *Golfing in Ireland* came out, Ireland has blossomed into one of the world's most popular golf destinations. The boom actually began in the late 1980s, with golfers—particularly American golfers—lured by magnificent, uncrowded golf courses at bargain-basement prices. Word spread among the golfing cognoscenti that Americans could pay next to nothing, walk onto often empty links golf courses, golf that is almost impossible to find in the United States, and experience the kind of game previously associated with such legendary, crowded, and prohibitively expensive Scottish links as St. Andrews and Royal Troon.

Travel agents, tour operators, and golf magazines are cashing in on Ireland's popularity. Bord Failte—The Irish Tourist Board and the Northern Ireland Tourist Board (NITB) spent the last five years of the twentieth century promoting golf with a nearly frantic level of enthusiasm. Entrepreneurs, eager to ride the wave, invested substantial sums. Since 1990, more than a half-dozen major new golf courses opened in Ireland—including the European Club in county Wicklow, Old Head in county Cork, and Ring of Kerry in county Kerry. Other facilities have expanded or upgraded. And more golf-related development is on the drawing board.

The numbers alone are impressive. There are nearly 380 golf courses throughout Ireland. Damian Ryan, golf executive at Bord

Failte, says the number of golfers rose from less than 175,000 in 1994 to more than a half-million in 2000 with players arriving from all over Europe, Japan, South Korea, South Africa, Australia, New Zealand, Canada, and the U.S.

A key to Ireland's change in international status—from little more than a poor and sometimes backward country beset with sectarian strife in the 1960s and 1970s to its emergence as a prosperous modern nation—was the European Union's involvement in shoring up the Irish economy. The E.U. actively promoted Ireland as a venue for business development. It encouraged industrial and high-tech expansion and relocation. Perhaps most importantly, it poured money into the country's infrastructure, which included several golf-course projects. Additional support facilities for the game and its visiting players, such as hotels, restaurants, shops, and golf schools, have followed at breakneck speed.

Tourism has long been the principal industry in the Irish Republic. Tourists in general and golfers in particular have been able to avoid the areas of violence and discord. And for the most part, much of the Republic has been insulated from events in Northern Ireland and along the Dublin-Belfast corridor.

Northern Ireland, on the other hand, has been less successful in attracting tourists, especially from North America, because of "the troubles," the Irish euphemism for the sectarian violence that regularly dominated world headlines right through the 1990s. The prospect of peace, born September 1, 1994, when the outlawed Provisional Wing of the Irish Republican Army announced a unilateral cease-fire, brought high hopes that the six counties of Northern Ireland would be able to reap the economic benefits of peace. Subsequent uncertainty helped persuade tourists that Northern Ireland was still a war zone. The tensions that resumed in 1996, culminating in the apparent collapse of the peace process in the summer of 1999, was a setback for the tourist industry in Northern Ireland. And as this second edition goes to press, a permanent resolution still appears elusive.

As an old Ireland hand, I can simply report that I have never experienced an injection of local politics into golf—either in the Republic or in Northern Ireland. The news and current events were, naturally, discussed, but as I recall, I was usually the person to start the discussion. As a golfer and a tourist, I have never felt anything other than safe and secure while playing such courses of Northern Ireland as Royal Portrush, Royal County Down, or Portstewart, or while traveling to them. It has been my experience that the key figures on both sides of the conflict are not golfers and almost everybody on both sides of the border connected with golf or tourism would be ecstatic if the whole thing would just go away.

Politics notwithstanding, golf is big business all over Ireland. And for those of us who knew it before the boom, there is a down-side to all the golf-related activity. Some of the big-name courses are so crowded—especially in the summer months, the height of the tourist season—that getting a tee time can be difficult. Not surprisingly, the golf boom has spurred a substantial increase in green fees at almost every course in Ireland, a trend that is likely to continue. I hasten to add that golf in Ireland remains a relative bargain, especially for Americans—with the exception of a few newer courses that have deliberately decided to charge the rates you'd expect at major American or European golf resorts.

Both the Irish Republic and Northern Ireland are friendly places that not only want to rake in American tourist dollars but that actually like Americans. That has not changed. The pace is slow, the people are charming, the air is clean, and the golf is wonderful. That hasn't changed much either.

Every golfer knows that "local knowledge" can shave strokes off the score. What follows are some tidbits of local knowledge, culled from experience, that you likely won't learn from your travel agent, Bord Failte, the NITB, or anywhere else.

Passports

I probably don't need to include this, but you'll need a valid passport. They won't let you on the plane without one. You won't need a visa unless you plan to stay for more than three months.

Planning

It is essential to plan your trip well in advance, especially if you want to go sometime during the peak tourist season—July, August, and September. Booking your airline, hotels, rental car, and, of paramount importance, your tee times a month or more ahead of your departure date will save you countless headaches. A spur-of-the-moment golfing trip used to be possible, but not anymore, not with Ireland's tremendous global popularity, especially among Europeans. The month of August can be especially busy as that is when entire businesses in France, Italy, Germany, and elsewhere in Europe close for summer vacation.

My usual approach is to pick dates and make airline reservations. Booking in January or February is not too early. I then reserve my tee times and follow with hotels. Weekends can be especially difficult as more and more golf clubs are reserving large blocks of time or even entire days for their own members on Saturday and Sunday. Courses such as Dooks, Wicklow, Blainroe, County Louth, and Cork Golf Club are virtually closed to visitors on weekends. The majority of Irish golf courses have adopted the American practice of charging more to play on Saturday, Sunday, and holidays than during the week.

As a rule, it's generally easier to cancel a reservation than to try to get one when the booking ledger is jammed. Beware, however, that a growing number of the most popular Irish golf courses—including Tralee, Old Head, Waterville, Portmarnock, and Royal County Down—have taken to requiring a deposit, in advance, to hold your tee time. If, for some reason, you should cancel, many of those courses will not provide a refund.

Old Ireland regulars will tell you wistfully about the days when you could get off the plane, have no trouble finding a place to stay, and walk onto any golf course in the land without advance planning. You can still do that in April, May, October, and the winter months. But in June, July, August, and September, those days are long gone.

Several organizations are available to help in your planning, if your travel agent does not happen to be an expert on Ireland. Ireland Reservations Direct is a one-stop shopping center for places to stay and can book accommodations across a wide spectrum, from first-class hotels to hostels. It's approved by both Bord Failte and the Northern Ireland Tourist Board, so it can help in both areas. The toll-free U.S. telephone number is 1-800-398-4376.

There are two central tee-time reservation services—one for the southwest and the other for the northwest. The Swing office can book times at Ballybunion, Ceann Sibéal, Lahinch, Dooks, Killarney, Tralee, Waterville, Dromoland, and Shannon. The telephone number from the U.S. is 011-353-66-7125733; fax is 011-353-66-7123651; e-mail is swing@iol.ie.

To play Connemara, County Sligo, Enniscrone, Donegal, or Ballyliffin,contact West Coast Golf Links at 011-353-91-794500; fax 011-353-91-794502; e-mail wclgolf@iol.ie.

Airlines

The primary air carrier from the United States to Ireland is the Irish national airline, Aer Lingus, a comfortable, reasonably efficient, minimum-frills airline that rests somewhere in the top-middle of the international airline pack. My preferred route is from the U.S. to Shannon Airport on Ireland's west coast. The overnight flights take about six and a half hours from New York's JFK, Newark, or Boston—just enough time to have a cocktail and a little dinner, take a nap or watch the movie, and freshen up before landing. Aer Lingus also has direct flights to Shannon from Chicago and Los Angeles.

Aer Lingus has daily flights from JFK, Newark, and Boston to Dublin, which is an effective route if you plan to concentrate on Ireland's east-coast golf courses from county Down to county Wicklow.

Shannon Airport is one of my favorite airports in Europe. Passport control and customs—which pose varying degrees of discomfort and inconvenience virtually everywhere—are about as easy and pleasant as they can be. As airports go, it is small, clean, easy to get around, and efficient. It also boasts one of the world's finest and largest tax-free shops. In fact, travelers are well advised to budget a little extra time before the flight home to do some last-minute shopping at the airport.

Shannon used to be one of the world's busiest airports, the primary refueling stop on trans-Atlantic flights from North America to Europe. But with the advent of long-distance jets, it now serves mostly as a gateway to western Ireland.

Delta flies to Shannon and Dublin out of Atlanta but the flights are not scheduled every day and the schedule varies seasonally. Continental has connections through Newark.

If it's an emergency or you have an enhanced sense of adventure, Russia's Aeroflot, a vestige of the old Soviet models of comfort, efficiency, and charm, flies several times a week out of Washington's Dulles. Despite the political changes, Aeroflot retains the old Kremlin (low) regard for on-time performance. When it does function as scheduled it gets you into Shannon around 2:00 A.M. Aeroflot also flies irregularly from New York's JFK and Chicago's O'Hare.

There are scores of flights from various North American cities on a variety of different airlines that connect through London to Belfast, Dublin, Shannon, or Cork, but there are serious drawbacks to going that way, the most serious of which is that you must travel through London's Heathrow Airport. That, alone, is enough to make me think twice.

Going through London is a colossal waste of time. Not only do you fly all night to get there, but once you get to London it takes hours to get through passport control and customs, take a shuttle bus to the departure terminal, and catch the short-hop flight across the Irish Sea. And, of course, there's always the unspeakable joy of being processed through one of the Heathrow International Arrivals Terminals along with at least a quarter of the population of the known world. Heathrow's expansion in the late 1990s helped ease some of the arrival miseries, but it remains an ordeal. It may just be coincidence, but it seems that passengers arriving on British Airways flights are processed more quickly and efficiently than passengers arriving on airlines of other countries.

Air fares can vary widely and the number of flights changes seasonally. A good, reliable travel agent is as valuable an ally in booking your trip as a good caddy is when playing the Old Course at Ballybunion. If you are heavily into doing it yourself, you can give Aer Lingus a call, toll free in the U.S. at 1-800-223-6537.

Tourist Information

Bord Failte—The Irish Tourist Board and the Northern Ireland Tourist Board are friendly, courteous, and helpful. Both are knowledgeable and willing to go out of their way to obtain information for you. A phone call can provide all manner of useful information—from what kind of converter you will need for your hair dryer to what's the most scenic driving route from Sligo to Derry. As I have prepared both editions of this book, they've both fielded dozens of off-the-wall questions for me with skill, speed, and a hefty dose of Irish charm.

Both have toll-free numbers in the United States. Bord Failte is 1-800-223-6470. The NITB is 1-800-326-0036. Bord Failte also has an e-mail address: user@irishtouristboard.ie.

Guided Tours

An offshoot of the Irish golf boom has been a proliferation of companies that purport to provide tours for visiting golfers. Like dandelions sprouting in spring, entrepreneurs smelling money to be made have popped up to cash in. You can hardly open a golf magazine in North America or Europe without finding a panoply of tour operators. Some specialize regionally. Others pledge to prepare a customized itinerary. Some work only with groups. Others say they will plan trips for individuals. I have talked with a few players who say they have had very satisfactory experiences. Others report less enjoyable results, ranging from fury to rage. For the most part, my advice is *don't!*

If you decide you want to entrust your care and feeding to a stranger, don't take what they tell you on the phone at face value. Take the time to check out the tour operators with extreme caution and skepticism. Ask for references and follow up on them. And make sure you get details in writing about what golf courses you will play, what level of accommodations and food you can expect, and what is and is not included in the price of the package.

One of the biggest general complaints I've heard about golfing tours to Ireland is that the tour operators make verbal promises they do not keep. You have very little recourse unless you have something written with which to seek recompense. In response to complaints from travelers, the Ireland Golf Tour Operators Association was founded in the late 1990s. The association has attempted to offer consumers a measure of quality control and a central location through which to funnel complaints. Unfortunately, any self-policing organization with voluntary rules is effective only when members adhere to the rules. Americans are cautioned that consumers often do not enjoy the same rights—to obtain refunds, to cancel, and the like in Ireland as they do in the United States.

Getting Around

Unquestionably, the best way for golfers to get around Ireland is by car. Plan to rent one. Then hold on to your wallet and get ready for sticker shock!

It's expensive. It may, in fact, be the most expensive single item on your itinerary. It may not rival a complete set of Waterford crystal stemware, but it's in that neighborhood. Rates are substantially reduced in the "off season."

I have used most of the major rental-car companies, all of which are represented at Shannon and Dublin airports, and can report very little difference in prices. Year to year and season to season, they all offer various discounts and packages. Several companies offer solid discounts if you pay for your car a month or more before you leave home. Occasionally, Irish and European companies offer slightly better rates than their U.S.-based counterparts. Have your travel agent check the rates at Payless, Murrays Europcar, Sixt, and Dan Dooley (which is the only one with a toll-free North American number—1-800-331-9301).

The best advice is that a little rate shopping can save you some money. (It is not out of line to be dunned $50 to $60 per day for a standard-shift subcompact. If you want a bigger car or an automatic transmission, brace yourself!)

The least expensive cars come with standard transmissions. That means you shift with your left hand. It's a very awkward feeling at first. The clutch, brakes, and accelerator have the same configuration as in the U.S.

Once you get over the initial jolt of the cost of renting your automobile, steel yourself for the price of petrol (that's gasoline). You can probably fill up your car at home three or four times for what one fill-up will cost you in Ireland. In addition, they sell it in liters (which is like a quart) and watching the numbers change on the gas pump is like watching an electronic game tote up the score.

Insurance

Before you rent your car, check with your own American insurance company about whether you should also purchase the rental company's collision and damage policies. Coverage varies, and while some U.S. policies will cover you in Europe, many won't. It adds to the cost, but the peace-of-mind factor makes it worth it. Some credit-card companies also provide car-rental insurance and it's a good idea to check before you leave the U.S. about whether the coverage extends to cars rented in Europe and if so, how much coverage there is and what is and is not covered.

Rules of the Road

Be advised that the Irish drive on the left and pass on the right. The traffic approaches you from a different side than you're used to, so you look to the right first, then to the left.

The best rule is to drive carefully, especially until you get the hang of it. The police—the Garda in the Republic—have little sense of humor about driving mishaps. Under Irish law, in almost every accident the rule is "hitter pays."

I am obliged to tell you that the laws against drinking and driving are very strict in both the Irish Republic and Northern Ireland. Ireland's roads are crowded, and the Garda frequently set up checkpoints to inspect for everything from drinking to seatbelt use. (Seatbelts are mandatory.) Be advised that if you're involved in any kind of an accident after drinking they can fine you heavily, revoke your license, impound your car, put you in the slammer, or carry out any combination of the four.

Livestock

The narrow, winding backroads of Ireland, and even some fairly major roadways, are more rural than almost anything you'll ever encounter in the United States. Even the main highways are mostly two lane and feel constricted to Americans used to interstates and freeways. Divided highways ("dual carriageways," they call them) exist only around major population centers, such as Dublin, Cork, Limerick, and Galway.

Be cautious when driving the serpentine backroads! Cattle and sheep are still herded regularly across them, from farmyards or barns to pastures, or from one field to another. They have the right of way. Don't honk! Don't be impatient! They'll let you pass just as soon as they've gotten where they're going, and not before. An old-timer in county Sligo warned me many years ago to budget an extra fifteen minutes "for sheep" on almost any journey. It remains valid.

The Irish also have a passion for horses. In some places you are likely to encounter horses and their riders, even on major roadways. Drivers are expected to give them a wide swath. The same is true for walkers and bicycles.

Distances

Most of the maps you receive when you rent your car will have some rough estimate of mileage on them. Ignore it. Every skill you have developed over the years for figuring out how long it's going to take you to get from one point to another is out the window in Ireland.

If, for example, you determine that it's about 70 miles from Limerick to Killarney, forget how long it would take you to drive 70 miles at home. In the U.S. you'd probably estimate it will take you a little over an hour. In Ireland it will take you two hours and longer if you happen to hit the regular sheep sale or market day in Castleisland or get stopped for road work anywhere along the route. On the narrow two-lane roads, you slow down to a crawl at every little town on the way. (You'll find the roads are better and wider in Northern Ireland, but you won't make an appreciably better pace.)

Road Signs

Distance signs in the Republic are usually in kilometers; in Northern Ireland they are in miles. The signs are uniformly smaller than those we are used to in North America. You know you are in Northern Ireland when the Gaelic names for towns disappear from the signposts.

Parking

Parking takes a little getting used to. Many towns have restrictions about where you can park. Parking meters are less common than "parking discs." In most major cities and towns you'll find parking-disc vending machines in most public parking lots and on streets that require them. The location of the machines is usually well marked. Follow the instructions regarding how much money to deposit to buy a disc with the proper amount of parking time on it.

A few places still use the older system in which you purchase little paper coupons on which you poke the appropriate boxes (date, time, and the like) with the point of a pencil, allowing you to park for a particular period of time. If you see them on dashboards of other cars but can't figure out where to buy one, ask. People are usually very helpful. In the places that still use this system, the signs that say Parking Discs Sold Here are often small, easily missed, and obscured among the other window signs for cigarettes, candy, soft drinks, and the like.

Money

For as long as I've been going to the Republic of Ireland, the unit of currency has been the Irish punt, which they call a "pound." In Northern Ireland, it's the British pound, which they also call a "pound." It was a pretty easy system to catch on to. There was about a 10 percent difference in value between the two currencies and in towns along the border, exchange was easy. Many establishments took either and were happy to do the conversion for you, albeit at a rate beneficial to them.

On January 1, 1999, however, an economic upheaval was begun. A brand-new currency—the euro—was born with the goal of becoming a single unit of currency for all of Europe capable of competing in the international arena with the U.S. dollar. The euro started trading on the international currency exchange, as scheduled. The coins and paper money are scheduled to be put into circulation in 2002. The political gyrations, angry debate, and financial firestorm surrounding the switchover in some countries have been profound. Britain was engaged in a sometimes furious internal debate over whether to abandon the pound sterling in favor of the new euro. And as we go to press, Britain does not plan to adopt the euro before 2008, if at all.

On the other hand, the Republic of Ireland was quick to sign on and announce its intention to scrap the punt in favor of the euro when the general switchover takes place in January 2002.

It's a good idea to take some Irish money with you when you leave home. It's especially smart if you're arriving on Saturday or Sunday, when the banks are closed. If you forget, the foreign currency exchanges at Shannon and Dublin airports are open most of the time and can tide you over.

Changing money is not difficult. There are foreign currency exchanges all over the place. The commercial establishments bear the sign Bureau de Change. Hotels, stores, and restaurants will often change money for you as well, but they'll charge you such outrageous rates that they would have been expelled from the Temple in biblical times. Banks invariably have the most favorable rates and they are usually posted in the window, so even among banks you can save a buck or two with a little window shopping.

Most hotels, restaurants, and shops take major credit cards. Pubs and some golf courses do not.

Bills and Tips

Most of the bigger hotels and some restaurants add on a service charge. Most restaurants will tell you how much the service charge is right on the menu; 12 to 15 percent is pretty standard. The price of virtually everything includes a Value Added Tax or VAT. It's 12.5 percent in the Republic and 17.5 percent in Northern Ireland.

In restaurants, if there is no service charge, tip as you would in the U.S. If there is a service charge, I usually leave a little extra if the service has been outstanding—something on the order of 5 percent. In hotels I virtually always leave a little tip for the housekeeping staff, about one Irish punt or one British pound per night. Hotel bellmen get one punt or pound per bag, about the same as in American hotels.

In most pubs, you serve yourself unless you're seated at the bar. The bartenders do not usually expect a tip.

Caddies, on the other hand, make their living from tips. Most pro shops or caddymasters will offer you a list of the going rates, which you should confirm with your caddie before you tee off. After the round, the rate plus 15 to 20 percent is pretty standard. (I'm always a little more generous if I've had a particularly good round.) If for some reason you take a taxi ride, get a haircut, or go to a beauty shop, tip about the same as you would at home.

Telephones

To call the Republic of Ireland from the United States, use the international code followed by the country code (011-353). Then you need the city code. If the city code is preceded by a zero, you ignore the zero. The local phone number can be four, five, six, or seven digits long. Let's say you want to call the Wicklow Golf Club and you see the number listed as (0404) 67379. To dial from the U.S., dial 011-353-404-67379.

In 1999, the British phone system undertook a major overhaul in Northern Ireland. Calling Northern Ireland from the U.S. is the same as calling Britain. The country code is 44. To call any number in Northern Ireland from the United States, you dial 011-44-0801- and the local number.

For some reason, the telephone system has always been unnecessarily and often maddeningly complicated in Ireland. General phone service was much later arriving than in the rest of Europe. Well into the 1960s, it was common for an entire village to have only one or two telephones. The direct-dial concept is truly high tech. Until the mid-1970s most phone service outside of Dublin was operator assisted, and in remote places, such as the Dingle peninsula, there was no phone service after noon on Sunday at all, until the operators came back on duty Monday morning.

It is virtually always less expensive to call back home to the United States or Canada from Ireland with a calling card, rather than using your hotel operator or the Irish phone system to place the call.

Emergencies

Nobody goes on a golfing vacation with the anticipation of something awful happening. But it can happen. In the event you need emergency help, the telephone number in most of the Republic and Northern Ireland is 999.

Climate

The Irish climate is cooler than most of the U.S. in summer and be advised that it can rain—and often does—every day. In fact, Ireland has about 240 days of rain a year. That doesn't mean that it's like Burma in monsoon season. The rain often comes and goes in a matter of hours, if not minutes. "It's a fine, soft day" is a common phrase. That means it's raining, but not very hard, usually a little harder than mist and certainly not enough to cause you to cancel your golf game. In fact, rain is rarely, if ever, an excuse for canceling a golf game.

Daytime highs in the summer are usually in the 60s, occasionally into the 70s, and the temperature drops into the mid- to low 50s at night. But there are rare exceptions. In 1995, Ireland experienced its hottest, driest summer in decades. "It's the worst heat wave I can remember," said Lindy O'Hara when I called to book a room at Coopershill House in county Sligo after a week of record-setting 80-plus degree days. Nobody knew what to pack that summer, but the assumption is that it won't happen again for several more decades.

The locals will tell you that you can golf all year in most of Ireland, but take that with a grain of salt. It can—and does—snow regularly during the winter months in the northern and eastern parts of the country and more often than not it is rainy, blustery, and downright nasty in December, January, and February all over the place. In addition, many Irish hotels, especially outside the major cities, simply close from about mid-November until mid-March because the trickle of tourists is so slight that it's more cost-effective to shut the doors than to pay the staff for that period.

What to Pack

For the most part it is an informal land, although, until recently, it was more European in its attitude toward clothing than American. That has changed to a degree, but not to the point that blue jeans or halter tops are acceptable as widely as in the U.S. Casual dress in Ireland remains a little more formal than Americans are used to. While a tie is required only in the most upscale of restaurants, men should wear decent slacks, a shirt with a collar, and a sweater or sports coat. A sweater and nice slacks or a skirt are advised for women. In most major hotels and resorts, a coat and tie for men and a dress or skirt and blouse for women are in order.

For golf, packing can be a bit tricky. The weather conditions can vary from short-sleeve weather to heavy-sweater weather in a matter of hours. While laboring through a bit of icy rain, verging on sleet, one August day at the Wicklow Golf Club, the local chap I was playing with quipped, "You can have all four seasons in a single round."

Logic will tell you that it's cooler in the north than in the south and the golf courses on the Atlantic side of Ireland are subject to more severe winds and weather than the courses on the Irish Sea.

You'll wear a sweater most days, so take several in case they get wet. Also pack plenty of socks. I also usually take one or two extra golf towels, as things tend to dry very slowly in the Irish climate.

Golf Equipment

A few essentials for the golfer include waterproof shoes, several all-weather golf gloves, a tight-fitting rain hat (when it rains it is often windy too), and a full rain suit (jacket and pants). A golf umbrella is less valuable than good rain clothes. In some of the winds you'll encounter, you can imagine putting up your umbrella and taking off like Mary Poppins.

You can jettison a lot of the junk you may keep in your bag at home. For example, you probably won't need bug spray. And sun block is optional. (Nobody goes to Ireland for a suntan, but it can be windy and the sun does shine from time to time. So if you're fair skinned and sensitive, use your own good judgment about sun block.)

Take lots of golf balls! On the treacherous links courses along the Irish coast, you will be hitting to tight and hidden landing areas and—unless you're Greg Norman or Tom Kite, in which case you wouldn't be reading this anyway—you will lose balls. Even after hitting a good shot you can lose a ball. You'll probably lose more balls than you ever imagined. Of course, you can buy them in Ireland, but they are extraordinarily expensive and the selection is sometimes quite limited.

Pack lots of tees. There are only a couple of golf courses I know of in all of Ireland that give them away. Some will sell you a small packet of tees, but you'll discover that most of the time they are made of plastic. I simply hate plastic tees. While they don't break, they make a disconcerting "thwock!" when you hit the ball from them.

Take your own pencil, pen, crayon, or charred stick. While it's changing gradually, most courses will not provide pencils with the scorecard. (Some Irish courses still have two scorecards, one for men and the other for women, so be sure to get the right one.)

Ball markers or a few dimes are useful. Irish coins are the size of hockey pucks.

Golf Carts

The golf buggy (what we call a cart) is making inroads at many of the bigger, newer golf courses, but buggies remain the exception rather than the rule. If you feel that you can't play without riding, inquire when you book your tee time, and reserve one at that time. The hottest new golf product in Ireland seems to be battery-powered trolleys (pull-carts). They can be rented at many of the bigger courses. Most players opt to carry their clubs, rent a trolley, or hire a caddy. Before you get there and suddenly discover you're a pack-mule, consider the weight of your golf bag. A light bag makes it easier, especially given the hilly topography of most Irish golf courses. If your bag is not equipped with a cover, buy one before you leave home, as it will help keep your clubs and grips dry in the rain.

Caddies

Caddies can be arranged at many, but certainly not at all, courses. Only a very few actually have caddies standing around waiting for bags to carry. As the demand for caddies has increased, you'll find they are often teenagers trying to make a little extra money during the summer. They have little knowledge of the game and will not help you much, except with such basics as where the next tee is. Check when you book your tee time about availability.

Tee Times

It is absolutely critical to book your tee times as soon as you can, especially during the summer months and especially on weekends.

Some courses, such as Old Head, Ballybunion, Lahinch, and Royal County Down, fill up two to three months in advance. In 1996, for example, two months before my departure I tried to get a Saturday tee time in August at Lahinch and was told the only time open was 4:58 P.M. I opted to change my itinerary to play another course on Saturday and do Lahinch on Friday.

I plan my entire itinerary around my tee times. Once I've decided on my travel dates and gotten my plane ticket, I list the golf courses I want to play and group them geographically. Then I phone for tee times, up to two months in advance for such popular courses as Old Head, Ballybunion, Tralee, Lahinch, and Royal Portrush. Even some of the less famous courses book up early. Many reserve much or all of the weekends for members or competitions. Almost all have a specific weekday—Tuesday, Wednesday, or Thursday—restricted, at least in part, to women members.

Some top courses demand a deposit to confirm your tee times. For example, the last time I played Portmarnock, they had billed my credit card for full green fees and pocketed the money before I left home for the airport. When I inquired about their refund policy, the young woman in the office informed me that when advance payment is made and the tee time is subsequently canceled they generally do not give a refund. The story was similar at Old Head. The young man who took my reservation said a 50 percent deposit was required and the cancelation policy was that they would give me another tee time on another day—no refund. Consider this a grim warning about Ireland's consumer protection laws!

Once tee times have been reserved, it's relatively easy to pick accommodations in reasonable proximity.

Courses, Shots, Etiquette, Etc.

LINKS VS. PARKLAND

Irish golf courses are divided into two general categories: inland or parkland courses and seaside or links courses. Not every seaside course is a links course, but virtually every inland course is a parkland course. A few new courses are amalgamating the qualities of both, but this hybrid has not been given a moniker yet.

Parkland courses cover a broad spectrum, but most are very

much like golf courses all over the United States. Few, however, are as well manicured and maintained as the average American country club, golf resort, or even the lion's share of public and daily-fee golf courses. The biggest visible difference between parkland and links courses is that parkland courses have trees and shrubs with more clearly defined fairways and roughs than the links layouts. Links have a wilder look.

For visiting Americans, links golf is the heart and soul of the game and it is showcased at its finest in Ireland.

There are many definitions of what a "links" golf course is. It is clearly coastal, built on wind-hardened sand, which generally allows extraordinary drainage. Traditionalists will tell you that a links has never been used for any agricultural purpose. (By that definition, several famous Irish links would not qualify, so for practical purposes the definition has been modified.) Linksland, as the golf-course architects call it, is the buffer between the sea and habitable, arable land. Links golf puts the emphasis on natural hazards, such as dunes and rocks, gullies and palisades. The topography is usually rolling and hilly, sometimes craggy, with huge variances between fairway and rough. Some links play right along a sandy beach; others are constructed high atop coastal cliffs.

The hardy coastal grasses often provide extremely tight lies in the fairway and can produce monstrous difficulties in the knee-high rough. In between, there is usually a short cut of rough—a few yards of grass that's longer than in the fairway. But the deep rough simply cannot be ignored. On links courses, deep rough means uncut, unkempt, and often unplayable. When it is not a sea of grass and weeds up to the tummy of a tall sheep, it is given over to such nasty and unfriendly plants as gorse, buckthorn, and heather, not to mention rocks, scrub-brush, moss, and sand.

On links, the wind is almost always a factor, from gentle breezes to gales. There tend to be very few, if any, trees. At first glance, the landscape can appear stark, but there is enormous beauty on virtually every links golf course in Ireland. The visiting American golfer must exercise caution not to let the glorious landscapes interfere with what is surely one of the greatest golfing experiences in the world.

I have dealt with a few parkland golf courses—mostly those that are uniquely Irish in character or those that have garnered a substantial measure of fame or acclaim for one reason or another. Generally

American golfers don't go to Ireland to play what they play every weekend back home. They go to Ireland to sample the wind-blown, sometimes wild links golf courses that dot the Irish coast and that are the quintessence of what the game was in its earliest and purest form. American golfers want to play the fabled links of Ireland, such legendary courses as Ballybunion's Old Course, Lahinch, Royal County Down, and Royal Portrush. They are also eager to sample the newer links designs including the Old Head, The European Club, Arnold Palmer's Tralee, and Connemara.

SPECIAL SHOTS

The almost constant wind and the extremely tight lies you will encounter in most links fairways require some techniques far different from those commonly used in the U.S. Players who regularly compete on links courses have an arsenal of low, running shots. American golfers traveling to Ireland would be well advised to learn a pitch-and-run or bump-and-run shot before leaving home. If you don't learn one before you arrive, you will probably invent one before you leave. A knockdown shot is also incredibly useful.

Given the nature of links courses and the fact that the wind is in play on most holes most of the time, you'll save yourself countless strokes if you learn to approach the pin low and rolling. A high lob-wedge or sand-wedge lofted toward the pin on a calm day, on American greens that hold, is a thing of beauty. On wind-blasted, weather-hardened links courses in Ireland, such a shot can be blown to the Aran Islands or worse. Likewise, a high and floating tee shot is seldom rewarded and your slice or hook will be exaggerated beyond recognition by the wind.

The deep rough will probably cost you a stroke. If you don't exercise proper care, it can cost you more than that. If you can find your ball in the deep rough on links courses—which is always problematic—your best option, usually, is to take a medium to short iron and get it back into the fairway as expeditiously as possible. This is especially true for women. But even the strongest men will find it difficult to get any distance out of the long rough.

Gorse, buckthorn, and heather are nasty, ball-eating flora. For the most part if you hit into some, don't try to hit out. Take an unplayable lie, accept the penalty stroke, and move on.

In addition, with very few exceptions, the greens are hard and do not hold. A shot played to the pin can easily squirt out of bounds, into pot bunkers or deep rough or even the ocean. Many links veterans putt from as much as twenty-five feet off the green.

WINTER RULES

If you are playing with the locals, it's summer rules all the time, even in winter. Don't even think about moving your ball, regardless of your lie. If you're playing with other Americans or by yourself you can do anything you want.

PACE OF PLAY

One of the biggest complaints about Americans is that they stand around too long on the putting greens. Unless you're qualifying for the Irish Open, putt the damned ball and move along! The same thing goes on the fairway. Hit the shot and walk on.

LOST BALLS

Keep your eye on the ball. If your ball is lost, Rule 27 applies. If you haven't memorized Rule 27, here it is: "A ball is 'lost' if it is not found or identified as his by the player within *five* minutes after the player's side or his or their caddies have begun to search for it."

If there's a group right behind you, it's usually the thing to do to ask them to play through while you look for your ball. The British and the Irish are much better than the Americans about letting people through. We could learn something. So could a large number of Europeans and Asians who seem not to understand the concept.

METRIC MEASURES

Be prepared to convert meters to yards. The logic escapes me, but some Irish golf courses are measured in yards and others are measured in meters. There seems to be no particular pattern or reason that determines how a course is measured. For example, Tralee and County Sligo have meters on their scorecards; Waterville and

Old Head have yards. Most courses in Northern Ireland are measured in yards.

For American golfers, the metric system can be perplexing. I
came upon it unexpectedly the first time I played in Ireland. While
it's common in much of Europe, I'd never thought of golf in
meters. What does it mean when there's a 150-meter marker? What
does that do to my club selection? What does a 163-meter par 3 really
mean? I think it's overkill, but some golfers even carry small pocket
calculators for precise conversion. (One meter equals 1.094 yards or
39.37 inches.) If you're computing in your head, add 10 percent to
the number of meters to come up with yards.

I find this conversion table satisfactory:

10 meters = 11 yards
50 meters = 55 yards
100 meters = 110 yards
150 meters = 165 yards
200 meters = 220 yards
250 meters = 275 yards

FAIRWAY MARKERS

There is no standardized approach to distances indicated by stakes
or other fairway markers. On some courses it is from the marker to
the *front* of the green; on others it's to the center. Most will have a sign
or a notation on the scorecard. Only a handful of courses, mostly the
newer and more American-style ones, have anything other than 150-
yard or -meter stakes. Many courses, however, now have "stroke
savers"—little booklets that will delineate distances from various hazards or landmarks. They will generally cost you a couple pounds.

SOFT SPIKES

Ireland is wasting no time catching up with the American golf
trend requiring players to wear "soft spikes." It is far from universal
across Ireland, but many top courses have made the switch, others
are encouraging a voluntary change, and in the summer of 1999
there was an abundance of signs on locker-room bulletin boards
stating that soft spikes will soon be the rule.

RESTROOM

Go to the bathroom before you tee off. Many Irish golf courses are laid out in the traditional Scottish manner: the front nine plays *out* and the back nine plays *in*. In other words, unlike most American courses, there is no point at which the golfer returns to the clubhouse between the first and eighteenth holes. Only a few of the newest courses have built restrooms on the field of play. It's not something most people think about until it's too late.

BETTING

Most golf clubs in Ireland have local competitions almost every weekend. The rules vary widely regarding whether visitors may compete. Some restrict competition play to club members and invited guests only. Almost all clubs have an "open" week, or weeks, at some point during the summer, which means that anybody with an established handicap can pay the entry fee and play. Most of these open competitions are scored using the Stableford system. American visitors should make sure they understand the scoring rules, as the pure Stableford system used in Europe is quite different from some of the variations that crop up at American clubs usually in the guise of a modified Stableford known widely as "quota points."

When they are not playing in an organized event, many Irish golfers, like many Americans, like to make a little wager on the game from time to time. The games are similar to those played on almost every golf course in the United States, although sometimes the local names for the bets are highly colloquial. It is not considered rude to inquire about the rules and terms before you enter into any wager and frankly, it's foolish not to.

It is also a good rule of thumb never to bet with or underestimate a youngster wearing blue jeans, a tattered sweater, and sneakers and using a set of totally unmatched, out-of-date clubs. This young person will clobber you until you bleed.

I once met up with such a young man on the eighth green at the Mallow Golf Club in county Cork. I'd followed him for several holes before we joined up and was smirking to my arrogant, self-satisfied American self about his odd and awkward swing. He'd been a champion hurler, he told me. That didn't mean a thing to me, except that he'd once played an incomprehensible, field-hockey-like, Celtic sport. When we got to the par-4 ninth hole, which in those days measured only 323 yards, he made me a true believer.

We stood on the tee and waited and waited until the threesome (they call it a "three-ball") ahead of us cleared the green. I thought it was absurd to wait, until this young man teed up his ball and with his odd and awkward swing launched it into the bunker to the right of the green. "Damn! I pushed it," he said.

CHAPTER 2

The Best

Every golfer is a self-proclaimed expert. Regardless of playing ability, every golfer who's been playing longer than a month assumes that his or her capacity to judge a golf course, assess the playing conditions, and grade the subtleties is the final word. Seldom do two of these experts employ the same criteria, come up with identical judgments, or agree on any listing that purports to represent the best golf courses anywhere—whether in Ireland, Virginia, California, or Saskatchewan. A discussion of the toughest holes, most challenging layouts, or most appealing designs is likely to spark a lively disagreement. It seems to be as much a part of the game as speculating on who will win the Masters or the U.S. Open. A little eavesdropping in almost any golf-course bar in the country will provide ample evidence of this.

There is good reason that every golf magazine on the planet regularly offers some kind of listing of "the best" courses, "the best" holes, "the best" greens, "the best" resorts, and on and on. There is often some duplication, but they are never identical.

I deliver no claim that the following list is anything other than subjective, arbitrary, and highly opinionated, based on a substantial level of experience. My general conclusions are the result of golfing trips to Ireland that began in 1985 and are leavened by my profound love for the game. In preparing the second edition of this book, I expanded and changed the list because of new golf-course construction, redesign, and return visits to many of the courses listed in the original book. Comments from readers, especially those who disagreed with my conclusions, and fellow golfers also brought about some changes for this edition.

I'll start with some general observations. For the visiting American, the interior of the country offers far fewer great golfing opportunities than the coast. That is not to say there are not some respectable golf courses there, but most are parkland style and very much akin to what Americans play all the time at home. The reality is that Americans build better parkland golf courses than anybody and that's why European, Asian, and other golfers from around the world flock to places like Orlando, Phoenix, and Williamsburg to play some of the great ones.

In Ireland, it is the links golf courses that offer the unique challenges and delights the American golfer can't get at home, unless, of course, he or she belongs to one of the few true links courses in the United States such as Shinnecock Hills, on New York's Long Island, where they played the 1995 U.S. Open. For the American player, links golf is the primary reason to visit Ireland. The Irish coast is dotted with some of the greatest links in the world.

In the west and south, the U.S. visitor can pick from a gourmet menu of remarkable links from county Cork to county Derry, and sample such delights as Old Head, Tralee, Lahinch, Ballybunion, County Sligo, Donegal, and Ballyliffin to name just a few. Along the north coast in Northern Ireland, there's Castlerock, Portstewart, and Royal Portrush, the last being a regular venue for such tournaments as the Senior European PGA Championship. Ireland's east coast, along the Irish Sea, is home to such fabulous courses as Royal County Down, County Louth, and The European Club. While all links golf courses have certain similarities in appearance, design, and topography, each, too, is delectable and wonderful unto itself. Each has its own distinct personality, its own character.

If you have only a short time in which to experience Irish golf, you can have yourself a wonderful time by simply booking into Killarney (a splendid little town with plenty of good hotels, restaurants, shopping, and evening entertainment) and playing the courses within an easy drive, starting with Dooks a few miles away overlooking Dingle Bay, and adding Waterville, Tralee, Ceann Sibéal, and the legendary duo at Ballybunion. By all means plan a day trip to Kinsale in county Cork to play the brilliant links at Old Head, opened in 1997. On your last day, drive to Lahinch, play Old Tom Morris's masterpiece, stay the night in the town, and still make it to Shannon Airport the next day for your flight.

My personal penchant for links golf and my belief that links golf is what lures Americans to Ireland is not meant to diminish Ireland's other courses. There are some charming parkland courses that will test the ability of the most skilled players.

In some cases, Irish golf course architects have employed the best of both styles to create distinctly Irish hybrids. The scenic and challenging Ring of Kerry Golf Club in county Kerry and Alister MacKenzie's brilliant Cork Golf Club are both world class. Blainroe Golf Club in county Wicklow and the long, tough Shannon Golf Club in county Clare (about a three wood from the Shannon Airport runway) are fine examples of hybridization in Irish golf-course design.

I have tried not to let my own shortcomings as a player have too great an impact on the courses profiled here. As you might expect, I play some courses better than others and score better on some than on others. For example, I've never broken 85 on Arnold Palmer's beautiful but diabolically difficult layout at Tralee, though I intend to keep trying. And the expanded course at Wicklow has me completely baffled. I can't seem to find the greens and when I can I can't putt them. On the other hand I managed to score very well the last few times I've played the Old Course at Ballybunion and I seem to play consistently well at Rosses Point (County Sligo Golf Club). Even a blind squirrel finds a nut now and then.

I have also endeavored throughout to note any unique configurations, challenges, obstacles, or features of the various courses for women. On Old Head, for example, the women's tee placement is brilliantly thought out. It is one of the best tests of the game in all of Ireland for women, bringing hazards into play and requiring an assortment of shots and course management specifically suited to the abilities of women players.

I will also draw your attention to those places where the needs and skills of men are paramount and women are a poor afterthought, even though women are charged the same green fees.

Where scorecards are simulated, I have selected the markers from which the good, average golfer is most likely to play and, where necessary, converted from the metric measures. Some courses—such as Waterville, Lahinch, and Royal Portrush—prohibit players from using the championship markers unless they are playing in a championship event.

Green fees at Irish golf courses, as with virtually every golf course in the United States, change yearly, and sometimes seasonally. For this edition I have adopted the following chart from which you can get an idea what you will pay to play the courses I discuss. As with American courses, the bigger-named places and the more popular venues generally charge a higher fee than the more remote or less famous tracks. Because of the different currencies involved, the prices are in U.S. dollars, but that will provide a good idea of what you can expect to be charged. Given the fluctuations of the international currency exchange market, the stronger the dollar the lower the actual price will be and conversely the weaker the dollar the higher the real price.

Green Fees (Per Person)

Very Expensive	$75 and up
Expensive	$50-75
Moderate	$30-50
Inexpensive	$30 and below

So, all that being said, the following are, in my opinion, the best, most challenging, and most enjoyable golf courses in Ireland for the average to good club player. I have listed the courses under this heading alphabetically by county, starting with the Irish Republic and following with Northern Ireland.

THE IRISH REPUBLIC

Players putting on the par-3 sixth at Lahinch. The hole called "the Dell" features a completely blind tee shot to a green surrounded high dunes.

County Clare

LAHINCH GOLF CLUB

A well-dressed American from Arizona, with expensive equipment, was overheard talking to his caddy while waiting to hit a shot to the fourteenth green one summer day. The frustration was evident in his voice. "Son, does the wind blow like this all the damned time?" he asked.

"Oh, no, sir," said his teenaged caddy without missing a beat. "Sometimes it blows much harder."

The many faces and moods of Lahinch are a product of the wind off the Atlantic, the blustery squalls that blow in from the sea, the hills and rocks that shape the landscape, and the sheer genius of its design. This magnificent golf course is justifiably called the St. Andrews of Ireland. It was originally designed by Old Tom Morris, one of the architects of the Royal and Ancient links.

It was redesigned in the late 1920s under the direction of Dr. Alister MacKenzie—the man who created Augusta National, Cyprus Point, and Royal Troon. It was MacKenzie who cultivated the sand-hills previously believed unusable and who mapped out the devilish and sometimes devastating amalgam of bunkers that litter the course. Those bunkers, at first glance, appear to be haphazard; the fact is that they are so cleverly and strategically placed that it verges on the supernatural.

The golfer is left with little doubt about what's ahead from the moment he or she walks up to the first tee. The huge tee box is right next to the clubhouse, where the famous Lahinch goats huddle if bad weather is approaching. The goats scatter across the course if the weather is fair. The first flag flutters in the wind, up a substantial hill, amid dunes and bunkers some 375 yards away. That wind is usually in your face and starting off with a par (4 for men and 5 for women) is a proud accomplishment.

The 497-yard, par-5 second hole plays from an elevated tee to a hidden green that's blind on the first shot and, unless your first shot is struck well, can be blind on the second shot as well.

On the scorecard map, it looks as if the par-5 fifth hole is a straight-away snap, only 476 yards from the tee box. But brace yourself when you get there. The narrow ribbon of fairway is guarded by steep hills on both sides and then it just ends. Your blind second shot—or maybe your third—plays over a mountain that looks like something Hannibal might have scaled with his elephants. Follow the little path around the alp, and the green seems relatively easy once you've negotiated all the problems between it and the tee.

While you're still gasping from the fifth, you approach the par-3 sixth—one of the most famous holes in golf. It is a vestige of Old Tom Morris's original design. They call it "the Dell." It plays only 150 yards, but the green is completely invisible from the tee. A whitewashed rock is positioned on the hill guarding the front of the green in such a manner as to give the golfers a target. The rock is moved daily according to where the pin is placed.

For years, professional and amateur players—as well as every golf writer alive (and many who have since passed on)—have debated about "the Dell." I believe it may be the most unique golf hole I've ever played, or seen for that matter. And, while there has occasionally been talk of changing it, I submit that it has served splendidly since 1893, and today's players should quit whining and aim at the rock.

The 383-yard, par-4 seventh hole looks gentle enough from the tee, but beware—there are two bunkers big enough to swallow a truck in the left-center of the fairway, within driving distance of most golfers. The diabolical placement of the tee boxes brings these deep craters into play for everybody. Women have not been exempted from the threat in any way. A shot to the right-center of the fairway is rewarded with a good look at the green.

The short par-4 thirteenth, which measures only about 267 yards, offers the big boomers an opportunity for an eagle or a birdie, although the moonscape of dunes and moguls leading up to the elevated putting surface presents the prospect of an imperfect shot being directed into the deep rough or sand fairly easily.

That little hole sets the stage for one of the finest finishing stretches in all of golf.

The 481-yard fourteenth, a par 5, plays to a huge expanse of landing area that serves both the fourteenth and fifteenth holes. A long drive that may appear safely left leaves an approach to the green that's nearly impossible, usually requiring a short lay-up to a spot where the flag is visible. The green is guarded on the right and left by steep and treacherous hills and deep, impenetrable rough. The straight approach is through a trough about as wide as a dinner plate. A shot that lands on the hard, unforgiving green is likely to find its way well off the back or side.

The par-4 fifteenth (a par 5 for women) presents a similar set of difficulties only in the opposite direction. The design simply guarantees that you will play one or the other of these monstrous holes into the wind.

Club selection on the par-3 sixteenth is critical. Don't be too short, but don't go for the flag either. The tee shot must land just short of the putting surface and release to the hole.

The par-4 seventeenth and the par-5 eighteenth are two of the best finishing holes anywhere. The eighteenth plays across the fifth fairway for men. For women it's a par 4 because their tee box is placed more than 140 yards in front of the men's markers on the clubhouse side of the fifth hole.

Lahinch is a microcosm of the way golf was intended to be played. Long, straight shots off the tee are rewarded and errant shots are punished. Well-struck shots to the greens will yield birdies and pars; poorly struck shots will find serious trouble and relegate the perpetrator to bogies and doubles.

It is not the longest course you'll ever play. It's only 6,443 yards long from the white markers, 5,466 yards for women. But length is only one of many criteria that make up a great golf course. Lahinch is one of the finest, fairest tests of the game anywhere. Every hole is an example of design excellence; every green presents a challenge, from severe undulation to subtle breaks. The weather is a factor virtually every time you play the course. Shot making and club selection are paramount; creativity and concentration pay dividends; a sure, true putting stroke can go a long way toward repairing self-inflicted damage done on the way to the greens.

If your scorecard approaches par (72 for men and 74 for women), you can go into the clubhouse for a pint or a tot with the satisfaction of knowing that you've played one of the world's best golf courses well.

Lahinch has a comfortable, modern clubhouse and one of the best-stocked pro shops in Ireland. It has a large practice green on which you are well advised to spend a few minutes before you tackle the links.

Across the road from Alister MacKenzie's jewel is the Castle Course, a shorter and substantially easier golf course than the Old Course. It was expanded from nine holes to a 5,600-yard, par-70 track in 1975. The "new" course, as many locals still call it, is also a classic links with some challenging holes and interesting greens. The topography is a little flatter and the fairways a little wider than on the Old Course. If it were anywhere other than in the shadow of the great championship course, it would be worth a special detour just for its own sake.

If you've got the energy after you've taken on the Old Course, or if you're spending a couple of days in the area, it's a very pleasant diversion and simply not to be missed. In fact, the last four holes on the New Course are every bit as good as some across the street.

LAHINCH GOLF CLUB (Old Course, links, par 72)
Location: About 15 miles west of Ennis, on the outskirts of Lahinch town
Facilities: Practice green, pro shop, caddies usually available, bar, restaurant
Green fees: Very Expensive
Telephone: (065) 81003   Fax: (065) 81592
E-mail: lgc@iol.ie

hole	par	yards	hole	par	yards
1	4	375	10	4	421
2	5	497	11	3	133
3	3	148	12	4	457
4	4	416	13	4	267
5	5	476	14	5	481
6	3	150	15	4	441
7	4	383	16	3	179
8	4	349	17	4	418
9	4	352	18	5	500
out	36	3,146	in	36	3,297
			TOTAL	72	6,443*

*white markers

SHANNON GOLF CLUB

Not many people would think of building a championship golf course between the Shannon River and the main runway at Shannon International Airport, but that's exactly what the famous golf-course architect John D. Harris did, and the result is astonishing. The Shannon Golf Club is less than a mile from the terminal, a bad slice from the jet fuel tank farm, and a sold three wood from the runway.

I have watched this course mature over the years. The trees used to be small, even scrawny, less a real hazard than an annoyance. It was easy to get out of the thin, infant woods if you happened to hook or slice a shot. Forget that now. The trees are big and dense, forming walls that frame the fairways. What has developed over the

Looking across the back nine at Shannon Golf Club.

years since the course was opened is one of the best golfing tests in Ireland. The course is more a parkland-style course than links, although several holes have distinctly linkslike characteristics.

The front nine is a monster, playing to a par 38 and measuring 3,589 yards from the white markers, 3,803 yards from the championship tees, with three par 5s to stiffen your spine. There is only one par 3 on the outgoing side. (For women it's even more daunting, with four par 5s on the front nine.)

My favorite hole is the 498-yard, par-5 eighth hole that plays along the main runway at the airport. Its status as a personal favorite has nothing to do with its merits as a golf hole nor with its relative difficulty or level of playing interest. It has to do with the fact that one day back in 1989, when the ground was hard and the hole was playing downwind, I managed to belt about a 275-yard drive followed by a 225-yard two iron across the small pond that guards the green. It bounced short of the putting surface and rolled right into the hole for a double eagle. For that reason alone the eighth hole at the Shannon Golf Club will always hold a special place in my heart.

The rest of the front is nothing to sneer at. The par-5 second hole, a gentle dogleg left, has a forest and three devilishly placed bunkers along the left, in a position to gobble up a drive that cuts the corner too much.

The par-4 third—which is a par 5 on the ladies' card threads its way between two dense stands of pines. The fairway is about as wide as my driveway and a shot that catches the trees will almost certainly cost you a stroke or more. The sixth hole—another par 5—is a dogleg right that is guarded down the right side of the fairway by trees that, again, make cutting the corner a dangerous option.

The par-4 seventh hole—which plays 369 yards from the white tees—requires a long tee shot that carries water, swampland, and marsh grasses to a narrow fairway. (It's rated the toughest hole on the ladies' card and with good reason. Women must hit a long, accurate drive in order to set up a second that will reach the green, which is 350 yards away from the red markers.)

The ninth hole is a long par 4 that's rated the toughest hole on the course. It plays 458 yards right along the runway and the perimeter of the airport to a tiny green. The out-of-bounds line is drawn dangerously close to the left side of the fairway from tee to green.

For my money, the best hole on the golf course is the par-3 seventeenth. This is a mean, unforgiving, arduous hole that plays 216 yards from the white markers and leaves virtually no room for error. Any shot that is short or right finds the rocks or the marshy shoreline of the Shannon estuary. The hard green does not hold particularly well and a shot at the flag stick runs the risk of skipping off the back side of the putting surface. I've seen good golfers play this hole with everything from a four iron to a driver depending on the velocity and direction of the wind. And I've seen more golfers taking penalty strokes than I've seen pars.

The 490-yard, par-5 finishing hole is a fine way to end the round. There is a small road that is more than halfway to the green. "You'll never get there," said a local lad I was playing with one day. And he was right.

But one day, PGA champion Greg Norman played there. Norman played it from the 511-yard championship tees and blasted a drive about 370 yards across the road. That left him only a nine iron to the green. "I was standing in the locker-room door," a longtime member of the club told me. "I said to my chum, 'That's a good second,' when his ball came to rest. I couldn't believe it was his drive!" They've erected a marker on the spot where his ball finally stopped rolling.

The modern clubhouse features a friendly bar and there is a well-stocked pro shop.

SHANNON GOLF CLUB (parkland, par 72)
Location: About a half-mile from the passenger terminal at Shannon Airport
Facilities: Practice green, pro shop, rental clubs, a few riding carts, bar, restaurant
Green fees: Moderate
Telephone: (061) 471849   Fax: (061) 471507

hole	par	yards	hole	par	yards
1	4	373	10	3	154
2	5	493	11	4	414
3	4	407	13	4	332
5	4	320	14	4	346
6	5	501	15	4	393
7	4	369	16	4	378
8	5	498	17	3	216
9	4	458	18	5	490
out	38	3,589	in	34	2,926
			TOTAL	72	6,515*

*white markers

County Cork

CORK GOLF CLUB

The name Dr. Alister MacKenzie is synonymous with the best of classic golf-course design. Some say he is the best that ever was; others challenge that. Nonetheless, if he is not the undisputed sovereign, he is certainly among the most prominent of nobles in the hierarchy of golf-course architects. His imprint is on such shrines as Augusta, Royal Troon, and Lahinch. Cork Golf Club is the product of his talent and, while subordinate to the shrines, it is nothing less than a brilliant example of the old Scot's work. It is a nearly flawless golf course that will leave you well pleased after your first round and send you away with a yearning to return again and again.

The locals call it "Little Island" because it resides on the banks of the river Lee, instead of by its real name, a common practice in Ireland. In fact, some know it by no other name than Little Island and look puzzled when asked for directions to Cork Golf Club. The land on which Dr. MacKenzie was commissioned to ply his magic was once, in part, a stone quarry by the river and while it is a parkland course, several of the quarry holes that play along the water have a distinctly linkslike look to them. And even the traditional parkland holes feel like links turf, firm and dry, lending themselves to the kind of shot making required on the coastal courses. MacKenzie's familiarity with linksland helped him make extraordinary use of the terrain, creating a montage of splendid holes.

The feel of Little Island is the result of careful maintenance and mother nature. "It never gets too soft regardless of the weather or the season," said the club's pro, Peter Hickey. "It's built on porous limestone with a shallow depth of soil, so it drains away very quickly."

The openers offer a gentle introduction to the course, using elevation changes and trees to create their character. The par-4 first climbs to a raised, contoured green, followed by a par 5 that provides a glimpse of the river from elevated tees. The short par-4 third, on which many players eschew their drivers for fairway woods or long irons, is extremely tight from tee to green.

The long par-4 fourth hole begins the journey to the heart of the course. It is the first of the quarry holes, one that would make you think you were playing a traditional links. Your tee shot must clear

The view from the elevated green back down the twelfth fairway at Cork Golf Club.

a bit of the river in order to find the well-mounded fairway. The river then forms the right boundary of the hole; to the left are deep grass indentations, rocks, hills, and high rough; the green is elevated. It's the hardest hole on the course for men, the number-three stroke hole for women.

The par-5 fifth—the hardest hole on the course for women, measuring a daunting 513 yards from the red markers—is another linkslike hole with the narrow green snuggled tightly against the riverbank and protected by trees and deep rough on the left.

One of MacKenzie's most intriguing gems is the very short par-4 sixth, which is a transition from the linkslike riverside to the steep, rocky cliffs that are the remains of the quarrymen's labors. Your tee shot is blind, playing over or between hills and trees. From the tee, the invisible green sits directly below the white house with red trim atop the cliff, but it is folly to aim directly at it. A midiron over the stand of trees to the left of the tees will provide a fine approach to the green; a shot that drifts to the right will find all manner of trouble. The long, thin, multitiered green rubs up against the towering quarry wall. The sides are protected by gorse and deep rough. The front entrance to the putting surface is a narrow chute.

The outgoing nine finishes with a long, demanding one-shot hole that plays from a terraced set of tees to an incredibly difficult green that features a series of tiers and a basin in the middle. Once you're on the putting surface—which is no mean feat in itself—you will find that you can face a putt with three or more breaks to it, depending on pin placement and how close you managed to hit.

The tenth hole returns to linkslike terrain, with the tees on a series of hills and a fairway that is festooned with moguls. The par-5 eleventh plays uphill with the remains of the quarry along most of the right edge of the fairway. It can be reached in two shots by a few men, but it's a real test for women. For men it is rated the easiest hole on the course, while it is the number-four handicap hole on the ladies' card, playing 462 yards with gravity working against you. "It's a lovely hole," said pro Peter Hickey, "but it's deceptive."

The short par-4 twelfth, which plays to a green perched high on the hillside overlooking the quarry and river, leads back to the more traditional parkland terrain. Your tee shot on the par-3 thirteenth plays from a hillside, through a chute carved from dense forest, to a green well below.

In the early part of the twentieth century, when Dr. Alister MacKenzie was building his masterpieces, crude length was less important than the level of skill required to negotiate a hole successfully. An example of design aimed at highlighting skill over power is the severe dogleg-right, par-4 sixteenth. Your drive is blind and must clear a hedgerow. It needs to be long enough to open the small, elevated, and undulating green but not so long as to get into the trees beyond the dogleg's turn. Despite the fact that it's only 339 yards from the white markers it requires a pair of precision shots to look at a birdie putt.

The finishing holes—both solid par 4s—provide an enormously satisfying conclusion to the round. The golf course is a superb test of the game for both men and women, difficult but at the same time extremely fair. Good shots are rewarded; bad shots receive gradations of punishment depending upon how far they happen to stray. The backbone of MacKenzie's design is the incredible variety of par 4s that range from a diminutive 265 yards to a muscular 440 yards. The par 3s and par 5s, three of each, provide flesh and sinew. The greens are moderately fast, true, and immaculately maintained.

In short, Little Island is a must. With me it was an unrepentant, unflinching love affair from the first time I played it. Even when I'm not in Ireland, it stays with me, generating pleasant memories, like an old friend.

CORK GOLF CLUB (parkland, par 72)
Location: About five miles east of Cork city off the N25 at the
    Little Island exit
Facilities: Practice ground, pro shop, putting green, bar, restaurant
Green fees: Expensive
Telephone: (021) 353451   Fax: (021) 353410

hole	par	yards	hole	par	yards
1	4	366	10	4	392
2	5	484	11	5	492
3	4	265	12	4	313
4	4	440	13	3	163
5	5	551	14	4	416
6	4	298	15	4	400
7	3	173	16	4	339
8	4	409	17	4	366
9	3	186	18	4	404
out	36	3,172	in	36	3,285
			TOTAL	72	6,457*

*white markers

OLD HEAD GOLF LINKS

On a foggy July day in 1999, a foursome of golf's megastars—Tiger Woods, Mark O'Meara, Payne Stewart, and David Duval—stepped to the first tee at Old Head and set out to tame this much ballyhooed and hyped new golf course. It was the week before the British Open and the four were in Ireland playing a few links courses in preparation for the tournament at Carnoustie, across the Irish Sea in Scotland.

It was quite a scene, the stellar four with their considerable entourage around them trailed by a gaggle of star watchers, golf fans, and local newspeople, setting off on the long, uphill par-4 opener. When it was over, the stars had managed the 7,121 yards

Looking back down the spectacular par-4 eighteenth hole at Old Head Golf Links toward the lighthouse and the ocean.

(from the intimidating championship tees) shooting around par. Woods reportedly fired a 71, one under par. They all gave Old Head very positive reviews, according to the local press, calling it "challenging" and "fun"—heady stuff for a course that had just opened in 1997.

Even before the bulldozers had finished their work preparing the ground for the course, its corporate parents had started generating publicity about it. By the time it opened, Old Head had garnered more international ink and airtime than all of the other big-name, glitzy Irish courses combined. Naturally, all this hoopla—along with green fees that placed it among the most expensive places to play in Europe—piqued my journalistic skepticism. Too often, it had been my experience, such publicity and prices raise expectations that turn out to be, as they say in Texas, all hat and no cattle. But this was not so with Old Head!

Never in my golfing experience have I played a young course that is so good. Architects Joe Carr (the Irish amateur champion) and Ron Kirby created magic on the Old Head of Kinsale, that windswept tongue of land that juts out into the Celtic Sea. For centuries, there has been a lighthouse at the Old Head, a guide for sailors. The lighthouse is still there, now both a nautical beacon and a landmark to tell golfers that this is the place. The golf course is spectacular. And all the advance hyperbole in reality falls short of describing just how good, how challenging, how fair, and how delightfully playable this golf course is.

The two opening holes, both solid par 4s, introduce you to what will follow. The dogleg-left second hole begins at the top of a hill, next to the ruins of the sixteenth-century lighthouse, and plays downhill and along the palisade that falls into the sea. The new lighthouse, built in 1900 and dominating many of the holes at Old Head, looms in the distance.

The views from the third and fourth tees—a par 3 and par 4 respectively—are absolutely breathtaking with the waves crashing against the rocky cliffs, ships plying the choppy water in the distance, and the lighthouse at the extreme tip of the rugged landscape. It's almost enough to distract you from the task at hand, negotiating the mounds, rocks, and bunkers that stand between you and the greens.

Then it's time to put on your climbing shoes. The par-4 fifth hole looks serene enough, but it plays directly up a steep hill, to an elevated, contoured green. Your eye does not tell you just how steep the hill is. The par-5 sixth—which would seem reachable in two, given its yardage—continues up the same hill. (Tiger Woods reached it in two shots, according to the caddy accompanying the twosome playing with my wife and me, but how many of us can hit a ball like that?)

The par-3 seventh and the par-5 eighth offer the best scoring opportunities on the outgoing nine before the dogleg-left ninth leads you to the windswept western side of the Old Head. (Much of the front nine is laid out on the eastern side of the head, the sheltered side. "The guys in the pro shop said it's always windier on the back nine," said one of the two women from California who were playing with us. That turned out to be an understatement.)

The downhill, dogleg-right tenth hole is a par 5 that almost always plays into the wind and gives you the illusion that you will drive your ball right down into the ocean. You won't. The key is to avoid the steep hills and deep rough along the right side. The solid par-3 eleventh demands accuracy and control to find the well-protected, contoured green, which leads you to perhaps the most spectacular hole on Old Head.

The long par-5 twelfth is a risk-reward hole from all of the men's tees. It demands a carry from narrow tee boxes carved on a ledge on the side of the palisade, across an expanse of space with the ocean hundreds of feet below, to the other side of the chasm. A ball that fails to clear the rocky cliff face will never be seen again. Women do not have to carry the abyss but must keep their tee shot on the ribbon of fairway guarded by the cliff on the left and steep mounds on the right. The green is then down a steep hill, in a bowl among the dunes.

Two long par 4s lead back to the cliff and the splendid par-3 sixteenth, which features a drop into the ocean along the right and towering sandhills along the left. The postage-stamp-sized green is cradled between steep grassy hills.

The par-5 seventeenth, called "Lighthouse" on the card after the landmark directly behind the green, starts with a blind tee shot that must avoid the palisade along the right length of the hole and the hills on the left. The good news is that the hole generally plays with the wind; the bad news is that it is monstrously long. (It's rated the hardest hole on the course for women, playing 437 yards from tee to green from the forward markers.)

The finisher plays with the lighthouse at your back, uphill to the magnificently appointed clubhouse. The panorama from the big, rolling green will generate a memory of this world-class golf course, in this breathtaking place, that will live with you as long as you play the game.

Every aspect of the facility—from the clubhouse to the etiquette observed by the grounds crew to the design of the golf course—has achieved a level of excellence that rivals such golf Meccas as Pebble Beach, Cascades (at The Homestead), and the TPC Stadium Course at Sawgrass. Every golfer has been considered. The construction of the women's tees, for example, is inspired. The four sets of men's markers provide an enjoyable and challenging golf experience for every player from Tiger Woods (who played the 7,121 yards from the black tees) to a high handicapper who will be tested aplenty from the gold tees (which play nearly 1,700 yards shorter, at 5,439 yards). Men whose handicaps are in single digits or in the low teens will likely want to play the blue markers; women whose handicaps are in the midteens or lower may want to move back and play the gold tees.

The fact is that Old Head Golf Links is on the cutting edge of where Irish golf is headed. It is almost as if the golf boom of the 1980s and 1990s was simply setting the stage for Old Head to lead the way into the twenty-first century. The design is brilliant, from the first tee to the eighteenth green. The sophisticated use of bunkers, mounds, rocks, deep rough, and the natural terrain to dictate the way the course must be played transcends most of what has gone before. The mix of holes—five par 3s, five par 5s, and eight par 4s—and the attention to detail in their design create an unparalleled golf experience.

OLD HEAD GOLF LINKS (links, par 72)
Location: About seven miles south of Kinsale ,follow the signs
Facilities: Practice green, practice tee, pro shop, caddies, riding
　　carts, bar, restaurant

Green fees: Very Expensive
Telephone: (021) 778444   Fax: (021) 778022
E-mail: info@oldheadgolf.ie

hole	par	yards	hole	par	yards
1	4	420	10	5	493
2	4	387	11	3	182
3	3	163	12	5	498
4	4	407	13	3	228
5	4	410	14	4	429
6	5	489	15	4	328
7	3	182	16	3	186
8	5	496	17	5	600
9	4	449	18	4	411
out	36	3,403	in	36	3,355
			TOTAL	72	6,758*

*bluemarkers

County Donegal

BALLYLIFFIN GOLF CLUB

In the summer of 1993, PGA superstar Nick Faldo—who at that time reigned as both British and Irish Open Champion—paid a visit to Ballyliffin Golf Club and declared it the most natural links he'd ever seen. Faldo is credited with comparing Ballyliffin's Old Links, the northernmost golf course in Ireland, with Royal Dornoch, the fabled links in extreme northern Scotland that was once home to the brilliant golf-course architect Donald Ross.

I suspect Donald Ross (one of my favorite golf-course designers, the man responsible for, among other great courses, Pinehurst No. 2, where they played the 1999 U.S. Open) would have approved of the Old Links. He probably would have felt right at home there, for

The elevated, undulating green on the par-3 fifth at Ballyliffin's Old Links, with Glashedy Island in the background.

like Royal Dornoch, there are many plateaued and turtleback greens that are difficult to approach. Like Royal Dornoch, it's a tight, demanding, old-fashioned links golf course. Also like Royal Dornoch, it's a wild and windblown bit of land, with rolling mounds and moguls, deep basins and pot bunkers, high sandhills and rocks, and what looks like an ocean of deep grass from which extracting a mis-hit golf ball can be a nearly impossible feat.

In fact the first hole on the Old Links is called "the Mounds," which is an understatement. It is almost impossible to find a level place anywhere from tee to green on the par-4, dogleg right. The long, tight par-4 second leads to the spectacular third hole, called "Glashedy" after the rocky little island visible just offshore where seals sun themselves. It looks from the tee as if the green is so close to the ocean that a big wave could wash your ball away. The strip of fairway, an elongated S, is less than 25 yards wide in some places, and where the fairway ends, tall grass and precarious mounds await errant shots.

One of many delightful holes on Ballyliffin's Old Links is the one-shot fifth. The elevated green is cradled among towering dunes that form a horseshoe around the short grass, leaving only a narrow opening in front. Do not let the length of the hole on the scorecard mislead you into taking too little club. A short shot runs the risk of being rejected back down the severe incline in front of the green. The view, looking back toward Glashedy Island and the ocean, is almost enough to distract you from the task of getting your ball into the cup once you're safely on the putting surface.

The par-4 sixth plays to a long, kidney-shaped green that is extremely well protected by bunkers, mounds, and deep grass on all sides. The par-3 seventh presents a formidable challenge for most women. It's 147 yards from the red markers and requires a tee shot that carries almost all the way. The par-4 eighth features an elevated green that sits on a little plateau and makes a run-up or bump-and-run approach extremely difficult.

As with all the other par 4s on the golf course, the ninth is extremely tight with a narrow belt of fairway embraced on both sides by unforgiving foliage that lives in remarkably undulating ter-rain, a reflection in miniature of the hills of the Inishowen Peninsula that loom behind the green like a movie set. My wife, Barbara, noted that the par 4s are a strenuous challenge to women, and even long hitters like her will be required to use two woods to reach many of them in regulation.

After you enjoy a quick refreshment at the magnificent clubhouse, completed just in time to host a new year's gala welcoming the new millennium, a pair of par 4s, the short tenth and the demanding eleventh, lead you back into the ball-striking challenge that is the Old Links at Ballyliffin. The long par-3 twelfth is named "the Dell," the same as the famous blind par-3 at Lahinch. This one-shot hole is not blind from the tees, but it is long and tough. The solid three-shot fourteenth plays right along the coast and features a blind tee shot. From the men's tees the view of the crashing surf is spectacular.

The risk-reward par-4 fifteenth is rated the toughest hole on the course for men and women and invites you to hit across as much of the dogleg as you dare, if you keep mindful of the thatch of gnarled grass that awaits any shot not landing in the fairway. (Barbara, who came up short of the green in two, pointed out that the fifteenth is 395 yards from the red markers, par 5 length for women on many other links in Ireland.)

The par-3 seventeenth supplies an unsurpassed putting challenge. It's the most contoured, rolling green on the Old Links and demands an accurate eye and a steady hand to limit yourself to just two putts. Picture a raised relief map of Switzerland and you've got an idea of what you face.

The closing hole is a lovely, long par 5, uphill dogleg left, that requires three good shots to put yourself in position to finish with a birdie or par. Looking back down the fairway from the final green on this classic, traditional links, you are left with the indelible image of the Inishowen Peninsula, the surf, the strand, Glashedy Island, and the distant mountains. In general, this is a long, difficult golf course and ego notwithstanding, men with handicaps above fifteen should seriously consider playing the gold tees. It's more than 325 yards shorter and provides a better scoring opportunity without diminishing the layout in the slightest. For women, this is a tough test at 5,398 yards and a par the same as the mens.

The course is a relative newcomer when compared to the many nineteenth-century golf courses in Ireland. The Old Links opened in 1948, right after World War II, but somehow it feels as if it's been there forever.

In 1995, a second eighteen opened at Ballyliffin. The delightful, new Glashedy Links was designed by Pat Ruddy and Tom Craddock (who have combined their talents on several other Irish golf-course projects including Druids Glen and the second nine at Wicklow). It is very similar to the Old Course in look and feel, although it is constructed on slightly higher terrain and is a little flatter than the traditional seaside linksland on which the Old Links is built.

If you can play only one of the Ballyliffin courses, opt for the Old Links, but you will not regret making the time to play both fine golf courses. You will also not go wrong staying for at least one postround drink or even a meal in the marvelous clubhouse.

BALLYLIFFIN GOLF CLUB (Old Links, links, par 71)
Location: About fifteen miles north of Buncrana in the village of
    Ballyliffin
Facilities: Practice green, practice tee, pro shop, riding carts, bar,
    restaurant
Green fees: Expensive
Telephone: (077) 76119   Fax: (077) 76672
E-mail: ballyliffingolfclub@tinet.ie

hole	par	yards	hole	par	yards
1	4	393	10	4	334
2	4	422	11	4	395
3	4	354	12	3	206
4	5	491	13	4	426
5	3	176	14	5	535
6	4	378	15	4	435
7	3	211	16	4	344
8	4	409	17	3	160
9	4	389	18	5	554
out	35	3,223	in	36	3,389

TOTAL   71   6,612*
*white markers

DONEGAL GOLF CLUB

About five miles south of Donegal town, down a narrow little road that leads to the ocean, separated from the rest of the world by a strip of dense forest, is the Murvagh Peninsula. Along the shores of Donegal Bay is a promontory of dunes and coastal grass out of which the famous Irish golf-course architect Eddie Hackett was commissioned to create the links golf course that now occupies the land. In the late 1950s the Temple family—founders of Magee & Company, the famous Donegal tweed makers—donated the property to the golf club and the golf course opened in 1960.

Not to overstate the obvious, but this is one long track: nearly 7,200 yards from the championship markers and a grueling 6,830 from the white tees, playing to a par 73 and featuring five par 5s. Even the par

Steep mounds and deep rough await any shot that strays from the fairway at the long, demanding Donegal Golf Club.

3s are long. Only one plays less than 180 yards, and that simply provides a little relief between two big par 5s. In short, Donegal Golf Club requires length and accuracy as well as a superior short game in order for you to shoot in the vicinity of your handicap.

The scope of the golf course is evident from the first tee, but at the same time the opener—a 523-yard par 5—draws the golfer into the sublime beauty of the place. The Blue Stack Mountains of Donegal rise majestically across a shimmering inlet of Donegal Bay behind the first green. The hole itself is a slight dogleg right and is largely flat and gentle. It is rated one of the easier holes on the card. Enjoy it! The real test has yet to begin.

The second hole, a long, narrow, straight par 4, is rated the most difficult hole on the men's card. It plays some 415 yards from the white markers to a green that's deceptively difficult to hit.

The last five holes on the front side are among the best five back-to-back holes in Ireland. The par-3 fifth—which is named *Valley of Tears* on the scorecard—is 186 yards from the white markers to the long, undulating, narrow green, and it's all carry. The elevated green is guarded in front and to the right by a steep drop-off that guarantees a recovery shot from tall grass and weeds—if you can find your ball at all. Anything to the left or too long comes to rest in a series of steep dunes. It is not rated the most difficult hole on the card, but any golfer who walks to the next tee with a par should be well pleased.

The seventh hole is my favorite. The hole, a dogleg left along the strand, plays 385 yards from the tee to a green that remains hidden on both the drive and the approach shot. The green itself is tiered and tricky.

The par-5 eighth is a testament to the length of this course—a mere 546 yards down a ribbon of fairway cut between the dunes. Catch your breath on the par-4 ninth, a dogleg right that requires only a drive and a short iron to set up a birdie opportunity.

The back nine is the easier of the two but still tests your nerve as well as your shot-making ability. On the 550-yard, par-5 twelfth, a nasty little ditch intersects the fairway about where your second shot lands. It can present a truly unpleasant surprise if you don't know it's there, because you can't see it from where your drive lands.

The par-4 fifteenth is about as wide as my belt and requires a tee shot that is hit with surgical precision.

The par-3 sixteenth is 229 yards long (yes, and it's 240 yards from the championship markers). It is an understatement to say it demands a long, accurate shot. It is justifiably rated the second toughest hole on the course. A driver is not an unusual club selection for the tee shot.

The eighteenth—which is aptly named *Bogey Hill* on the score-card—features a blind tee shot over a ridge of grass and trouble. A successful shot will leave you a mid- to short iron to the big, undu-lating green. A shot that fails to clear the ridge will provide ample evidence of why the hole is named as it is.

In general the greens on Donegal Golf Club are exceptional—fast and true. They require concentration because of subtle and sometimes unseen breaks. They also hold slightly better than many other links courses, although that in no way implies that you can play for the pin. It merely means that if the pin is back, you can land the ball on the putting surface and not have it roll off into Donegal Bay or beyond.

DONEGAL GOLF CLUB (links, par 73)
Location: About five miles south of Donegal town, follow the signs
    west from the N15
Facilities: Practice green, practice tee, pro shop, bar, restaurant
Green fees: Moderate
Telephone: (073) 34054   Fax: (073) 34377

hole	par	yards	hole	par	yards
1	5	523	10	4	350
2	4	415	11	4	372
3	3	189	12	5	550
4	4	416	13	3	159
5	3	186	14	5	524
6	5	517	15	4	405
7	4	385	16	3	229
8	5	546	17	4	353
9	4	335	18	4	376
out	37	3,512	in	36	3,318
			TOTAL	73	6,830*

*white markers

County Dublin

PORTMARNOCK GOLF CLUB

There are few other golf course in Ireland that have gotten more press over the years than Portmarnock, and certainly there is no other club that takes itself quite so seriously. There's an air of superiority the moment you enter the pro shop. It's as if they're doing you an extraordinary favor to let you pay your hefty green fee and play there. (They charge women a little less than men and should. They treat them as second-class citizens in almost every way. The club steadfastly refuses to accept women as full members.)

Portmarnock has hosted an impressive list of big tournaments, and golf writers in Ireland, Britain, and the rest of Europe seem to have nothing but good things to say about it. I take exception. The fact that it was ranked 38th in *Golf Magazine*'s 1995 list of the world's 100 greatest golf courses simply boggles my mind. The course offers none of breathtaking grandeur of Rosses Point, Royal County Down, Tralee, or Portstewart; it is devoid of the design and layout brilliance of Lahinch, The European Club, and either course at Ballybunion; it requires none of the shot-making prowess you must have to score at Royal Portrush, Old Head, or County Louth. In short, while it's not a bad course by any stretch, it's no match for a lot of other Irish golf courses.

Portmarnock plays shorter than its 6,839 yards would suggest. It is relatively open and extraordinarily merciful to errant shots—especially when compared to other great links courses, such as County Louth, Lahinch, or Royal Portrush.

The first, second, and third holes are gentle par 4s that require only that you hit halfway-decent tee shots and avoid the trouble on the right. The fourth is, perhaps, the most interesting hole on the golf course and is rated the hardest. It's a 435-yard par 4 that is protected by a berm along the left side of the fairway and a series of strategically placed bunkers on the right. (For women it's a 387-yard par 4, also rated the hardest hole on the course.)

The par-4 fifth features a blind tee shot over a mound in the middle of the fairway, but safely over it, you'll only have a mid- or short iron to the green.

The best of the par 3s is the 141-yard twelfth hole, which requires an accurate shot to a pear-shaped green that's pitched severely back toward the tees. If you fail to hit enough club and the pin is back, you may find yourself well into three-putt range.

The 549-yard, par-5 thirteenth requires three good, solid shots to get to the green.

If there's one hole on Portmarnock that has drawn the attention of players and writers alike it is the dogleg-left, par-4 fourteenth, which plays toward the Irish Sea to a green that's perched on a plateau. The approach shot demands a precise bump-and-run that must be hard enough to climb the hill to the putting surface but not so hard that it rolls off the back of the green.

The two par-4 finishing holes are open and forgiving and will provide a good chance to score well as you head to the clubhouse. (The seventeenth is a par 5 for women and plays to 405 yards.)

If there is a golf course in Ireland that is bad news for women, this is it, not because of its difficulty, but because of its attitude. On at least seven holes, women are not provided with a tee box of any kind. Their tees are simply plunked down, haphazardly, in the fairway somewhere in front of the men's markers. Little or no time or care is taken to assure that the teeing ground is level or that the markers are properly placed. Women are clearly an afterthought. It is disgraceful that a golf club that takes itself so seriously cannot treat women better. In fact, it is the only big-name club in Ireland that relegates women to such inferior and shabby status.

Portmarnock features an additional nine holes, which look very similar to the regular eighteen. That track is played twice to make up a full round and has three par 5s and two par 3s for an eighteen-hole par of 74 and a total of 6,717 yards.

The pro shop rates as one of the best stocked anywhere in Ireland.

PORTMARNOCK GOLF CLUB (links, par 72)

Location: About ten miles north of Dublin city center, just off the Malahide Road in the village of Portmarnock

Facilities: Practice green, practice tee, pro shop, caddies usually available, bar, restaurant

Green fees: Very Expensive

Telephone: (01) 846-2968   Fax: (01) 846-2601

E-mail: secretary@portmarnockgolfclub.ie

hole	par	yards	hole	par	yards
1	4	372	10	4	364
2	4	357	11	4	415
3	4	377	12	3	141
4	4	435	13	5	549
5	4	380	14	4	375
6	5	583	15	3	183
7	3	171	16	5	514
8	4	379	17	4	434
9	4	417	18	4	393
out	36	3,471	in	36	3,368
			TOTAL	72	6,839*

*white markers

County Galway

CONNEMARA GOLF CLUB

Getting out to the Connemara Golf Club takes you through the rugged and forbidding land that is Connemara. The fields are festooned with rocks and provide only enough grass for a few hardy sheep or the famous Connemara ponies. The bare hills are dotted with whitewashed cottages, some with thatched roofs, where shepherds or fishermen try to scratch out a living from an inhospitable land. To get to the golf course, you turn west at the village of Ballyconneely—about halfway between Clifden and Cashel Bay—and drive until you think you're going to fall into the Atlantic.

The modern clubhouse overlooks the golf course and the ocean from atop a small hill. The first tee and starter's shack are on the right as you pull off the one-lane road into the parking lot.

Connemara Golf Club's ninth green to the left, the practice green to the right, against the backdrop of the shimmering North Atlantic.

If the Connemara Golf Club were a person it would be thoroughly schizophrenic. The original front nine is Dr. Jekyll; the original back is Mr. Hyde. The front is fairly gentle, reasonably open, and relatively forgiving. There are hidden troubles on the front—the rocky patches in the deep rough can bounce an errant shot into the depths of heartbreak. The greens are difficult to read. But for the most part the front is where you make up as many strokes as you possibly can.

My favorite hole on the front nine is the par-3 sixth, which plays 191 yards from the men's white tees, usually straight into the wind. The green is a mass of undulations, protected by rocks, deep grass, and small dunes on all sides.

The eighth green is the toughest one on the front side and sits 457 yards from the tee. To register a par 4 takes two long accurate shots and all the putting skill you can muster.

Nonetheless, if you're striking the ball well and are able to get the hang of the greens, it is well within reason to expect to be shooting to your handicap at the turn.

But once you've teed off on the long, par-4 tenth, you're headed into the jaws of a monster. In fact, there isn't a short par 4 on the entire back side and they are all measured in degrees of difficulty from hard to harder. The tenth hole, for example, plays from an elevated tee to a difficult green 419 grueling yards away.

The twelfth is rated the hardest hole on the course for both men and women—436 yards from the white markers and 348 yards from the ladies' tees. The hole plays uphill all the way; the fairway is narrow; the trouble is severe on all sides.

The brutal 197-yard, par-3 thirteenth—which requires a long carry over a vale of rocks, gorse, long grass, and lost golf balls to a small, hard green—sets the stage for a homestretch that features three par 5s and a pair of testing, arduous par 4s.

The par-4 sixteenth is guarded by three little ponds and plays to a slick green. It's not unusual to watch approach shots slide off that green in all directions. In fact, both its grain and pitch are toward the ocean, away from the approaching golfers.

The two finishing holes—both par 5s—are generous from the tees. You can unload a big drive on both without too much trouble around the fairway. But the seventeenth green is devilishly difficult, perched high above the fairway between two hills. It's guarded by dunes and bunkers on the approach, and even if you're capable of covering 512 yards into the wind in two shots, it's a bad gamble. For long hitters, par is best achieved by two long shots and an accurate chip.

By the time you've played from the elevated tee, down into the coastal valley, and back uphill to the eighteenth green, you've earned a pint and a rest. And if you've shot to your handicap on the back, you can take a large measure of satisfaction as well for having mastered nine holes that are among the most difficult anywhere.

An additional nine difficult holes were built in 1997, matching the rigors of both existing nines and expanding the attraction of this wonderful, if remote, Irish links.

CONNEMARA GOLF CLUB (links, par 72)

Location: West of Ballyconneely, off the coast road from Clifden to Cashel Bay

Facilities: Practice green, a few riding carts, bar, restaurant

Green fees: Expensive

Telephone: (095) 23502   Fax: (095) 23662

E-mail: links@iol.ie

hole	par	yards	hole	par	yards
1	4	362	10	4	419
2	4	400	11	3	165
3	3	159	12	4	436
4	4	366	13	3	197
5	4	374	14	5	503
6	3	191	15	4	382
7	5	527	16	4	404
8	4	457	17	5	512
9	4	376	18	5	520
out	35	3,212	in	37	3,538
			TOTAL	72	6,750*

*white markers

County Kerry

BALLYBUNION GOLF CLUB

The village of Ballybunion hugs the Atlantic coast, just south of the point at which the Shannon River meets the North Atlantic. It boasts no major industries, hotels, stores, or restaurants. But it does boast two of the world's most famous and outstanding golf courses and draws enthusiastic golfers from all over the globe eager to sample the fare. The clubhouse walls are adorned with pictures of some of the best-known visitors, including Pres. Bill Clinton, Tiger Woods, Mark O'Meara, and Tom Watson.

They've had a golf club at Ballybunion since before 1900; the first nine-hole track was completed in 1906 and extended to eighteen holes in 1927. But until Tom Watson spouted off in the early 1980s about the wonders of the Old Course, it was largely unknown outside of Britain and Ireland. Watson declared it one of the finest links golf courses in the world and that opened the floodgates. Now, of course, buses full of golfers from all over Continental Europe, Britain, Japan, and the United States converge on that famous, intimidating, windswept piece of real estate.

On the Old Course advance reservations are absolutely essential in the summer months and even then starting times are an approximation; occasionally it is possible to get a late reservation on the Cashen Course, which is hardly privation. This is a golf facility at which caddies are available most of the time without advance notice, though telling them when you book your tee time that you want a caddie may assure you of getting one who's older than twelve and who knows more about the layout than where the next tee is located. Demand occasionally outpaces supply.

The clubhouse is one of the best in Ireland in terms of pro-shop, restaurant, bar, and locker-room facilities. Beware the pro shop! The prices on shirts, sweaters, hats, and the like bearing the Ballybunion logo are somewhere in the ozone layer.

The Old Course

PGA veteran and champion Tom Watson is still a regular at the Old Course. He often uses Ballybunion to warm up and get ready for the British Open. In fact, Ballybunion Golf Club took advantage of Watson's affection for it in the fall of 1995, when the club commissioned him to do some redesign work on the Old Course. In addition to some relatively minor changes, he did some major work on the seventh green and the approach to the eighteenth.

"This isn't a guy who says, 'Bring in the bulldozers and let's tear things up,'" said a longtime club employee as we stood over the work being done on the finishing hole. "These are subtle changes, like lowering the hill in front of the green to give you a little better look at the flag." Watson's changes did not meet with universal approval. Some golf writers and professionals argued that he changed the character of the finishing hole too much. Others, however, say the changes enhanced both the playability of the hole as well as its aesthetics.

The first tee on the Old Course may be one of the most photographed golf holes in the world. The tee overlooks the town cemetery, an ancient burial ground that has also claimed more than its share of errant golf balls, including one from no less a golfing legend than Jack Nicklaus. The 366-yard, par-4 opener is a dogleg left, curving past the cemetery to a long, narrow, well-trapped green—a nice hole, but nothing like the war stories you hear about the place. "Ha!" you might be tempted to sneer, marking a 4 or 5 on your card and puffing out your chest. Don't gloat yet.

The next hole shatters any illusions you may have harbored about the difficulty of the Old Course. The par-4 second hole—rated the toughest hole on the course for men (only the fourth most difficult for women, because it's a par 5 from the red markers)—is as narrow as a pair of shrunken blue jeans. The tee shot plays across a small creek to a landing area that narrows precipitously the longer you hit. A pair of strategically placed bunkers will catch a tee shot that is less than perfection. If you don't get to or beyond the bunkers, your chances of par have been substantially reduced. The elevated and sharply pitched green is protected by steep hills and deep rough that create an ascending bowling alley effect, with trouble on all sides except for a dead-on approach—which, of course, brings more bunkers into play.

Even if you play the second reasonably well, don't heave a sigh of relief yet! The par-3 third hole plays a solid 211 yards from the middle tees and requires a superbly placed tee shot. For women it plays a massive 184 yards and tests the shot-making ability of even the low handicappers.

The fourth and fifth holes are sheer tests of will, back-to-back par 5s that require precision shot making. They both play around 500 yards and demand huge, well-placed drives even to consider going for the greens in two. Many midlevel golfers find a three wood a preferable option, setting up second and third shots that make par reasonable. The fourth hole, a dogleg left, plays straight in to a green about as wide as my living room. The fifth is a double dogleg (left on the tee shot and then slightly to the right near the green).

That leads to the devilishly difficult par-4 sixth hole, a 344-yard dogleg left to a plateaued green. If your tee shot is too long, you're into deep grass. The narrow approach is to a long, narrow green, with the strand and the water behind it. The seventh plays right along the water, demanding that golfers dodge a midfairway bunker and a pair of Sahara-like sand traps that guard the green.

The par-3 eighth is a short little hole (137 yards from the white markers and only 118 yards for women) but it plays to an uncharitable pear-shaped green that is just as likely to yield a slide into the rough or one of the bunkers as it is to cough up a birdie.

The 400-yard, par-4 eleventh hole is often rated as one of the best par 4s anywhere. It features a tight, hourglass-shaped fairway, guarded on both sides by dunes, scrub-brush, and deep rough. It plays to an immensely well protected, narrow green. Straight and short is infinitely better than long and to the right or left. Approaching on your third shot and hoping to get it up and down is the wiser option than trying to be too bold. An errant shot all but assures a bogie or much worse. If you're in position to get on in two, take enough club. There's less trouble in back than in front.

The par-3 fifteenth ranks as one of the tougher holes on the Old Course for men, requiring a long, pinpoint shot (197 yards from the white markers), but for women it's a short, easy little par 4 (only 186 yards, just 2 yards longer than the par-3 third on the front).

The par-5 sixteenth, a dogleg left, is short enough (only 475 yards from the white markers) that a big hitter might think it's an easy two-shot for a birdie. But the steep hills guarding the left of the fairway from the tee make placing your ball in scoring position extremely difficult. The hole then plays to the well-guarded green from one of the narrowest little fairways you'll ever see.

The par-4 seventeenth—a dogleg left—plays along the coast and is another brilliant and treacherous test, protected along its right length by the Atlantic beach and on the left by a row of hills as tall as small buildings that stand like sentries. There is one unpleasant little pot bunker at the left front of the green that can waste a stroke if the approach is improperly played. The hole's 362 yards should not leave you with the impression that this is an easy birdie hole. It's not.

That leads to the eighteenth. The exhilarating finishing hole is a 360-yard par 4 with the tee backing onto the ocean and the green tucked at the far end of a champagne flute. In front of the narrow

The par-4 seventeenth at Ballybunion's Old Course is one of the world's most famous golf holes. The approach to the green is pinched by the ocean on one side and towering dunes on the other.

alley that leads to the green is a bunker they call "the Sahara," which says all that need be said. Tom Watson's redesign of the hole shaved off the top of the hill that protects the right front of the green. It was his contention that it made the flag more visible and allowed for more precise approach shots.

There is ample landing area for your drive, but the approach to the green demands a shot that propels your ball over the sand to a green that's like an inverted cereal bowl protected by towering hills on three sides. Once you're safely on the green, your troubles are far from over. The green has more undulation than a belly dancer and more break than you want to ponder.

Women should be aware that the approach to the green requires a long carry to the putting surface, and while that grassy lane provides some bailout room, it provides precious little safety from the grassy dunes on all sides.

The biggest visual drawback to the Old Course is the unparalleled view of the trailer park that graces the first hole, but that's nitpicking and the scenery—which at many other points is wonderful—is secondary to the golf course, which is among the very best.

For women it's a lively par 74, with four par 5s on the front side, playing out to a 38. It is difficult but fair and much thought has been given to how the course plays from the red markers. For men, it's relatively short, only 6,200-plus yards from the white tees, but length is not the key to the greatness of the Old Course at Ballybunion. Once you've played it you will understand why it belongs in any conversation about the world's finest golf courses.

The Cashen Course

Old-timers still call it "the New Course," and if the Cashen Course at Ballybunion were anywhere else, it would certainly garner a lot more attention than it does. As it is, it is too often mentioned as an aside to its older and better-known sibling. For my money, the Cashen Course is a substantially more difficult test of the game than the more popular and more famous Old Course. In fact, many golf writers agree that the Cashen Course is one of the toughest golf courses anywhere. Some have even suggested that in a strong wind it verges on being unplayable, even though it's less than 6,000 yards from the white markers.

Difficulty should not be confused with overall excellence. The Old Course is a superior golf course because it is fairer to golfers at all levels of play. Frankly, if your handicap isn't ten or less for men (twenty or less for women), the enjoyment level achieved from playing the Cashen Course can be mitigated by its sometimes ferocious challenges.

Nonetheless, over a jar (glass of libation) or two in the pub after your round you will doubtless hear discussions of which course is better. I confess a perverse fondness for the Cashen Course's sometimes bullying character and its sheer brutality. There's a naked face of aggression and even intimidation that the golf course reveals to the golfer on almost every shot. Tackling it is often more a battle than a game.

The tenth green at Ballybunion's Cashen Course is elevated and guarded by dunes and bunkers. The difficult par-3 eleventh green is cradled among the hills in the distance.

You look down that bleak, undulating, windswept first fairway and know that this golf course has a chip on its shoulder. In reality, the elevated green is only 484 yards away from the white markers and as a par 5 it is quite easily reached in two shots. Solid play will be rewarded.

The Cashen Course was designed by Robert Trent Jones and, when he first set foot on the grassy dunes and rocky outcrop-pings, he is reputed to have declared that bit of land, bounded by the Atlantic on one side and the river Feale on another, the best linksland he'd ever seen. The course itself has been something of a work in progress since it opened. In 1998 and 1999 it was lengthened and the order in which several holes are played was changed.

The par-4 second hole plays from the top of one sandhill to an elevated green cut from another. It's followed by a short par 3 that requires pinpoint accuracy in order to place your tee shot on the small green that is surrounded by dunes and bunkers. This is rated the easiest hole on the course for men and among the easiest for women. But if the wind is blowing and your shot is a little off line it's among the easiest double bogies I've ever seen.

In general, the greens on the Cashen Course are some of the hardest to approach in the world. For example, the par-4 seventh features a trip to the beach for any shot that strays left and there are hills to the right. It plays to a tiny, narrow green by a cliff and—like the third hole—requires laser guidance and a computerized launch system to get the ball close in regulation.

The par-5 eighth hole lurks in the shadows like a thug, ready to mug you. It's 585 yards from tee to green and requires three long, accurate shots. By contrast, the 451-yard, par-5 ninth hole—like the first hole—is reachable in two. For women, however, the ninth is played as a 338-yard par 4 and is rated the most difficult hole on the course with good reason. Any woman who walks to the tenth with a par is playing very solid golf.

The tenth hole is simply a lovely little test as well as a breathtak-ing aesthetic feast for the eye. It's a short par 4 that plays down a canyon of three- and four-story-tall hills to an elevated green that backs onto the Atlantic. The tee shot is blind; the approach is tough; the green is difficult.

A pair of solid par 3s (the twelfth hole is a short par 4 on the women's card) follows and takes you to one of the most challenging holes in Ireland—or anywhere else. The tee shot, over a hill, is blind and the thirteenth fairway is narrow and fraught with peril. The green sits 374 yards away from the tee, a dogleg left. The approach shot is hindered on the left by sheer-faced dunes that almost form a wall. On the right is a drop-off that leaves a nearly vertical recovery shot of up to 40 feet. The green itself is undulating and tricky.

The par-5 fifteenth, a dogleg right, again plays down a canyon of steep and unforgiving dunes. And despite the fact that it's only 476 yards long, it is designed in such a way that it is nearly impossible to hit a tee shot into a position from which the superbly protected green can be reached in two.

The par-4 eighteenth is a treacherous finisher that plays uphill through a narrow little chute to a hilly, tricky green. For women it is a par 5. And anybody who walks away with a par can be well satisfied with his or her finish.

The best advice for anyone playing the Cashen Course is bring plenty of golf balls. On one typical October day in 1996 (it was drizzling but relatively calm with occasional blustery stretches) I was put with three guys from Tokyo and among the four of us we lost eighteen golf balls. As we walked to the clubhouse, the youngest of my partners—a solid player with a 6 handicap—shook his head. "That's the hardest course I've ever played," he said.

BALLYBUNION GOLF CLUB (Old Course, links, par 71)
Location: About a mile from the center of Ballybunion town
Facilities: Practice green, practice tee, pro shop, rental clubs, caddies, bar, restaurant
Green fees: Very Expensive
Telephone: (068) 27146   Fax: (068) 27387
E-mail: bbgolffc@iol.ie

hole	par	yards	hole	par	yards
1	4	366	10	4	336
2	4	394	11	4	400
3	3	211	12	3	179
4	5	504	13	5	466
5	5	496	14	3	118
6	4	344	15	3	197
7	4	400	16	5	475
8	3	137	17	4	362
9	4	430	18	4	360
out	36	3,282	in	35	2,959
			TOTAL	71	6,241*

*white markers

BALLYBUNION GOLF CLUB (Cashen Course, links, par 72)
Green fees: Expensive

hole	par	yards	hole	par	yards
1	5	484	10	4	312
2	4	359	11	3	140
3	3	141	12	3	194
4	4	325	13	4	374
5	4	303	14	4	355
6	3	143	15	5	476
7	4	373	16	3	145
8	5	585	17	5	476
9	5	451	18	4	361
out	37	3,164	in	35	2,833
			TOTAL	72	5,997*

*white markers

CEANN SIBEAL

The extreme western end of the Dingle Peninsula, where the rocky land meets the Atlantic, was once a favored retreat for early Irish Christian monks, who sought solitude and spiritual wholeness. The ruins of some of their beehive-shaped rock huts and their Ogham Stones—pillars into which the earliest known examples of the Gaelic language were chiseled—draw tourists and religious scholars alike to that sometimes awesomely beautiful and sometimes wild and storm-lashed part of the world. The landscape bears witness to the attraction for those early hermit monks. The face of God is revealed in countless forms, from its most tranquil to its most violent and baleful.

In many ways, the west end of the Dingle Peninsula remains a land where time has stood still. Shepherds still tend their flocks, dogs herd the cattle from the fields to their barns, and Irish remains the spoken language at home, in the shops, and on the village streets. English road signs disappear completely and are replaced with things like directions from An Daingean (Dingle town) to Baile an Fheirtéaraigh (Ballyferriter), a lovely little hamlet in the rocky hills near the promontory called Ceann Sibéal.

In Irish Gaelic, "ceann" means "head," and "Sibéal" is the Gaelic spelling of the woman's name Sybil. It's pronounced "cown shi-BEEL" and back in 1924 the geographic landmark gave its name to Golf Chumann Ceann Sibéal, the westernmost golf course in Europe. It is a largely undiscovered gem, a wonderful and challenging track replete with treacherous bunkers, undulating greens, hills, rocks, deep rough, and a devilish little stream that winds its way across, around, and parallel to ten of the eighteen holes.

"It'll break your heart," said my friend William Power, an enthusiastic golfer from county Wicklow. "You'll hit a great shot only to discover your ball down in the water."

The first hole introduces you to the creek—the locals call it a "burn"—on your second shot. Unseen from the fairway, it lurks right in front of the green. The opener is a tough par 4 that plays 396 yards from tee to green.

The par-3 second and fifth both play more than 200 yards and demand length and accuracy. From the red markers women face a testing 141-yard hole and a relatively easy 118-yard one-shotter, respectively.

The par-5 sixth hole—the only par 5 on the front side—is a real challenge, playing a massive 565 yards and rendering even the long ball hitters powerless to reach it in two shots. The green is well protected and a par here should bring a smile.

The 427-yard, par-4 ninth hole (380 yards on the ladies' card) is considered the toughest hole on the course for both men and women, and justifiably so. The tee shot over that devilish creek must be long enough to let you reach the green on your second shot, but not so long it slides through the left-to-right dogleg. The green is tremendously well protected with hills and bunkers.

The creek intersects the par-5 eleventh just about perfectly to catch an imprecise drive. At 523 yards it's a long way to think about

A devilish little creek, called a "burn," meanders throughout the links at Ceann Sibéal. Here it has thwarted an approach to the par-5 thirteenth green.

getting on in two; at 483 yards from the red markers it's difficult for women to get on in three.

The most interesting hole on the course follows the gentle little par-3 twelfth. The par-5 thirteenth is only 479 yards from tee to green, but presents the golfer with a fascinating smorgasbord of choices, depending on the direction and severity of the wind. Played straight down the middle, the hole requires a tee shot with a long iron or a fairway wood, to the point where the dogleg turns almost ninety degrees to the right toward the elevated green.

If conditions are right, a big hitter can think about cutting the corner, which is a farmer's field where sheep graze. To fly over the out of bounds safely requires a carry of about 175 to 190 yards. It's more than 220 to reach the fairway, but it sets up a midiron to the green in two. The peril, however, is that a shot that's too good can find that creek as it meanders across the fairway and up the right side.

The par-4 seventeenth plays through a field of dunes and leads to the par-5 eighteenth, the third par 5 on the back side. It's a satisfying finisher that plays uphill to a wide but shallow green.

Ceann Sibéal is a wonderful test of the game for golfers of every level of ability except the rankest beginners. For women, it is an especially fine and fair test. The designers gave an unusual amount of thought to the placement of the ladies' tee boxes and the result is unique. The 245-yard, par-4 eighth, for example, is reachable with a driver and midiron. On the other hand most women will need two solid wood shots to reach the 380-yard, par-4 ninth in regulation. The red markers play 5,749 yards, and it is a certainty that women players will use virtually every club in the bag.

A pint in the pleasant bar that overlooks the golf course and the ocean is a fine way to reward yourself before you drive those narrow, winding roads back to wherever.

CEANN SIBEAL (links, par 72)
Location: West of Ballyferriter at the western end of the Dingle
    Peninsula
Facilities: Practice green, pro shop, bar, restaurant
Green fees: Moderate
Telephone: (066) 915-6255   Fax: (066) 915-6409

hole	par	yards	hole	par	yards
1	4	396	10	3	197
2	3	201	11	5	523
3	4	376	12	3	156
4	4	378	13	5	479
5	3	202	14	4	342
6	5	565	15	4	405
7	4	425	16	4	373
8	4	370	17	4	371
9	4	427	18	5	504
out	35	3,346	in	37	3,350
			TOTAL	72	6,696*

*white markers

DOOKS GOLF CLUB

They've been playing golf at Dooks since 1889, earning it a place among Ireland's oldest established golf clubs. The course is a little difficult to find. Heading west, toward Waterville, you take a right from the Ring of Kerry Road about four miles from the town of Killorglin and just before you enter the village of Glenbeigh. Despite the signpost on the main road, the red clubhouse is so far up a narrow, winding little track that you think you're going to end up in Dingle Bay before you reach it.

Dooks makes absolutely nobody's list of the best courses in Ireland, except mine, but that's their problem. For me it's one of the unsung gems of Irish golf. For the good to average club player, Dooks is a premier example of links golf. It's not so difficult that it intimidates, but it requires a well-stocked arsenal of golfing skills. It is far more difficult than it looks. In addition, it's a beautiful place, sandwiched between Macgillicuddy's Reeks reaching to the sky in the south and Dingle Bay to the north. In all, Dooks is a thoroughly enjoyable golf course to play.

The topography, from a distance, appears to be relatively flat, gentle, and open, but on closer inspection it reveals rocks, dunes, scrub-brush, heather bowers, and washes that characterize the coastal land in that part of the country. It is not as daunting as Lahinch, Tralee, or Rosses Point, but I challenge anyone who dismisses it as too easy or tame to produce a scorecard with subpar numbers on it. As with most links courses, aggressive play is rewarded less than precise shot making. Even single-digit handicappers will be forced to use almost every one of their fourteen clubs before the round is finished.

The test begins at once. The par-4 first hole—which measures 419 yards from the championship markers—is a gently curving dog-leg left with a green you can't see from the tee. The drive plays up what appears to be an innocuous little hill. But if the shot is too low, it can drift into the deep rough. If it's too long and crests the hill, it cascades into a field of what skiers would call heavy moguls. A hook (for the right-handed player) brings the out of bounds into play. A slice guarantees a huge second shot, probably from unfriendly rough and from a stance with the ball well above your feet (possibly above your knees).

Finishing a round on the eighteenth green at Dooks Golf Club with Dingle Bay and the Dingle Peninsula in the distance.

Unless you've smacked a long straight drive, the green may remain hidden on your approach shot too. That can jump-start your pace-maker, when you discover that the green is about the size of a subcompact car and the back edge is cut about six inches from the out-of-bounds fence.

The short par-3 second hole is fairly easy, unless of course you miss the shallow, little domed green, in which case a double bogie is very much in the picture. The third and fourth holes are a pair of par 4s that presage the incredible variety of trouble that lies ahead. Once again, course management will produce better scores than naked aggression.

The par-3 fifth hole—one of three par 3s on the front side—is a lovely one-shot test, well guarded by steep dunes and deep rough. The championship tee sits 194 yards from the green.

The long par-5 eleventh hole requires men and women to clear a no-man's-land of thorny gorse and hip-deep rough before approaching a narrow little Band-Aid of a green. The rest of the back side offers a variety of hills, vales, and tiered and bowl-shaped greens. In 2000, the fourteenth hole was lengthened and made considerably more difficult with the opening of a big, undulating new green that is guarded by a gaping bunker in front.

My favorite is the finishing hole—one of the best in Ireland. The 494-yard, par-5 eighteenth plays uphill from the tee. Your drive is guaranteed to roll sharply to the left if it is not hit right of center, and on the other hand if it is hit too far to the right it will almost certainly find deep rough. There is a marker post visible from the tee box. My advice is to aim slightly to the right of that, unless of course you are like Chi Chi Rodriguez and can pick which sprinkler head you're going to land on.

The green is not visible from the tee, nor from wherever that tee shot comes to rest. Certain points on the fairway may give you a glimpse of the flag, but the green itself is shielded by two huge dunes, something like the grassy humps of a giant green camel. To score requires a long, well-placed drive followed by a lay-up that comes to rest about fifty yards in front of the camelback dunes. Your second shot can be anything from a five wood to a six iron, depending on the wind and the length of your drive. You do not want to play right up to the camelback dunes because they are preceded by a nasty little gully that you can't see until you're almost standing on the edge of it. The approach shot is then a wedge or sand iron over the dunes to the pin.

Big hitters can reach this hole in two, but a long, low shot that clears the dunes will clear the green too. A high second shot risks not clearing the dunes at all and hanging up in their thick, soft grass. The best birdie opportunity comes from a well-struck chip shot.

My one complaint about the layout of Dooks is that the eighteenth green is about 400 yards, on the far side of the first fairway, from the clubhouse. Not only do you have to schlepp your clubs down to your car, but you have to dodge golf balls while you're doing it. It's a minor thing.

Dooks wasn't expanded to eighteen holes until 1970. The name is a word in Irish Gaelic meaning "rabbit warren." The golf course is the natural habitat of the natterjack, an endangered toad, which is the club's symbol.

In the winter of 1994, Dooks undertook an ambitious expansion program. They built an addition to the pleasant bar, added a fine little pro shop, and constructed a large practice green. A subsequent series of upgrades included several strategically placed bunkers and other relatively minor adjustments aimed at improving the playability of the links. No matter what handicap you carry, you can count on a pleasant golfing experience at Dooks.

DOOKS GOLF CLUB (links, par 70)
Location: About four miles from Killorglin (toward Waterville), turn right off the Ring of Kerry Road just before the village of Glenbeigh
Facilities: Practice green, pro shop, bar, restaurant
Green fees: Moderate
Telephone: (066) 976-8205   Fax: (066) 976-8476

hole	par	yards	hole	par	yards
1	4	419	10	4	406
2	3	131	11	5	531
3	4	300	12	4	370
4	4	344	13	3	150
5	3	194	14	4	375
6	4	394	15	3	213
7	5	477	16	4	348
8	4	368	17	4	313
9	3	183	18	5	494
out	34	2,810	in	36	3,200
			TOTAL	70	6,010*

*championship markers

KILLARNEY GOLF & FISHING CLUB

On the edge of the wonderful town of Killarney, on the banks of the brooding lake called Lough Leane, across from the point at which the mountains—Macgillicuddy's Reeks—meet the water, there are two lovely golf courses—Killeen and Mahoney's Point. In 1999, a third course, called Lackabane, was opened across the Killorglin Road, a long track measuring more than 7,000 yards from the championship tees. It's a par 72 for men, 73 for women. The three make up the complex known as the Killarney Golf & Fishing Club.

For many years, from the club's founding in 1893 until the 1960s, there was only one golf course there. Some argued that it was the best parkland course in Ireland. In 1955, PGA champion Gary Player made his first appearance outside South Africa at the old course in Killarney. But if one course was good, two would be better, said some club members and the second course was born. The holes were divvied up between the two tracks and new holes filled in the blanks. Some old-timers still say they ruined a great course by making two lesser ones, but for those of us who never played the old layout, the argument has little merit.

The popularity of the place and of golf itself dictated both the need and the financial viability of the series of expansions—the second eighteen holes, followed by construction of a splendid modern clubhouse, capped by the third eighteen.

Despite my personal penchant for the links courses along Ireland's coasts, these are two fine golf courses, worthy of play. Lackabane has the potential of rivaling the other two, but as this edition goes to press it remains a little raw and immature. If you're staying any length of time in Killarney—and I heartily recommend that you do so—these courses provide a wonderful breather from the arduous nearby links challenges at Tralee, Waterville, Ceann Sibéal, and Ballybunion.

Killeen Course

One of the most picturesque starting holes anywhere is the 332-yard, par-4 first hole on Killarney's Killeen Course. It's a dogleg right that plays along the shore of Lough Leane. With the water lapping almost at its fringe on the right and protected by bunkers on the left, the first green requires an accurate approach in order for you to score.

The lake comes into play on two of the next three holes. The 179-yard, par-3 third hole requires an accurate tee shot across a dimple of the lough. And the short par-4 fourth hole—352 yards—penalizes any shot that strays too far to the right.

Trees guard the fairway along most of the par-4 fifth hole, a 469-yard double dogleg. The hole is a par 5 on the ladies' card and rated among the easier holes. But for men, it's rated the hardest hole on the course. The approach shot requires pinpoint accuracy. An errant shot can easily send your ball down a steep hill into bogie or double-bogie country.

My favorite hole is the par-3 tenth, which is guarded by a small pond, with a wonderful view of Macgillicuddy's Reeks rising beyond

The first green at Killarney's Killeen Course sits on the shore of Lough Leane.

Lough Leane. It's only 164 yards long, but failure to take enough club assures a penalty.

The par-4 seventeenth heads you for home. It's a slight dogleg left that plays a mere 356 yards. The only real trouble is to the right of the green, which is guarded by a stand of ancient evergreens.

The par-4 eighteenth plays toward the lovely clubhouse and watching players approach and putt is a favorite sport of those in the bar enjoying a postround drink. With a small pond protecting the green, the hole is pretty, but easy.

The Killeen Course plays to a par 72 for men and par 74 for women.

Mahoney's Point Course

The Mahoney's Point Course is shorter than Killeen—6,374 yards, compared with 6,579 yards, measured from the men's white markers—but it is the more picturesque of the two, providing delightful views of the lake and mountains from more than half the holes. While the lake only comes into play on the final two Mahoney's Point holes, the course is a solid test with more hills and contours than its twin.

It is tight, and it seems to get tighter each year. Most of the course plays through stands of mature old trees and unforgiving shrubbery that assure that wild shots are punished severely. On both Killeen and Mahoney's Point, the greens are well maintained and loaded with plenty of subtle breaks. They are also difficult to hold and a chip shot directly to the pin can wind up well off the putting surface.

The 542-yard, par-5 eighth—protected by giant old trees along both sides of the fairway—requires three solid golf shots. It is a fine hole. The best test on the course for women is the par-4 fourteenth. It looks serene and easy but plays hard. It is a 307-yard challenge that requires a long, accurate second shot to a well-protected green in order to secure a birdie or par. For all golfers, the downhill sixteenth, a solid par 5 with the lough and mountains behind the green, is simply gorgeous. The seventeenth and eighteenth are delightful finishing holes, with Lough Leane in play along the right length of both.

The demanding par-3 eighteenth plays 177 yards for men and 136 yards for women—and it's almost all carry. The lake protects the front and right of the undulating green; the rest of it is surrounded by jungle. It is a superb way to complete your round, and a par should send you to the clubhouse smiling—although the scenery alone is enough to do that too.

Par for men is 72; par for women is 74.

KILLARNEY GOLF & FISHING CLUB (Killeen Course, parkland, par 72)
Location: Just outside Killarney town on the Killorglin road
Facilities: Practice green, pro shop, a few riding carts, bar, restaurant
Green fees: Expensive
Telephone: (064) 31034   Fax: (064) 33065
E-mail: kgc@iol.ie

The par-3 eighteenth hole at Killarney's Mahoney's Point Course is one of the most spectacular finishers in the country.

hole	par	yards	hole	par	yards
1	4	332	10	3	164
2	4	350	11	5	494
3	3	179	12	4	425
4	4	352	13	4	429
5	4	469	14	4	355
6	3	160	15	4	398
7	5	480	16	5	454
8	4	392	17	4	356
9	4	363	18	4	427
out	35	3,077	in	37	3,502
			TOTAL	72	6,579*

*white markers

KILLARNEY GOLF & FISHING CLUB (Mahoney's Point Course, parkland, par 72)
Green fees: Expensive

hole	par	yards	hole	par	yards
1	4	346	10	4	367
2	4	422	11	4	450
3	4	432	12	3	183
4	3	150	13	5	465
5	5	480	14	4	376
6	4	380	15	4	269
7	3	172	16	5	476
8	5	542	17	4	372
9	4	315	18	3	177
out	36	3,239	in	36	3,135
			TOTAL	72	6,374*

*white markers

RING OF KERRY GOLF & COUNTRY CLUB

When you pull into the parking lot at Ring of Kerry Golf & Country Club, halfway up a mountain on the banks of Kenmare Bay, you know you are in for something very special. The first look back down the mountain reveals a breathtaking scene—the bay with its shimmering water, rocky islands, and the Caha Mountains looming on the other side of the water, all framing a splendid-looking golf course. Your drive up to the clubhouse tells you that the fairways and greens are superbly manicured, the bunkers are wellmaintained and raked, and you are in for a serious test of Irish golf.

By definition, Ring of Kerry is a parkland course, but there are hybrid elements to it. The turf has a linkslike firmness. The mounding, contours, and rocky clusters on the fairways and in the rough, along with nasty patches of gorse and tall grass (typical of links golf courses), make the layout unusual. Add to that the mountain feel of the place (the only place in all of Ireland that offers the kind of mountain golf similar to that which defines such fine U.S. courses as Cascades in Virginia and Castle Pines in Colorado). And finally mix in an abundance of trees, sand, and water to complete the picture. From the standpoint of location, design, topography, and sheer golfability, this is one of the most unique golf courses in Ireland.

It first opened for play in late 1998, designed by champion player Eddie Hackett, one of my all-time favorite Irish golf-course designers. It's a par 72, par 37 on the front—which is actually the shorter of the two nines—and par 35 on the long, tough back side. There are four sets of tees, but unless you're a low-single-digit player the championship blue markers (just shy of 7,000 yards) can well be avoided. Only single-digit-handicap women will really want to move back to the gold markers. My wife, a good player, found the reds (at 5,552 yards) a thoroughly satisfying challenge.

From the first hole, Ring of Kerry will demand your finest shot-making skills, cutting you no slack from the moment you ascend to the opening tee and launch your drive over the lake and up the mountain. The hole measures only 351 yards from the white markers, but it's a steep climb from tee to green. In addition, you have to beware of the stream that intersects the fairway about 100 yards in front of the elevated green and which is invisible until you're nearly standing in it.

The second hole, also a par 4, continues the climb to a multi-tiered green that is all but surrounded by serpentine bunkers. And the comparatively tame par-3 third leads you to a demanding pair of back-to-back par 5s. The long fourth features a pond on the left, just beyond driving distance, that is invisible from the tees. About 85 yards in front of the putting surface there is a gaping bunker that creates the optical illusion that the green is closer than it really is, and it masks the two greenside bunkers that lie in wait for a shot that comes up short.

When you look at the card, your assumption will likely be that even a short hitter will be able to reach the fifth green in two shots, but not so fast! First, your tee shot must split the two fairway bunkers that are just about driving distance for everybody. Then, to give you pause about your second shot, a small rocky pond has been designed about 60 yards from the green, with a deep bunker between the water and the domed, undulating putting surface.

The par-4 sixth, with water on both sides of the fairway, offers a spectacular view of Kenmare Bay and the mountains. For men, the lake on the right is a substantial obstacle; for women, the placement of the red tees has largely taken the lake out of play and at 265 yards it presents a good scoring opportunity. The dogleg right plays to an enormous green that is segmented into three lobes.

The par-3 seventh plays from elevated tees across a heavily mounded wetland and a stream to an elevated and severely contoured green. In fact, the green is so mounded and contoured that it is simply unfair. I am not sure there is a single place on it you can put a reasonable pin placement. The first time my wife and I played the course, we followed a foursome from Cork city. We stood on the tees and watched while one of the men struck his ball no fewer than six times on the green, each time only to have it reach the top of the ridge on which the cup was cut and then roll twenty, thirty, and more feet back to him until it ultimately rolled off the front of the green. I am told that the seventh green is slated for a redesign to level it out a bit. As it is, it's like miniature golf and damages the overall impact and playability of what is otherwise an absolutely sensational golf course.

Once you've finished the seventh you're back into serious stuff.

The *L*-shaped par-5 eighth with a blind tee shot over a ridge is down-hill most of the way. Women should ignore the marker post and aim their tee shots just to the left of the bunker that sits nearly in front of the red markers. The green is hooked almost ninety degrees behind a series of bunkers and an inhospitable wasteland. The short par-4 ninth, with its huge, contoured green, offers a good scoring opportunity at the end of the outgoing side. The biggest problem on the ninth is the lake that runs the entire length of the right side.

Ten and eleven—a long par 4 and a long par 5, respectively—take you back over the lake, up the mountain, and then back down again. The double dogleg eleventh, the number-one handicap hole, begins your descent toward the banks of Kenmare Bay. Your tee shot—which is blind—must both find the fairway and be long enough to prevent you from encountering a blind second as well. There are trees to the left and deep grass on high mounds to the right. The hole opens up and flattens out but then constricts as you head uphill to the elevated and superbly bunkered green. The par-4 twelfth plays downhill to a long, thin green at the base of the hill.

The long, par-3 thirteenth features elevated tees and a drive across a thatch of deep grass and a stream. The hole is over 200 yards for men and a substantial 163 yards for women. The long dog-leg-left, par-4 fourteenth is guarded down its right length by a stream, with the entrance to the green pinched by several bushy old trees on the left and a huge bunker on the right. A stream intersects the par-4 fifteenth at just about driving distance for everybody, but you can't see it from the tees. Your tee shot is blind and either you hit a big one and clear the stream or you take less than a driver and lay it up to the crest of the hill.

Two long, straight par 4s—both tight, demanding, and playing to greens that are all but isolated from the rest of the world by sand—lead to the lovely one-shot finisher. The eighteenth requires all players to clear a lake with their tee shots and find an elevated, extremely well contoured green. (The green is not as unfair as the seventh, but it is certainly one of the most difficult greens in Ireland on which to putt accurately.) If you can finish with one or two putts on this monster, you've accomplished a major feat. Looking back from the multitiered green presents a wonderful panorama of the hole, the bay, and the mountains beyond.

My wife, Barbara, noted that the placement of the women's tees is incredibly well thought out and designed, giving women a fine look at every hole, even where it's a different look than that presented to men. She especially noted the eighteenth, in which a separate island tee box was constructed for women to provide a forced carry over water to the green, just as men face.

Overall the greens at Ring of Kerry are spectacular—superbly maintained, fast, and true. The bunkering is among the best in Ireland (or anywhere in the world, for that matter). The condition of the golf course is exceptional. The water is diabolical with streams, ponds, lakes, marshland, or any combination of them coming into play on fifteen of the eighteen holes. The golf course is sublimely difficult but at the same time extraordinarily fair, with the few exceptions herein noted.

The par-3 eighteenth at Ring of Kerry Golf & Country Club plays uphill, over water and bunkers, to a huge multitiered green.

The bottom line is that Ring of Kerry is a great golf course. Several of our golfing friends in Ireland predict lofty things for it. In fact, the golf course may well be the jewel in the crown of architect Eddie Hackett's lifetime of golfing achievements. Despite the fact that it is not a links, it is an example of the very best in new Irish golf-course design. It retains its Irishness, its Celtic temperament and flavor, its distinct character. And while there are American-style parkland courses that are not worth the time of a visitor from the United States, this Irish gem should be on everybody's short list of superior Irish experiences.

In addition, the lovely new clubhouse offers a well-stocked pro shop and a bar with the unparalleled vista that so dominates the golf course itself.

RING OF KERRY GOLF & COUNTRY CLUB (mountain/parkland, par 72)
Location: About four miles west of Kenmare just off the Ring of Kerry Road
Facilities: Practice green, pro shop, rental clubs, riding carts, bar, restaurant
Green fees: Expensive
Telephone: (064) 42000   Fax: (064) 42533
E-mail: ringofkerrygolf@tinet.ie

hole	par	yards	hole	par	yards
1	4	351	10	4	419
2	4	357	11	5	589
3	3	165	12	4	366
4	5	529	13	3	208
5	5	419	14	4	404
6	4	383	15	4	385
7	3	175	16	4	406
8	5	476	17	4	397
9	4	288	18	3	179
out	37	3,143	in	35	3,353
			TOTAL	72	6,496*

*white markers

TRALEE GOLF CLUB

Arnold Palmer, one of the great legends of the game of golf, had been looking to build a golf course in Europe for several years before a group of Irish business and investment people persuaded him to make the trek to Tralee in the mid-1980s. Upon walking the palisades that overlook the crashing surf and the golden beach at a little town called Barrow, Palmer reportedly said that he had never seen a more perfect place to build a golf course. The Tralee Golf Club was to become Palmer's first European course and one of the best he has designed anywhere. The links preside over the North Atlantic from atop a series of cliffs about a fifteen-minute drive west of Tralee town. The golf course is a testament to Palmer's skill as an architect, a skill born from his love of the game and his ability to attack it and master it as nobody had before he came along.

Palmer laid out the golf course against some of the most majestic and rugged coastline on earth—from the ruins of a Tudor watchtower that once guarded the entrance to a small bay to a gleaming strand that stretches as far as the eye can see.

Part of the movie *Ryan's Daughter* was filmed on that bit of coastline. Some legends say that Saint Brendan—the Irish saint many people believe sailed to North America long before the Vikings—was born near the site of the links.

The weather is always a factor at Tralee. A mild, sunny day can turn into a roaring storm in a matter of minutes, barreling in like a locomotive from the ocean and then blowing out again just as quickly.

The front nine is comparatively flat and gentle, although it plays about 150 yards longer than the back and demands 36 shots to achieve par. The back nine has only one par 5 and is a par 35 for men. (On the women's card it has two par 5s and is a 36.)

The straight-away, par-4 first hole lulls you into a false sense of security. From there it's on to the treacherous and often devastating par-5 second. The wind off the North Atlantic is nearly always in your face as you negotiate the 565-yard curving dogleg right along a palisade that runs from tee to green. If you try to bite off too much of the dogleg on your drive, you're into the rocks. If you bail out too far to the left, you may find yourself stymied on your second shot by a rock wall that once restrained sheep. You will, almost certainly, have two more woods to the green.

The smallish green perches next to the cliff, requiring a well-considered approach. It looks flat and tame from the fairway but gives way to gorse and heather if you stray a wee bit too far right. Of course, if you really slice one it's rocks or beach.

The par-3 third hole—Tralee's signature hole—has been a continuous problem. The original hole was designed to play across a terrifying expanse of rocks (and surf at high tide) to an undulating green. The degree of trouble between player and green diminished exponentially from the championship tee to the ladies' tee, although there was more than enough trouble for everybody. The ideal tee shot was to the left; the fairway sloped sharply onto the surface of the green. A bold shot directly at the pin ran the risk of careening off the back of the green toward the ruins of that Tudor watchtower. (The oceanside cave in *Ryan's Daughter* is directly under the original third green.)

Sadly, the picturesque third was closed so frequently from 1993 through 2000 that a second one-shot hole that officials call "just temporary" was built adjacent to the fourth tees. It seems that when Atlantic storms battered the coast, sea water washed across the original green and killed the grass. After replanting it several times, the club finally constructed a sea wall in an effort to hold back the water, but the problems persist. Unfortunately, without the signature hole, the drama of the front nine is diminished and players are left with an inferior substitute.

The sixth, seventh, and eighth holes are known as "Palmer's loop"—a blind, serpentine par 4, a tricky little par 3, and a treacherous seaside par 4. The third hole of the loop, the eighth, is a sharp dogleg left, with the coastal rocks and crags eager to devour shots that risk cutting too much of the corner. The hole measures 371 yards but the elevated tee creates an optical illusion of shortness. Don't be misled. Many players opt for an iron aimed straight, about 190 or 200 yards out, just short of the hills. That leaves a five or six iron to the undulating green that breaks severely to the bay.

The eighth hole offers a substantial advantage for women because the angle of their tee eliminates much of the dogleg. Nonetheless, most women would be well advised to play for the hills, just below the high rough. That shot will run sharply to the left. A shot straight down the fairway runs the risk of the hillside drawing it so far left it finds the rocks.

Catch your breath on the long, straight, uphill, par-5 ninth because you'll need all your strength, and a good measure of your courage, for what faces you after the turn.

The long eleventh hole, for example, is the only par 5 (for men) on the back. Your tee shot is into a valley; long hitters can think about starting up the hill, if the wind is at your back, which it often is. Then it's up the steep hill to a green that remains hidden until after most players have played their third shots. You don't see the green until you reach the white stone marker in the middle of the fairway at the crest of the hill. (The locals argue that on those rare days when the wind is against you, the eleventh is nearly impossible to par.)

That leads to the par-4 twelfth, a 440-yard monster that gobbles up golf balls and devastates egos. It is justifiably rated the most difficult hole on the course and may be one of the most difficult holes in the world. The jungle of weeds and tall grass on the right and a moonscape of rocks on the left require a tee shot that lands in an area about the size of my dining-room table. (We seat six.) The green is elevated, hidden from the tee, and sits in the crater of a dune. If your approach is even slightly off target to the left it careens down a nearly vertical embankment into an abyss from which some unfortunates have never returned. A shot slightly to the right is likely to lodge your ball in a tangle of deep rough on the hills that guard the green.

The twelfth is a par 4 for women as well, but unless you carry a handicap in the teens or below, you'd be very wise to play the hole conservatively, so you could walk away smiling with a bogie.

But relentless Tralee doesn't ease up there; it charges on as its designer did at the apex of his marvelous playing career. The thirteenth is a short little par 3 that plays from the top of a dune to a wide but shallow green sculpted from the side of a cliff. Between the tees and the green there is nothing but a chasm filled with deep grass, weeds, rocks, and gorse. If you should locate your ball in there, your chances of hitting the green without a howitzer are slim.

The fifteenth, sixteenth, and seventeenth holes play along the cliffs overlooking the sandy beach and ocean, usually dead into the prevailing wind. The sixteenth is a substantial (166 yards) par 3 that is simply a brutal test when the wind is in your face. I've seen many a good golfer hit a driver and come up short. The margin for error is slim and—like its one-shot twin, the thirteenth—it plays across a yawning expanse of wilderness.

The seventeenth lies in wait near the end of the round like an undertaker waiting for his next body. The hole requires a precise drive that stays left, balancing on a tightrope of fairway. The approach to the steeply elevated green, protected by high hills and deep rough, is a mid- to short iron, depending on the velocity of the wind. The view from the seventeenth green is worth all of the agony that can be connected with getting to it—in all directions there is surf crashing onto the shore, a golden ribbon of beach, pastures and fields in various shades of green, and distant farmhouses with peat smoke curling from their chimneys.

Arnold Palmer designed Tralee Golf Club among coastal dunes and sandhills. The par-4 seventeenth green, seen here, sits atop a high hill.

The par-4 eighteenth hole—which is long, but relatively straight and flat from an elevated tee—allows for a little decompression before returning to the clubhouse.

To Palmer's credit, the design pays special attention to women and presents them with hazards and rough that few American courses offer. My wife insists that Tralee is one of the best tests of the game in Ireland and possibly in the entire world for women golfers.

While Irish clubhouses tend toward the utilitarian, the new clubhouse at Tralee is extremely comfortable and pleasant. The second-floor bar and restaurant look out over the eighteenth green and the first tee, toward the cliffs and the strand. It is a charming place to enjoy a pint or a tot of whiskey after the round.

The pro shop is well stocked, by Irish standards. The locker facilities—Spartan when measured against American golf clubs—are luxurious in comparison to much of the rest of Ireland. Tralee boasts a few gas golf carts.

For the above-average golfer, the Tralee Golf Club is exhilarating. For the novice, it may be one to save until you shave a few more strokes off your handicap.

TRALEE GOLF CLUB (links, par 71)
Location: Eight miles from Tralee on the Fenit/Spa Road
Facilities: Practice green, pro shop, a few riding carts, bar, restaurant
Green fees: Very Expensive
Telephone: (066) 713-6379   Fax: (066) 713-6008

hole	par	yards	hole	par	yards
1	4	388	10	4	404
2	5	565	11	5	562
3	3	153	12	4	440
4	4	400	13	3	152
5	4	409	14	4	395
6	4	419	15	4	292
7	3	147	16	3	166
8	4	371	17	4	333
9	5	485	18	4	441
out	36	3,337	in	35	3,185
			TOTAL	71	6,522*

*white markers

WATERVILLE GOLF CLUB

For a while in the 1970s and 1980s it seemed as if every golf book and magazine you picked up had wonderful things to say about the links at Waterville. While it is a good golf course, I have not found it to live up to its press clippings. Perhaps it is a case of having been built up too much. Nonetheless it is worth playing especially if it is combined with a trip around the Ring of Kerry Road.

There is no question that Waterville is long—6,549 yards from the white markers with a par of 72. The back side is simply monstrous, with three par 5s that wind their way among the sandhills. It is a ruggedly beautiful venue, with the sun-dappled water of the North Atlantic lapping at the shore in the distance and with the cottages of herders and fishermen clinging to the Kerry coast. It has hosted some of the top tournaments in Ireland, including the Irish Professional Championship, although much of its thunder has been stolen by newer and often more American-style courses such as the K Club, Mount Juliet, and Druids Glen with which the European PGA players have fallen in love.

Nonetheless, Waterville is home to some interesting and difficult holes. My favorite is the 154-yard, par-3 twelfth, known as the "Mass Hole." Before the Irish revolution, when practicing the Roman Catholic religion was against the law and punishable by death, local citizens would trek out to a remote location near the coast. A priest would celebrate mass in a deep hole among the hills from which the congregants could not be seen from the town; a sentry would sound the alarm if a stranger approached.

The twelfth plays across the Mass Hole from an elevated tee to a fairly generous green. The golf is almost as nifty as the history. If you happen to boot your tee shot into the Mass Hole itself, you will struggle for a bogie or a double.

The par-5 eleventh—just prior to the Mass Hole—is a marvelous challenge by any standard. It requires a pair of long, accurate shots that thread their way between a range of sandy, gorse-laden hills that line both sides of the ribbon-thin fairway. The green sits elevated on a little mesa that requires an approach that is neither too short (it will roll back toward you) nor too long.

The par-3 seventeenth is one of Ireland's most famous golf holes. It plays 153 yards from an elevated tee to a little gem of a green that is surrounded by a jungle of dense and unforgiving grass, gorse, and weeds. The hole is called "Mulcahy's Peak," named for an Irish-American—John Mulcahy—who realized his dream of building this golf course.

Opened in 1972, Waterville is a newcomer when compared to some of its venerable neighbors where golf has been played for a century or more, yet it enjoys a fine reputation, especially among international golf writers. Unfortunately, the bulk of what has been written about Waterville deals with the course as it is prepared for tournaments. Very few people get to play it that way. I confess to more than a slight annoyance when I was informed that the championship markers were "not open" and that the ranger would enforce the fact that they were not available for play. They're never

A narrow ribbon of fairway cut between unfriendly hills leads to the green on Waterville's par-5 eleventh hole.

available unless you happen to be in some kind of championship and I think it's outrageous. I note, however, that several major Irish golf courses adhere to the policy of not allowing play from the championship tees except in certain tournaments.

My regret is that, at Waterville, the disparity between the championship layout and the white markers is tremendous, more noticeable than at any other big-name course, which makes it all the more objectionable. The famous seventeenth, for example, is 196 yards from the blue tees and only 153 from the whites. (It's a scant 100 yards for women and is simply too easy.) I submit that as long as it does not hold up play or damage the course, golfers should be allowed to play whatever tee markers they choose. They are, after all, paying a hefty price for the privilege of playing.

It took me considerable time to analyze why I am less troubled by not being able to play the championship tees at many other courses. Frankly, it makes less difference in how some of these other great courses are attacked, managed, and approached. For example at Lahinch, only about 250 yards in total length separate the blue and white tees; at the long, difficult Donegal Golf Club the difference is slightly more than 300 yards; at Royal County Down it's about 275 yards. But at Waterville, 690 yards separate the blue from the white tees. That is a huge difference.

While so much that has been written about Waterville focuses on the length, it is interesting to note that from the white markers Donegal, Royal County Down, Royal Portrush, Enniscrone, and Portstewart are all longer than Waterville.

In addition, it makes a substantial difference on key holes. On the par-4 second (rated the most difficult hole on the men's card) the blue tees are 44 yards behind the whites. On the eleventh hole the white tees are some 25 yards short of the championship markers and placement on the tee box makes a significant difference in the look of the hole. On the par-4 fourteenth, the difference is 40 yards or more from the front to the back of a lengthy tee box. On the par 3s, Waterville's signature holes, the difference in length is less significant than the placement of the tee boxes themselves. The championship placement gives the golfer a more interesting look at the hole.

I submit that the low handicapper or scratch golfer who plays Waterville from the back tees in a tournament, or who obtains a special dispensation from the pro, the taoiseach (the Irish prime minister), or the pope, gets to experience a magnificent, if grueling, test of the game. But we average humans, who are herded onto the course by the busload and merely pay the bills for the place, are not afforded the same privilege. The tales of the "great length" and the "extraordinary difficulty" of the links are disappointing exaggerations to those who are required to play the abridged edition.

Sadly, it is even worse for women. The regular front tees for women are at best an afterthought and at worst an insult. Some women justifiably complain that the 5,268 yards they play (more than 1,900 yards shorter than the men's championship tees) are a pale imitation of what the course ought to be, and there is no discount at the cash register despite the short change in yardage and challenge.

The women's par at Waterville is 73, compared with 72 for men. On Ceann Sibéal, The European Club, Donegal, and Connemara, women play substantially longer yardage with par of 73 or less. My wife points out that the care given to the obstacles and challenges presented to female golfers and the respect given their abilities by such wonderful courses as Tralee, Rosses Point, Lahinch, Portstewart, and Royal Portrush highlight even further the disparity at Waterville.

While this golf course is important in the history of Irish golf, I am dismayed at the perfunctory treatment given to the people who pony up their punts to play.

It does offer a comfortable and pleasant clubhouse in which to hoist a pint after your game and it has one of the best pro shops in Ireland.

WATERVILLE GOLF CLUB (links, par 72)
Location: About a mile from the Ring of Kerry Road on the north side of Waterville town
Facilities: Practice green, practice tee, pro shop, rental clubs, a few riding carts, bar, restaurant
Green fees: Very Expensive
Telephone: (066) 947-4102   Fax: (066) 947-4482
E-mail: wvgolf@iol.ie

hole	par	yards	hole	par	yards
1	4	395	10	4	475
2	4	425	11	5	477
3	4	362	12	3	154
4	3	160	13	5	480
5	5	525	14	4	410
6	4	343	15	4	365
7	3	155	16	4	330
8	4	410	17	3	153
9	4	405	18	5	550
out	35	3,180	in	37	3,369
			TOTAL	72	6,549*

*white markers

County Louth

COUNTY LOUTH GOLF CLUB

Almost everybody refers to the County Louth Golf Club simply as "Baltray," after the village near the mouth of the river Boyne just outside Drogheda in which it has been a landmark since 1892. "A couple of low handicappers from America swear it's the best links in Ireland," said my friend Brian O'Hara in county Sligo. That may be a stretch, but by any measure it is an extremely good golf course, a classic links that is very long, tight, and demanding. It is 6,612 yards, par 73, from the white markers and 5,873 yards, par 75, for women. Men encounter five par 5s; women have seven.

It is a traditional golf course that has been changed very little over the years. "It was redesigned in 1938 by Tom Simpson [a well-known golf-course architect of the day]," said club manager Michael Delaney, "and that's pretty much the layout we have today."

The course is straightforward and gimmick free. What you see is what you get, and what you get is a superior challenge to both your shot-making ability and your skills at course management. The fact is that length and accuracy are paid large dividends. The long, par-4 first hole—a well-bunkered, dogleg left—presages what is to come. If you don't keep your ball on the fairway, you are in for an arduous time of it; if you don't hit long and straight your score will be in the stratosphere; if you make the mistake of trying to chip directly at the flag (instead of playing a bump-and-run game) you'll end up in another area code.

Back-to-back par 5s follow, with a blind approach awaiting you at the third green. The putting surface is in a basin behind a pair of high sandhills. Aim at the marker post behind the green and you'll probably be putting. Getting on is easier than getting your approach close to the flag, which is a feat I have yet to master.

The fourth is the shortest par 4 on the outgoing side, but what it lacks in length it more than compensates for in topographical obstacles. You drive over a collection of intimidating hills into a field of moguls that guarantee something other than a flat stance for your approach.

The two par 3s on the front are fine one-shot holes, especially the seventh, which features an uphill tee shot to an elevated green. The

Deep bunkers protect the ninth green at County Louth Golf Club.

tees are sheltered from the wind, but the green is exposed, which makes club selection critical. The hole generally plays longer than the yardage would indicate, which is accentuated by the pot bunker fiendishly positioned in front of the putting surface. It is invisible from the tees, but it will snag a ball that comes up short.

The front side finishes with a pair of superb par 4s. The eighth is the most difficult hole on the ladies' card, playing 371 yards from the red markers. The ninth is the number-one stroke hole for men, while it's a relatively easy par 5 for women and offers a good chance for par or birdie.

The back side, the shorter of the two nines, opens with a solid par 4. The par-5 eleventh is a good birdie hole for men, a hole that most players can go for in two. For women, it's a massive 462-yard monster that will require three fine shots to be putting for a birdie. The twelfth is a wonderful par 4, featuring a blind tee shot that must thread its way among the dunes and sandhills. The entrance to the elevated green is pinched by a pair of dunes that require pinpoint accuracy for a successful second-shot approach.

At just 322 yards from the white tees, the fourteenth is the shortest par 4 on Baltray, but like its diminutive cousin on the front nine, it's a tricky, tough little hole. "People talk more about that hole than any other," said manager Michael Delaney. It's called *The Cup* on the card and that accurately describes what the green is like, a speck of a thing embraced and surrounded by hills and high grass. "Some people will try to drive the green, but you see a lot more sixes than threes," Delaney added with a broad grin.

The three finishers will examine just how good your game really is. The sixteenth is a long par 4 with a green that is well protected and hard to hit. The seventeenth is a long par 3, one of the few one-shot holes in Ireland—or anywhere else I can think of—where the men's white markers are closer to the green than the women's tee. (The hole is 169 yards from the whites and 173 from the reds.) It was at this point that my wife, Barbara, opined that Baltray is a substantially tougher course for women than for men. She also noted that a majority of the par 4s required her to hit two good wood shots to find the greens in regulation. The par-5 eighteenth is a solid three-shot hole for everybody.

While County Louth Golf Club has got a large and active membership and is a popular venue for players from Dublin and environs, I find it remarkable how undiscovered the course is, even among Irish golfers outside the immediate area. Few Americans have ever heard of it. Despite boasting more than a century in play, the venerable links simply hasn't garnered the kind of publicity its more famous neighbors—such as Portmarnock, a few miles south, and Royal County Down, a few miles north—have enjoyed. Nonetheless it is worth a detour to try your skill against this course they call Baltray.

COUNTY LOUTH GOLF CLUB (links, par 73)
Location: About five miles northeast of Drogheda in the village of
   Baltray
Facilities: Practice green, practice tee, pro shop, bar, restaurant
Green fees: Expensive
Telephone: (041) 982-2329   Fax: (041) 982-2969
E-mail: Baltray@indigo.ie

hole	par	yards	hole	par	yards
1	4	423	10	4	388
2	5	476	11	5	476
3	5	534	12	4	410
4	4	334	13	4	408
5	3	148	14	4	322
6	5	521	15	3	142
7	3	153	16	4	375
8	4	397	17	3	169
9	4	409	18	5	527
out	37	3,395	in	36	3,217
			TOTAL	73	6,612*

*white markers

County Sligo

COUNTY SLIGO GOLF CLUB

The grave of the poet William Butler Yeats lies "under bare Ben Bulben's head," as he said in his own epitaph, in the tiny Drumcliff village churchyard across a finger of Sligo Bay from the County Sligo Golf Club. You can see the cottages of Drumcliff in the shadow of the mountain Ben Bulben from at least nine of the eighteen holes at this venerable legendary links.

That mountain is the heart of county Sligo. The images of that part of the world, the metaphors, the Celtic mythology, and allusions to the people and the places of northwestern Ireland repeat themselves throughout Yeats' works.

Ben Bulben's character changes with the seasons and the sun. It broods. It smiles. It dominates the landscape. And nowhere is its presence more evident, more pervasive, more awe inspiring, than from the links of County Sligo Golf Club.

Until you get to the second green, the mountain is hidden from view like a timid child unwilling to come and play with the others. It's not until you climb to the fifth tee that its full impact assaults the eye like the village bully, taking the landscape under its command and demanding your attention as you see its full length and height looming across a shimmering slip of the bay. From the fifth hole on, the face of Ben Bulben oversees your progress on virtually every hole, every shot, until you again play over the cliff and back down the slope to the clubhouse on the short, par-4 eighteenth hole.

County Sligo Golf Club (which most golfers simply call Rosses Point) is visually deceptive. What the eye sees is not necessarily a true picture. The fairways look relatively flat, the bunkers look fairly shallow, and the rough looks manageable. The fact is, if you want to score well, you simply must stay out of the bunkers, avoid the rough at all costs, and keep the ball in the short grass. That is more easily said than done and requires profound concentration and skilled execution. The penalties for being too bold, for straying too far, or for trying shots beyond your capabilities can be severe. A bad gamble can result in a double bogie and sometimes in double digits.

The first two holes, both short par 4s, are misleading in that they play straight uphill, with the narrow fairways guarded by deep and nasty rough. The par-5 third hole, nearly 500 yards from tee to green, requires a long drive from an elevated tee over a daunting stretch of rocks and gnarled grasses. (Women are given a slight advantage in terms of the distance they must carry, but for men and women—with the exception of a few pros—it takes three good shots to get into scoring position.)

From the relatively easy par-3 fourth hole, you climb to the fifth tee. The fifth tee, with that unbelievable view of Ben Bulben, hugs the top of a sheer cliff, playing to a tiny green 468 yards away. It's a par 5 that's reachable in two shots if the wind is at your back and that can play like a par 6 if the wind is in your face. It is appropriately named *The Jump* on the scorecard. Your drive launches like a jet catapulting off the deck of an aircraft carrier and a good hit is rewarded with a little extra carry and a little extra roll on the straight, flat fairway.

The sixth, seventh, and eighth holes are wonderful par 4s, leading to the 151-yard, par-3 ninth, which requires an exacting tee shot. The tiered tees play across the side of an unforgiving hill of rocks, gorse, and deep grass to a green that seems arbitrarily to spit imperfectly struck golf balls into the punishing unknown. Pinpoint accuracy can yield birdies and pars, but banishment into the grass and weeds can produce double and triple bogies in the blink of an eye.

The par-4 tenth hole is tucked down a short path beyond the twelfth tee and can be missed if you're not mindful of where you're going. The tenth, named *Ben Bulben* on the scorecard, is a gentle dogleg to the right from an elevated tee that plays to a concealed green, the farthest point away from the clubhouse that you can get and the closest point to its namesake mountain.

The eleventh is one of the toughest holes on the links. It is a 400-yard, par-4 dogleg right. Your tee shot plays uphill and must be kept to the left side of the fairway, a fairway that is pitched like an oval sports-car raceway to the right. Every shot will roll right. A drive that is not left of center has a very good chance of rolling right off the fairway and down the even more steeply pitched hill at the edge into thigh-deep grass. If that happens, getting enough club onto the ball to get it to the green requires a level of strength few, if any, players possess.

Even a good drive that stays in the fairway sets up a long iron to a thin little green protected by rough in the back and bunkers,

steep hills, and scrub to the front and right. (You're better off drib-
bling a shot along the ground to the left than missing the green in
any manner, shape, or form to the front or right.)

The par-5 twelfth, again, is short and can be reached in two and
the par-3 thirteenth hole offers a brief respite before the finishing
five.

The 393-yard, par-4 fourteenth hole requires exceptional accuracy. Your drive must cross a ditch and an expanse of wasteland to a
landing area that is protected by trouble on all four sides. If you
must err on your approach to the green, take too much club and be
long. A short shot will find another stretch of ditch, gorse, heather,
rocks, and slag. Anything short and right will cost at least one
stroke, assuming you find your ball.

The fifteenth is about the same length as its predecessor, a par 4
that plays down a narrow funnel of fairway about as wide as a two-
lane road. Again the long, constricted green is heavily protected
and punishes imprecision.

The par-3 sixteenth measures 215 yards from the back tees, 188
yards from the white markers. Club selection depends on the direction and velocity of the wind, which more often than not comes
blustering off the ocean and into your face. The hole is guarded
along the right side for its entire length by a berm separating the
golf course from the beach. Across the berm is out of bounds.

With Ben Bulben looking over your shoulder, the par-4 seventeenth hole is spectacular. "It is one of the best golf holes in Ireland,"
said former European touring pro Sean Browne, now head pro at
Navan Golf Club in county Meath. It's a long, undulating obstacle
course that yields precious few birdies and sends more golfers than
you can imagine to the eighteenth with their heads hanging like
tired dogs.

The tee shot on seventeen plays downhill toward a gully. The
expanse to the gully is open and forgiving, save for the fact that if
you're too short (playing most of the time into the wind) you have
no shot to the hidden, tiered, treacherous green. That elevated
green is protected on three sides by sheer, rocky hills and in front
by an incline steep enough to send your ball right back toward you
if you come up short. Your tee shot should just make it over the
ledge leading to the gully, which channels your ball into a tiny landing

area, about the size of a beach towel. That gives you a glimpse of the flag stick. A tee shot that is too long slides off the fairway into that awful rough. A shot too far left leaves an almost impossible approach over a nasty, snarling little hill. A shot too far right finds the rough and leaves more than 200 yards straight uphill to the green with that slippery incline in front to negotiate.

The eighteenth tee shot is completely blind, not quite over the seventeenth green. It plays over a rocky cliff and then rolls downhill. A good drive will leave you a nine iron or wedge to the green, but a short drive will send you scrabbling like a mountain goat along the face of the cliff and leave you with an almost vertical recovery—if you can play your ball at all.

Many players consider the seventeenth at County Sligo Golf Club—with its blind tee shot and the green on a shelf midway up a severe hill—to be one of the hardest par 4s in Ireland.

Rosses Point is an all-around excellent test of the game. It requires a vast variety of shots, and calls on the player to think through each hole. While it is not the longest course in Ireland—measuring only 6,319 yards from the middle tees—it is among the most demanding.

It is also a friendly place, the course and the town. It is understandable why Yeats wrote of the area with such fondness. The bar and restaurant look out on the first tee and provide a popular gathering place. The pro shop is well stocked and usually offers a selection of fine woolen sweaters with the County Sligo Golf Club logo on them.

COUNTY SLIGO GOLF CLUB (links, par 71)
Location: About five miles from Sligo town, toward Donegal off
    the N15, and left at the sign to Rosses Point
Facilities: Practice green, practice tee, pro shop, a few riding carts,
    bar, restaurant
Green fees: Expensive
Telephone: (071) 77186 or 77134   Fax: (071) 77460
E-mail: cosligo@iol.ie

hole	par	yards	hole	par	yards
1	4	371	10	4	379
2	4	298	11	4	400
3	5	490	12	5	482
4	3	165	13	3	171
5	5	468	14	4	393
6	4	371	15	4	395
7	4	412	16	3	188
8	4	409	17	4	421
9	3	151	18	4	355
out	36	3,135	in	35	3,184
			TOTAL	71	6,319*

*white markers

ENNISCRONE GOLF CLUB

When I told my friend Brian O'Hara about this book, he immediately said, "You must play Enniscrone. It's an excellent course and the greens are superb!" He was right. In fact, the greens at Enniscrone are among the best in Ireland. They are wonderfully maintained, fast, true, and tricky. When legendary Irish golf-course architect Eddie Hackett redesigned the course, expanding it from a nine-hole to an eighteen-hole track in 1974, he paid special attention to the greens. Not only do they vary in size and shape, to fit the terrain, but they are full of contours and undulation.

Unlike the greens on many links courses, these greens hold surprisingly well. That does not imply that you should play for the pin. No sir. It simply means that you don't have to play every approach twenty to thirty yards short. If the pin is on the back half of the green, you can risk playing your approach shot to the front of the putting surface, depending how high you bring it in.

The golf course plays out to the tip of the Bartragh Peninsula, with Killala Bay on three sides, although the water is less a factor than the steep, treacherous coastal dunes. It sits at the edge of the village of Enniscrone. (It's occasionally spelled with an *I* on some older maps and road signs.)

Three of the first four holes are par 5s—551 yards, 535 yards, and 524 yards respectively. The first and second holes are relatively open and flat and lead the unsuspecting player to believe that Enniscrone is going to be an easy little walk in the park. But each succeeding hole becomes a little more challenging. The fourth hole is an especially testing par 5 for women. It plays 485 yards from the red markers and requires three long and precise shots to dodge trouble and reach the green.

By the time you stand on the elevated seventh tee, you know you're heading into the badlands with a posse on your tail and nothing but woe ahead. The seventh is a tight little par 4 that requires a well-placed tee shot that comes to rest somewhere between the rows of deep, nasty pot bunkers—five of them on each side—lining the fairway. If you're skilled enough to find the short grass, you'll have a midiron left with which to reach the green.

The seventh begins a difficult seven-hole stretch. These holes—which are made all the more devilish depending on the direction and velocity of the wind—offer a superb example of links golf at its finest. Each shot is critical to scoring. Errant shots are punished severely and well-considered and -executed shots are rewarded. Pars are highly satisfying; birdies are rare; bogies and worse appear with regularity.

The par-3 eighth is a wonderful little hole. It plays 170 yards across a deep valley to a green precariously balanced on a ledge with an escarpment above and left and below to the right.

The ninth is a splendid par 4. Men must hit a blind tee shot to a small landing area; women face a difficult tee shot that—while it's not blind—nonetheless requires careful placement in order to avoid the deep chasm in front of the green. The green itself is cut about halfway up a steep hill. A shot that is too short will not reach the target and runs the risk of rolling back down the severe incline; a shot that's too long will be smothered and imprisoned in the long grass.

The 338-yard, par-4 tenth also presents a blind tee shot, across a wilderness of deep grass and weeds. The dogleg right allows the truly long hitters to cut the corner and put the ball right in front of the green. Unless you're John Daly or Laura Davies, the better play is a long iron or fairway wood straight down the middle, which will leave a mid- to short iron to the green.

The twelfth is a 510-yard par 5 for men and is a thoroughly manageable par hole, but it is a 358-yard par 4 from the red markers and rated the toughest hole on the course on the ladies' card. It's a dogleg left and demands a huge shot from an elevated tee to set up a par.

The long par-3 thirteenth plays just over 200 yards straight uphill, with a tight out of bounds on the left. The undulating green offers a spectacular panorama, but don't let it distract you from the task at hand.

My favorite hole is the 373-yard, par-4 sixteenth. This severe dogleg right—almost a right angle—requires a tee shot that plays past the clubhouse. Trying to cut the corner is enormously risky, as the out-of-bounds line comes into play for nearly 200 yards before the hole opens up. The second shot plays up an ever-narrowing chute to an elevated green that's difficult to read.

The par-3 seventeenth plays from the top of one sandhill to the top of another, with virtually nothing in between from which you would want to try to hit a second shot.

The eighteenth features another blind tee shot over a substantial hill to a small landing area. The green, however, is large and relatively flat and offers good par and birdie opportunities for the player who has hit a solid drive.

The pro shop is well stocked; the clubhouse is modern and welcoming. If there is a drawback to Enniscrone it is that it has been discovered. It is a popular venue both for local golfing societies and for visitors from Europe and the U.S. Advance booking is essential, especially in the summer months.

ENNISCRONE GOLF CLUB (links, par 72)
Location: About ten miles north of Ballina in the village of
    Enniscrone

The narrow approach to the sixteenth green at Enniscrone Golf Club is straight uphill.

Facilities: Practice green, practice ground, pro shop, bar, restaurant

Green fees: Expensive

Telephone: (096) 36297   Fax: (096) 36657

E-mail: enniscronegolf@linet.ie

hole	par	yards	hole	par	yards
1	5	551	10	4	338
2	5	535	11	4	424
3	4	395	12	5	510
4	5	524	13	3	202
5	3	170	14	4	368
6	4	395	15	4	412
7	4	359	16	4	373
8	3	170	17	3	149
9	4	345	18	4	400
out	37	3,444	in	35	3,176
			TOTAL	72	6,620*

*white markers

County Wicklow

BLAINROE GOLF CLUB

The Irish Sea coastline from Wicklow town to Arklow town may be some of the prettiest country in all of Ireland. While there are stretches of rocks, towering dunes, and forbidding cliffs, there are also long stretches of golden beach bounded by lush farmland. About three miles south of the brutal, hilly challenge of the Wicklow Golf Club is a wonderful course that is about as opposite in character and design as you can get.

The Blainroe Golf Club is built along about a mile of the coast. Most of the front nine plays inland up and down a steep hill that rises more than three hundred feet above sea level and provides an unparalleled view of the Irish Sea and the surrounding landscape.

It is considered a parkland course, although the short par-4 four-teenth hole and the par-5 finisher play right along the water's edge and have the feel of links golf. While Blainroe has not been tapped for any major championships, it is a fine test, requiring course management, shot control, and careful club selection on virtually every hole. While only the hilly topography and the scenery will leave you breathless, golfers of all levels will have to use almost every club in the bag to score well. The club has a large private membership and members express considerable pride in their golf course.

The par-4 first hole is level, sanguine, and short. The next seven holes will test both your skill and stamina. The 433-yard, par-4 second—which begins your ascent up that dominating hill on which most of the front side is played—features a tight out of bounds on the left and bowers of trees on the right. The only place to be is in the fairway.

The dogleg-right, par-4 third plays to a long, narrow green. The side of the green slopes away almost vertically if your shot is errant to the right.

The back-to-back par 5s that follow—a 527-yard dogleg left and a 489-yard dogleg right respectively—are both intersected by a series of ancient trees and a formidable berm. They require well-placed tee shots if you want to think about going for either in two. While women are given a substantial length advantage on both, they must place their drives carefully in order not to be stymied by the trees for their lay-up second shots.

The fourth green is well protected by carefully placed trees and bunkers and the fifth plays to a tiny, elevated green. The fourth is rated as the hardest hole on the course on the women's card and has richly earned that position.

My favorite hole is the par-4 sixth. Its length—364 yards—is profoundly misleading. The blind tee shot plays along a left-sloping uphill fairway to an almost ninety-degree dogleg right. There is a stretch of out of bounds within a few yards of the right side of the fairway all the way up to the point that it turns toward the green. Cutting the corner is perilous at best, foolish for all but the biggest hitters.

Once you have a clear shot at the green it is straight up the hill at a severe angle. To make it even more treacherous, the green is sloped back toward the fairway at only a slightly gentler angle than the fairway itself. Do not get above the hole! The first time I played it, I put an overeager chip shot about ten feet beyond the pin and proceeded to roll my putt about 30 feet back off the green. The only reason it came to a halt was because it found a divot big enough to stop it. Memory—refreshed by long habit of keeping old scorecards—tells me that I rescued a seven, by virtue of sinking a six-foot putt.

The par-3 eighth is an easy little hole, but affords one of the finest coastal views anywhere. The elevated tee (which plays down a steep section of the hill to a fairly generous green) looks over the bulk of the front nine and the Irish Sea coast to the clubhouse and beyond. On a clear day you can see ships plying the waters offshore and sheep and cows grazing on the checkerboard of nearby fields. It is simply a lovely, pastoral scene well worth an extra moment or even a photograph if you happened to bring a camera along.

The par-4 tenth hole requires as much accuracy off the tee as any hole on the back side. It's a 378-yard dogleg right that calls for an opening shot through a chute of trees, across the driveway from the main road to the clubhouse. The shot must be played far enough to the left to take a clump of towering ancient trees out of play on your approach to the smallish green.

The par-3 fifteenth hole, for my money, is the hardest hole on the back side on which to score. It plays 228 yards from the championship markers, and the bulk of the shot must carry a small lake.

(Women get a substantial break, but still must carry the majority of 152 yards.) If you can find the green with your tee shot, par is fairly easy; if you miss the green, par is elusive.

The scorecard rates the sixteenth as the toughest hole on the course. It's a fairly straight par 4 that plays long, 458 yards. But it's a very makeable par, even with a wind. It is one of two par 4s on the men's card that are par 5s for women. The fact that it plays downhill and measures only 394 yards from the ladies' tees renders it reachable in two with a big drive in the center of the fairway.

The 491-yard, par-5 finishing hole is also straight and reachable, even for a moderate hitter, in two. (Women are given enough of a length advantage that two long shots will put you tight, if not on, and afford a great scoring chance.) The eighteenth and the short,

The par-3 eighth hole at Blainroe Golf Club plays from tees high on a hill—featuring a splendid panorama of the Irish Sea coast—to a green far below.

easy par-3 seventeenth offer good opportunities for a strong finish to your round at Blainroe.

On paper, Blainroe is only moderately difficult. Nonetheless, there are only three par 3s on the course, and two of them exceed 200 yards. The front side plays out to a par 37 over severely sloped and canted terrain. I usually play Blainroe about midtrip and thoroughly enjoy the change of pace. To play it is pleasing to the senses and it rewards good shot making.

The clubhouse bar offers a delightful view of the eighteenth green and the Irish Sea as you tuck into a pint after your round.

BLAINROE GOLF CLUB (parkland, par 72)
Location: About three miles south of Wicklow town on the coast
    road
Facilities: Practice green, pro shop, bar, restaurant
Green fees: Moderate
Telephone: (0404) 68168   Fax: (0404) 69369

hole	par	yards	hole	par	yards
1	4	362	10	4	378
2	4	433	11	4	391
3	4	422	12	4	428
4	5	527	13	4	398
5	5	489	14	4	333
6	4	364	15	3	228
7	4	371	16	4	458
8	3	212	17	3	123
9	4	368	18	5	491
out	37	3,548	in	35	3,228
			TOTAL	72	6,776*

*championship markers

THE EUROPEAN CLUB

Long before the time of Saint Brendan, even longer before the days when the Danish king, Sitric, ruled Dublin, there was a lovely stretch of sand dunes and coastal grassland along the Irish Sea at a place that came to be known as Brittas Bay. In the mid-1980s, an Irish golf writer, golf promoter, and golf lover named Pat Ruddy flew over that bit of real estate and had a vision. He saw a nearly perfect place to construct a links golf course. That vision is now a reality. The European Club, only open for a few years, is the first links to be built on the Irish Sea coast since the end of World War II.

Tall grass and deep bunkers await shots that stray from the fairway at The European Club. The par-3 second green is seen here in the foreground with the well-bunkered first hole in the distance.

What Pat Ruddy did was to borrow liberally from such legendary golf-course architects as Old Tom Morris, Harry Colt, and Dr. Alister MacKenzie, add elements used by such modern designers as Pete Dye and Robert Trent Jones, and stir it all together with his own genius to create one of the best golf courses in the world. The thought and creativity that went into the layout of The European Club is nothing short of a marvel.

From the incredibly skilled placement of bunkers to the huge undulating greens to the serpentine track along the coast, among the dunes and marshes, it's a knockout. Not only is it a delight to play, but some of the holes also feature a breathtaking feast for the eye.

This is not a course for the high handicapper or beginner. Quite simply, it is too difficult. For men it will test the shot making and strategy of the very best players, while it is fair and fun for the good-to-average club player. For women, however, it may be one of the world's most challenging golf courses on which to score well. Any woman who shoots to her handicap will have accomplished a major feat. The cards for men and women both reflect a par 71, with only two par 5s and three par 3s. The thirteen par 4s offer an enormous variety and will require players of both sexes to use virtually every club in the bag, and to invent some shots as well.

The pitch-and-run or bump-and-run shot is an essential tool, as is the ability to hit the ball long and straight off the tee. If you fear sand, take something to calm your nerves before you tee off. The par-3 second hole is a lovely example of the tricky bunkering all over the course. Three deep little bunkers guard the front of the smallish green and a long, narrow trap is just grinning there to catch any shot that strays too far left.

Some players call the 400-yard, par-4 seventh hole—rated the toughest on the course—"death row." It features a water hazard along its length to the right and a huge marsh to the left. Don't let your eye mislead you; the front edge of the marsh is far enough away that only a massive drive will reach it. If you are concerned you'll get there off the tee, hit a three wood or a long iron. But beware that such caution will leave you a long way from the well-protected green for your second shot. When the prevailing wind is against you, hit your longest club and hit it hard.

My favorite hole is the par-4 eighth, a long dogleg right that plays into a little valley between dunes. A good drive will open the elevated, undulating green for your approach. If you don't make it into the valley, however, consider a lay-up. Too much boldness will more often than not lead to a bogie, double, or worse. The approach to the green is through a funnel. A shot that's wide right, wide left, or too short lands in a wilderness of ball-gobbling long grass on hills so steep that if you can find the ball it may well be at shoulder level when you try to hit it. And once you get to the green, your troubles aren't over. Get your putter ready for a workout. The green is fraught with subtle and not-so-subtle breaks and bumps that can turn a twelve footer into a three-putt disaster with lightning speed.

The 400-yard, par-4 twelfth plays along the Irish Sea, a gentle dogleg left. There's a hidden indentation in front of the brilliantly protected green in which Pat Ruddy dropped two nasty little bunkers. That indentation creates the optical illusion that the green is closer to you than it really is as you select your club for your second shot.

The four grueling par 4s that complete the round conclude with one of the nicest finishing holes anywhere. It's a dogleg left that plays through a narrow strip of fairway to a green 385 yards away from the men's white markers. In front of the green is a lovely little manmade pond originating from a spring-fed marsh near the entrance to the clubhouse. The wide but shallow green is hard to hold and getting your approach shot close to the pin is quite a trick, especially if it's tucked to the left. A mid- to short iron over the water is a nail biter if your tee shot is less than precise. Many women end up playing the 345 yards more like a par 5, hoping to get a lay-up third shot close enough to save the par.

Every now and then, Pat Ruddy does something that baffles me. In 1998, he added two new holes to the layout—a pair of par 3s—one on the front and another on the back, so if you want you can play The European Club as a twenty-hole golf course. I'm not quite sure why. On the other hand he continuously strives to improve his course. While he was building the two new holes, he added several new tee boxes for women, rendering the course much more playable for them. A particularly brilliant design was the elevated ladies' tee on the seventeenth hole. It shaves off enough yardage to make the green reachable in regulation for most women, providing a new look and an entirely new dimension to the hole.

Over all, The European Club yields up pars and birdies only grudgingly and to have played it well produces immense satisfaction. Unfortunately the clubhouse does not have a bar, although you can get beer or wine, nor does it have a complete pro shop. Nonetheless, the brilliance of The European Club is the golf course itself.

THE EUROPEAN CLUB (links, par 71)
Location: Between Wicklow town and Arklow on the coast road
Facilities: Practice greens, restaurant, beer and wine only
Green fees: Very Expensive
Telephone: (0404) 47415   Fax: (0404) 47449

hole	par	yards	hole	par	yards
1	4	370	10	4	395
2	3	150	11	4	375
3	5	470	12	4	400
4	4	410	13	5	530
5	4	385	14	3	155
6	3	175	15	4	365
7	4	400	16	4	345
8	4	395	17	4	375
9	4	375	18	4	385
out	35	3,130	in	36	3,325
			TOTAL	71	6,455*

*white markers

WICKLOW GOLF CLUB

The par-5 first hole at the Wicklow Golf Club is as glorious a starting hole as there is. The elevated tee sits above Wicklow Head, looking out toward the ruins of the castle, which used to guard the entrance to Wicklow Harbor. Cargo ships can be seen gliding into and out of the busy port. The landscape is rugged. Just a glance previews the perils that lurk on each hole to challenge and bedevil the unwary.

The golf course, which has been there in some form since 1904, plays along the rocky dunes of the Irish Sea coast, a layout that is unlikely to offer more than a dozen flat lies or level stances in your entire eighteen holes. If you were a skier, you would say the moguls

The back nine at Wicklow Golf Club is constructed on the side of a series of craggy hills along the Irish Sea.

alone would qualify most fairways as expert slopes. The rough varies from extremely difficult to simply unplayable. Scrub-brush, rocks, lichen-covered boulders, dunes as tall as a three-story house, and deep, deep grass are the rule. Mischievously placed plantings of bushes and trees add to the difficulty.

The golf course is laid out on a series of hills that were once farm-land or pasture. The nature of the soil and the number of trees and bushes technically make it a parkland course. After several spirited discussions, I concede the technicality, but the course is right along the coast (like a links course), the turf is firm and it drains as if it were built on sand (like a links course), and the greens require more bump-and-run than lofted approaches (like a links course). I submit that, the technicality notwithstanding, the way the course feels and plays is quintessential links. The look of the place is, at least to an American visitor, like a links golf course. I have yet to find another parkland-type golf course that is anything like it. So for those reasons I include it and recommend it among the Irish links, even though the definition here will be challenged by some Old World purists. I yield to them only by calling it a hybrid.

For ninety years, the Wicklow Golf Club was a nine-hole track that you played twice to get in your eighteen-hole round. It always made my itinerary, even then. But in 1994 the brand-new second nine opened to unveil an absolutely stunning and brutally difficult par-71, eighteen-hole course. Unlike many new or expanded golf courses, the new holes at Wicklow were mature and well maintained from the first day play was allowed. They were not opened until they were primed and ready. The new greens proved to be true and fast, and have remained so. Unless you knew the history of the place, it would never occur to you that the second nine is so much younger than the first.

The golf-course architects—Pat Ruddy (designer of The European Club, just down the road) and Tom Craddock (who teamed with Ruddy on Druids Glen and the Glashedy Links at Ballyliffin)—and their grounds crew did nothing less then a spec-tacular job in designing, preparing, and nurturing the new holes.

I was bowed and humbled by the new nine the first time I played it. It was as difficult a test of the game as I ever experienced, and my opinion is unchanged, although maturity has taken some of the edge off and made the back nine at Wicklow substantially more playable. The old front nine, the original layout, retains the rugged charm that old timers like me found so attractive in the first place. It's like a quirky old friend. I have always liked the feel of those holes, their subtleties always ready to pounce upon you at the moment you least expect it. I like the trickiness of their design and the unperceived difficulties that only reveal themselves after you are up to your knees in them.

The second hole may provide the greatest challenge of any on the course for women. It is a 391-yard hole from the forward tees that plays more like a par 5 than a par 4 for most female golfers. The dogleg left hugs the coast and plays to a well-protected green at the edge of a small, rocky inlet.

For men and women alike, the front side is dominated by short par 4s that favor skilled shot selection over length and that reward cerebral prowess over brawn. The 277-yard third is an example. It requires a well-placed drive over a small inlet from one jut of land to a narrow fairway. The kidney-shaped green is jealously protected by high dunes and scrub bowers. A misplaced tee shot, right or left, renders a successful approach almost impossible.

One of my favorite tees anywhere is the fourth at Wicklow. It is so close to the edge of the Irish Sea that on a windy day when the tide is coming in you can feel the spray as the water meets the rocks. The 311-yard fourth is a deceptive and devilish hole that plays straight up a steep hill to a hidden green. Most of the locals use a lofted wood (like a seven) or a four or five iron to put the ball into position. Even the strongest hitters are overpowered by gravity and can't propel the ball up the hill to the green. A long shot that drifts right will reveal the fact that the fairway is angled in such a way that a shot that's too strong will almost certainly cascade down the far side of the tiny landing area into more unplayable misery. There is something of a bailout area to the left, but the grass is so tall that it is difficult to pull the club through the next shot with enough power to get the ball to its target.

The short par-4 fifth hole (which plays only 316 yards from the championship tees) reminds an overzealous big hitter that course management is sometimes the better option than muscle. The hole is pitched severely downhill and its shortness tempts even medium-length hitters, like a siren, to pull out the big stick and go for it. The problem lies in the fact that the green is canted away from you and behind the green the next point of dry land is Wales.

The 155-yard, par-3 ninth hole (one of the easiest holes on the course) plays close enough to the clubhouse that you can run in for something fortifying after you've scaled and descended the hills of the front side.

The back nine is longer and, if possible, even hillier than the front. A Rocky Mountain bighorn sheep would feel right at home. Golfers, brace yourselves!

The 369-yard, par-4 tenth hole is rated as the third hardest on the course and I'm not sure why. It's a gentle dogleg right that plays along the side of a hill to a long narrow green. A good drive can straighten out much of the dogleg and a good second ought to leave you a birdie putt.

The 191-yard, par-3 eleventh is the most difficult one-shot hole on the course. It plays from an elevated tee to a precariously situated green that leaves precious little margin for error. The carry includes a rocky gulch, a manmade pond, and a jungle of nasty and mean-spirited foliage that is unlikely to yield back your golf ball if you should mis-hit your tee shot. For women, this is an extremely difficult 166-yard hole that requires about a 140-yard carry from a tee that is less elevated than the men's.

The twelfth, thirteenth, and fourteenth—a pair of longish par 4s and a long par 5 (552 yards from the championship markers)—play out and back to the farthest points from the clubhouse. This used to be unhewn pasture on which sheep grazed. The rocky shoreline comes into play only with the wildest of shots, but on eleven and twelve the fairway slopes severely left, toward the Irish Sea. Coming back on thirteen the slope is to the right.

The thirteenth cuts women a little slack. The forward tees are nearly 60 yards ahead of the men's markers, leaving women only 295 yards to navigate. A creek and lake come into play in about the middle of the par-5 sixteenth hole, which leads to the lovely par-3 seventeenth. The tee shot must clear a manmade pond (one of three tucked down in the ravine from which the hole is cut) to a green protected by a cliff on the left and rear. There's water on the right front. The hole looks shorter than it plays. Do not be misled into hitting too little club.

The short par-4 eighteenth plays back to the clubhouse along the top of the hillside on which much of the back nine is designed.

The clubhouse offers a pleasant bar that's a local gathering place. There's a kitchen, but snacks and sandwiches are the normal fare. A pro shop was constructed in 1999, replacing the old starter's window by the first tee.

I have used championship yardage throughout this profile of the Wicklow Golf Club. Most men whose handicaps are 15 or below will feel comfortable playing the back tees on the front, but beware of the back. It is a grueling test from the blue tees. My advice is to try the blue markers if your handicap is 10 or less; otherwise, put your ego in your golf bag and play the whites.

Sundays are generally not open to visitors. The male club members have a competition virtually every Sunday, year round.

Nonetheless, the expanded and tremendously difficult Wicklow Golf Club is worth a special detour.

WICKLOW GOLF CLUB (parkland/links, par 71)
Location: About a quarter-mile south of Wicklow town just off
  Dunbur Road
Facilities: Pro shop, practice green, bar, snacks
Green fees: Inexpensive
Telephone: (0404) 67379   Fax: (0404) 66122

hole	par	yards	hole	par	yards
1	5	531	10	4	369
2	4	408	11	3	191
3	4	277	12	4	412
4	4	311	13	4	356
5	4	316	14	5	552
6	4	415	15	4	370
7	3	142	16	5	522
8	4	383	17	3	165
9	3	155	18	4	353
out	35	2,938	in	36	3,290

TOTAL   71   6,228*
*championship markers

NORTHERN IRELAND

They call it "Calamity" for what it can do to your score. The long par-3 fourteenth on the Dunluce Links at Royal Portrush Golf Club is one of the most difficult one-shot holes anywhere.

County Antrim

ROYAL PORTRUSH GOLF CLUB

Golf was first played on the rugged, windswept Antrim coastal dunes in the late nineteenth century. The golf club at Portrush was officially established in 1888. In 1947, the course was redesigned by the renowned architect Harry Colt, who was also responsible for such courses as Muirfield in Scotland and Rye in England. There, on the Antrim coast, Harry Colt created nothing short of a masterpiece, the eighteen holes now known as the Dunluce Links. In fact, he created such a masterpiece that in July 1951 the British Open Championship was played at Royal Portrush, the only time the British Open has been held in Ireland. It is a worthy venue and should be considered again.

For those of us who will never qualify for the Brisith Open, the Dunluce course lets you feel what it must be like, if only for a few moments. It's heady stuff to look out from the first tee at that kind of golf course. For men, it's a grueling par 72 that plays 6,650 yards from the white markers. For women it's a 6,129-yard par 76. Yet, while it is long and arduous, it is a fair test of the game for midlevel to world-class golfers of both sexes. It requires focus, along with the best shot making you can muster, to play to your handicap.

The greens are among the best in the world, undulating and contoured. While they roll true, a lapse in concentration can see a poorly struck putt go so far astray that the mind boggles. As with most links courses, the greens don't hold like the manicured putting surfaces most Americans are accustomed to and playing for the pin is always risky.

The 454-yard, par-4 fourth hole—a par 5 for women demands—outstanding accuracy, with the tee shot playing across a gully. The par-4 fifth hole plays 380 yards through a sea of towering dunes that can redirect an errant shot on a line never imagined when the ball was struck.

The toughest hole on the course—for men and women—is the seventh. It's a devilish par-4 dogleg left for men. It's a par 5 for women, and a tough par at that. It punishes errant drives and is unforgiving to approach shots that miss the target. Adding to the difficulty of the terrain is the huge number of deep, troublesome bunkers. Those bunkers litter the golf course in general but seem to be Harry Colt's revenge on the seventh in particular.

My favorite hole on the Dunluce course is one of the most devilish, treacherous, difficult par 3s I've ever played. They have named the fourteenth—appropriately—"Calamity" and that's exactly what faces a golfer who is too brave, too foolish, or too inept off the tee. It plays 205 yards from the men's white markers. Along its entire right length is a severe hill that will dispatch a short shot dead right into a thatch of gorse and weeds that eats golf balls. On the left, steep dunes catch shots that drift anywhere near them. There is more room to bail out on the left than is apparent from the tee, but to walk away with a par from Calamity is most rewarding.

The 415-yard sixteenth is relatively forgiving off the elevated tee, but the undulating green is well protected by nasty hills and bunkers. It's a par 4 for men, the first of three finishing par 5s for women.

The bunker on seventeen is about three stories tall and could swallow much of the infield at Yankee Stadium. The eighteenth simply requires long accurate shots and steady, controlled putting.

Some Americans who have seen the Dunluce Links on television in recent years say the course looks a little scruffy, fairly flat, and unimpressive. That is because the camera lens fails to capture the essence of links golf courses. The camera flattens the terrain and diminishes the rugged beauty of the place by compressing it into the limited confines of the small screen. In general, links simply don't translate well to the TV screen. This is especially true of the Dunluce Links. It is akin to what Bertolt Brecht suggested when he wrote of the man who carried a brick with him to show everybody what his house had been like.

Royal Portrush simply must be experienced. It cannot be explained. Pictures do not do it justice. Television misrepresents it. It is well worth the trek to one of the farthest points north at which golf is played in Ireland. It is a glorious and thrilling place in which to play the game, a golf course on which you will savor every par and birdie and delight in simply having played it.

There is a second eighteen at the Royal Portrush Golf Club—the Valley Course. If it were anywhere other than joined to the world-class Dunluce Links, the Valley Course would be a highly regarded championship golf course all by itself. The layout is difficult and the greens are every bit as formidable as those of Dunluce. The holes meander through the dunes and feature deep rough and tight fairways. Unfortunately, it lives in the shadow of its more famous neighbor. Nonetheless, while you're at Portrush, don't miss the opportunity to play the 6,050-yard, par-70 Valley Course as well.

ROYAL PORTRUSH GOLF CLUB (Dunluce Links, links, par 72)
Location: Just outside the town of Portrush on the road to
    Bushmills and the Giant's Causeway
Facilities: Practice green, practice ground, pro shop, caddies usually
    available, bar, restaurant
Green fees: Very Expensive
Telephone: (0801) 265-822311   Fax: (0801) 265-823139

hole	par	yards	hole	par	yards
1	4	381	10	5	477
2	5	493	11	3	166
3	3	150	12	4	389
4	4	454	13	4	366
5	4	380	14	3	205
6	3	187	15	4	361
7	4	420	16	4	415
8	4	365	17	5	508
9	5	476	18	4	457
out	36	3,306	in	36	3,344

TOTAL   72   6,650*
*white markers

County Derry

CASTLEROCK GOLF CLUB

A pilgrimage to Ireland's extreme northern coast, where county Derry and county Antrim meet, rewards the pilgrim with a selection of three of the best golf courses in the world. Everybody talks about the British Open course at Royal Portrush and the championship links about eight miles west of there at Portstewart. But it would be a shame not to include the brilliant and testing golf course at Castlerock as a member of that trinity. It's only about three miles as the birdie flies from Portstewart, but while you can see it from the Portstewart clubhouse, it's about a half-hour drive down through Coleraine town, across the river Bann, and back up to the coast.

Mounds, moguls, and bunkers are but a few of the hazards that lurk to snare imprecise shots at Castlerock Golf Club.

Castlerock is nothing short of a gem. The links caress the dunelands along the Derry coast like a fickle lover, providing golfers with breathtaking panoramas of the coastline and then punishing them with blind shots, deep rough, high sandhills, and a stream that makes its presence felt at the most inopportune moments. The golf course snakes its way over and around the dunes and grassy hills and provides a superior test of the game as well as a delightful balm to the senses. It is justifiably known for its narrow, ribbonlike fairways and its exceptionally true but tricky greens.

A pair of testing par-4 openers sets the stage for what is to come. Two solid shots and a chip will set up a birdie or at least a par on the 493-yard, par-5 third hole. The 472-yard, par-5 fifth hole, which plays along the railroad tracks, is reachable in two, even for medium hitters.

In addition to all of the other difficulties, the par-4 sixth—which only measures 336 yards—is guarded by that obdurate stream, hiding right in front of the green like a serpent ready to devour the golf ball of any player who fails to be bold enough in his or her approach.

The par-4, 407-yard seventh hole is rated the most difficult on the course for men. (For women it's a 394-yard par 5 and is rated one of the easier holes.) For players of either sex, a par requires the successful navigation of a long, undulating, narrow fairway to one of those tricky but plush greens.

The par-5 eleventh hole is the most difficult green on the course to approach successfully. Five gaping bunkers placed at strategic intervals protect a long, narrow oval of putting surface.

The most difficult hole at Castlerock for women (and at 510 yards all uphill, it's no snap for even the biggest male hitters) is the par-5 fifteenth. It measures 489 yards on the ladies' card and requires three huge, accurate shots to be on in regulation. A par on the fifteenth will send anyone smiling to the par-3 sixteenth tee.

The elevated tee on the 485-yard, par-5 seventeenth hole provides one of the most picturesque views in all of Northern Ireland, looking west to where—on a clear day—you can see the Donegal Peninsula jutting out into the ocean. The hole itself is reachable in two and offers the prospect of heading to eighteen with a birdie or better, but the green is surrounded by steep dunes and a battery of bunkers, including one fierce little devil that sits directly in front of the green, put there just to catch the shots of the unsuspecting, fool-hardy, or overly brave.

Castlerock Golf Club was established in 1901 between the ocean and the mouth of the river Bann and was expanded from nine to eighteen holes in 1908. The eighteen-hole championship Mussenden Course plays nearly 6,500 yards to a par 73, and requires an impressive arsenal of shots in order to play to one's handicap, although there are fine, ego-building scoring opportunities.

The course is an arduous and challenging track for women but a fair test of skill and shot making. It plays to a par 75 on the ladies' card, and has been a popular venue for women's tournaments for most of the century (except, of course, during World War II, when the place was turned over to sheep for grazing and for a while was in danger of being plowed up to be planted with crops). It has hosted the Irish Ladies Amateur Championship at least three times.

The lovely little nine-hole Bann Course (links, par 35) requires the use of virtually every club in your bag and it is well worth the extra time to play it.

The big, modern clubhouse and well-equipped pro shop are additional assets that make a trip to Castlerock a wonderful golfing experience.

By the way, the English refer to this county (and the city) as Londonderry. The Northern Ireland Tourist Board, which is an institution of the British government, insists that it is Londonderry and uses the name in all its publications. In the Republic, they are both Derry, and adding "London" simply injects a political spin into even the most innocuous of references. Many residents still use the historic name, Derry. I have opted for history over politics in this book and use Derry.

CASTLEROCK GOLF CLUB (Mussenden Course, links, par 73)
Location: In the village of Castlerock about six miles north of
   Coleraine
Facilities: Practice green, practice tee, pro shop, bar, restaurant
Green fees: Moderate
Telephone: (0801) 265-848314

hole	par	yards	hole	par	yards
1	4	343	10	4	386
2	4	366	11	5	485
3	5	493	12	4	420
4	3	184	13	4	363
5	5	472	14	3	182
6	4	336	15	5	510
7	4	407	16	3	145
8	4	400	17	5	485
9	3	193	18	4	330
out	36	3,194	in	37	3,305
			TOTAL	73	6,499*

*white markers

PORTSTEWART GOLF CLUB

It's hard to believe, as you look out at the ocean waves lapping at the shore and the peaceful seaside town of Portstewart, that only a few miles north of that spot Nazi U-boats used to hide, waiting to sink American merchant ships headed to Britain during World War II. And just across the river Bann, U.S. troops trained for the invasion of Normandy. That history seems remote from the sanctuary of Portstewart's lovely clubhouse.

Everything I had read and heard before I got there told me to expect a fine golf course. I did not expect the Strand Course (part of Portstewart's forty-five-hole golfing complex) to be as truly great as it is.

Your tee shot on the par-4 second hole at Portstewart Golf Club must thread its way between inhospitable hills to a narrow landing area.

The Strand Course was redesigned in 1990, with seven new holes. "They didn't go to some big-name architect to do it," said the club bartender proudly. "The secretary [manager] and a local schoolteacher—who was a fine player—and the groundskeeper put their heads together and did it themselves." And a brilliant job they did.

The golf course is laid out through the high dunes and hills between the seacoast and the river Bann. Par is 72 for men and 74 for women; it's 6,779 yards long from the men's white markers and 5,864 yards for women. For every golfer it is a daunting challenge that requires every ounce of skill you have to meet your handicap.

The first hole, a par-4 lazy dogleg right, tees off from a high hill that tempts the really big hitters to try to cut the corner. Unless you hit it like Greg Norman or Fred Couples, play it straight and then go for the green, which is 425 yards away. (For women it's a 399-yard, par 5.)

I like the second hole as well as any on the course. They call it *Devil's Hill* on the scorecard and with good reason. Your tee shot must thread its way between two towering dunes to a narrow fairway with a mountain to the left and a valley to the right. The elevated tee is 366 yards from the small, well-protected, and elevated green. (It's rated the toughest hole on the links for women.) The shot to the green must be precise. A slight variation to the left is caught by the hill, to the right your ball is sentenced to a dungeon of deep grass, gorse, and rocks.

The par-3 third hole requires a big, accurate tee shot (207 yards for men and 162 yards for women) to a lovely green. The par-5 fourth hole is a monster dogleg right. The blind tee shot must be kept to the left in order to allow a long lay-up past the trouble that guards the right side of the fairway.

The long par-4 fifth meanders along the contour of the river Bann, a dogleg left with a substantial landing area for your tee shot, but which narrows precipitously to an hourglass approach to the green. The tight dogleg-right seventh hole plays to a green that is guarded by a steep hill on the left and a gorge on the right.

The 384-yard, par-4 eighth hole features a blind tee shot and is a severe dogleg left. If it's not ninety degrees, it's close enough. Many players use something less than a driver from the tee to position the ball for a clear second shot from a plateau to the green below.

The par-5 thirteenth plays 500 yards along the river Bann and is a solid three-shot hole. It's followed quickly by the 485-yard, par-5 fourteenth, which tempts some of the long ball hitters to go for it in two. It's a risk-reward hole, with the slick, unreceptive green well protected in front. A shot that's too hot runs the risk of skipping off the back.

The par-3 fifteenth is a charming little one-shot hole that sets up a fairly easy par if you can hold the green. It also gives you a breather from the back-to-back par 5s and before you face the three splendid, long par 4s that take you home. (On the ladies' card, the seventeenth is a difficult 410-yard par 5.)

For men, none of the three finishing holes measures less than 420 yards and the eighteenth is 464 yards from tee to green. Each is a gentle dogleg. Sixteen and eighteen play to the left and seventeen is a dogleg right. Length and precision are required. On the eighteenth, strategically placed bunkers will catch a drive that fails to split the middle of the fairway. Just getting your ball safely on these three lovely but testing greens is no guarantee of par, unless you knock it close.

In general, the greens are a little less tricky than those up the road at Royal Portrush, but that is not to suggest they are easy by any stretch. They are subject to the influence of both the river Bann and the ocean, in the way they break and the direction of the grain. As with almost every links course, a shot square at the pin simply won't hold no matter how much backspin you can put on it. With the wind a constant factor as well, run-up shots generally yield the best scoring.

In addition to the Strand Course, the Town Course is a lovely little links that plays about 4,700 yards with a par of 64, and the Riverside nine plays to a par 32 and is some 2,650 yards. Both tracks are fun and pleasant, but it's the Strand that is the gem of Portstewart.

The clubhouse is a charming old two-story structure that houses a formal restaurant and a lovely barroom in which food is served. It's a friendly and welcoming place that provides a fitting end to the superb golfing experience that is Portstewart.

PORTSTEWART GOLF CLUB (Strand Course, links, par 72)
Location: 117 Strand Road, on the western edge of Portstewart

Facilities: Practice green, practice area, pro shop, bar, restaurant
Green fees: Expensive
Telephone: (0801) 265-832015   Fax: (0801) 265-834097

hole	par	yards	hole	par	yards
1	4	425	10	4	393
2	4	366	11	4	370
3	3	207	12	3	166
4	5	535	13	5	500
5	4	456	14	5	485
6	3	140	15	3	169
7	5	511	16	4	422
8	4	384	17	4	434
9	4	352	18	4	464
out	36	3,376	in	36	3,403
			TOTAL	72	6,779*

*white markers

County Down

ARDGLASS GOLF CLUB

The first thing you see when you turn into the parking lot at Ardglass Golf Club is the venerable old clubhouse, with the Irish Sea behind it and (on a clear day) the Isle of Man off in the distance. The clubhouse was a castle back in the fifteenth century; now it's a landmark.

The golf course is a wonderful, largely undiscovered jewel that is challenging to players of every level and pleasing to the senses. In the distance, to the southwest, the Mountains of Mourne loom on the horizon.

Looking back down the first hole at Ardglass Golf Club. The clubhouse used to be a castle.

Ardglass is relatively short—just a little over 6,000 yards from the white markers—and it plays to a par 70 for both men and women. Don't be fooled by the pleasant and salubrious landscape or the length of the track. There is serious golf to be played if you expect to score within the parameters of your handicap. "You'll use everything you're carrying," said the genial young assistant pro. "And if you can't keep it low into the wind, you're in for a rough round."

The test begins at the first tee, which generally plays into the wind. The narrow little green—which is hard to hit and harder to hold—sits up a long hill, 325 yards from the tee. Any shot that drifts too far left is gone, into the rocks, into the briny deep. There's plenty of room to the right.

The first four holes are a great introduction to Ardglass. They are laid out precariously along the cliffs and rocks that keep the sea from overtaking the land. They all feature small, well-guarded, and tricky greens that yield one-putts only grudgingly.

The par-3 second plays across a chasm into which waves crash and foam sprays. There's bailout room to the right; there's nothing but grief to the left.

The following two par 4s—with the sea crashing off to the left and with their tough greens—make the short and relatively easy par-3 fifth a welcome sight. The 494-yard, par-5 sixth hole, one of two back-to-back par 5s, features a stone wall along the left of the fairway from about 150 yards out to the green. Your second shot needs to carry a field of rocks and trouble to set up a chip and putt.

The best hole on the course is the par-3 eleventh, which was substantially redesigned in the fall of 1995. The elevated tee features a magnificent view of the village of Ardglass across a small inlet, with the Mountains of Mourne off in the distance. The green backs onto the strand and is protected by large, deep, and strategically placed bunkers. While it is less than 150 yards from tee to green, it generally plays into the wind and club selection is every bit as critical as how the ball is struck. The key is to take enough club to clear those hungry bunkers.

The 361-yard, par-4 sixteenth presents the player with a blind tee shot. The approach to a minuscule, domed green demands an almost perfect shot to get anywhere on the putting surface. It's a superb test for women, playing 354 yards from tee to green. Many women play it to put their second shot in front and finish with a bump-and-run approach to the pin and one putt for par.

The par-4 eighteenth, a nice, open, gentle finisher, plays downhill, back toward the clubhouse and a well-deserved pint or tot.

While Ardglass Golf Club is not going to make anybody's short list of PGA tournament venues, it is a superbly pleasant golf course. It is also an extraordinarily fair test of the game for women. For men of every handicap it requires skilled shot making and course management. In short, Ardglass is well worth a detour and is certainly not to be missed if you're already in the neighborhood.

ARDGLASS GOLF CLUB (links, par 70)
Location: In the village of Ardglass, about ten miles east-northeast
     of Newcastle
Facilities: Practice green, pro shop, bar, restaurant
Green fees: Moderate
Telephone: (0801) 396-841219   Fax: (0801) 396-841841
E-mail: ardglassgolfclub@hotmail.com

hole	par	yards	hole	par	yards
1	4	325	10	4	439
2	3	161	11	3	148
3	4	334	12	4	397
4	4	363	13	4	382
5	3	135	14	5	490
6	5	494	15	4	392
7	5	514	16	4	361
8	4	404	17	3	119
9	3	219	18	4	345
out	35	2,949	in	35	3,073
			TOTAL	70	6,022*

*white markers

ROYAL COUNTY DOWN GOLF CLUB

In the late nineteenth century, Newcastle was a quiet coastal town to which the gentry trekked in summer for their holidays by the strand. The Irish songwriter, Percy French, penned his most famous song inspired by the beauty of the place—"Where the Mountains of Mourne Sweep Down to the Sea."

In those days, golf was a game for the rich and, in 1889, a committee of rich men decided Newcastle would be an ideal place for a golf course. They offered the job to the legendary golf-course designer Old Tom Morris and paid him four gold guineas to lay out the links. And so it began. Not quite two decades later, Harry Vardon, one of the top golf-course architects of the day, redesigned the course into very much its present form.

A few writers and touring pros have complained that it's too old-fashioned for today's high-power, high-tech game. It's an anachronism, they say, with a handful of blind tee shots and several holes that are obscured on the approach. That's nonsense! If you want to play something fully modern, go down to Florida's Palm Beach area and play Tom Fazio's Emerald Dunes or Pete Dye's Cypress Links (which isn't a links course at all). They're only a few miles apart. But don't bother to travel to Ireland.

Royal County Down is a wonderful test of the game, a fair and pure challenge on one of the world's great links golf courses. From the white tee markers it plays to a par 71, just shy of 6,700 yards. Hold on to your hats, ladies! From the red markers it is a tough, arduous par 76 over 6,239 grueling yards. It is not a golf course for beginners of either sex, but for experienced players seeking to sample a world-class golf course, it is well worth the trip out to Newcastle.

One of Royal County Down's finest points is its great variety of holes. The par 4s, for example, range from the massive 473-yard third to the tiny 265-yard sixteenth. Three of the par 3s exceed 200 yards from tee to green, with the little seventh a mere 129 yards.

The par-5 first hole generally plays downwind and is, actually, one of the easier holes on the golf course. The 374-yard, par-4 second requires a good, solid drive that sets up a long iron to a green that's about as big as my computer screen. But they're just the doorman and the maid. The real introduction to Royal County Down takes place on the brutally long, intimidating par-4 third hole, one of the toughest golf holes in Ireland or anywhere else.

It requires a massive drive over all kinds of trouble to set up a long iron or even a fairway wood to the elevated, well-guarded green 473 yards away. Women get a bit of a break. On the ladies' card the third is a 424-yard par 5, but it still demands a very large tee shot. Failure to keep the ball in play will leave you feeling like the victim of a drive-by shooting.

On the risk-reward par-4 fifth, bite off as much of the dogleg right as you can, although the really big hitters should beware of four strategically placed fairway bunkers. A short drive, or one that

Royal County Down Golf Club is among the world's most photographed golf courses. This is a view across the second tee to the first green, with the breathtaking Mountains of Mourne in the background.

ventures too far left, will find a nasty bit of trouble beyond the fairway and a long way remaining to the safety of the green.

The front nine finishes with a pair of splendid par 4s. They are both par 5s on the ladies' card, and with justification. The eighth features a tiny domed green that's fast and tricky.

The ninth hole at Royal County Down is one of the most memorable holes in the world and is one of the most photographed holes in all of golf. Your tee shot is launched toward the Mountains of Mourne and disappears over a massive hill. When you get to the crest of the hill, before you start your descent, you have an unmatched view of the village of Newcastle silhouetted against the mountains with the Irish Sea and the golden strand along Dundrum Bay off to the left. The sight is breathtaking and the hole is simply spectacular.

The ninth hole plays 431 yards from the white markers, but women hit first on this one. It's 433 yards from the red tees and requires three very solid shots—almost always into the wind—to make par. Men can generally count on a pair of woods to reach the green in two, and if the wind is "fresh" (the Irish term for "hold onto your hairpiece") it can be two drivers and then it's no sure thing that you'll reach it.

The back nine heads out into the dunes again from the clubhouse with a lovely par 3 and a testing par 4 that demands a long accurate drive in order to set up a shot to the green. On the ladies' card the eleventh is rated second hardest on the course and features a blind tee shot.

The 422-yard, par-4 thirteenth is by far the toughest hole on the back side. It's a dogleg right that guarantees nothing but trouble if you stray from the fairway. The green is hidden behind a hill and surrounded by moguls and deep grass. The green is large and tricky and will just as easily yield a three-putt as let you snake one in from any distance.

The fifteenth is a 445-yard par 4 from the white markers, a 401-yard par 5 from the reds. Into a stiff wind this is another hole that can demand a pair of solid woods for men to get into the vicinity of a par; for women three long shots are needed to get on in regulation. The tee shot plays to a very small landing area at about the point where it doglegs to the right and then plays down an ever-narrowing fairway to a well-protected green.

The par-4 seventeenth features a small pond right in the middle of the fairway that is invisible from the tee. It is also out of reach for all but smashers like John Daly.

Finally, the 528-yard, par-5 eighteenth leads you home. It's a long way into the prevailing wind, down a fairway that's littered with bunkers. Again, the big green is easier to three-putt than to ace, unless you get your approach close.

Right next door to the fabled championship course is the newer and shorter Mourne Course, which plays about 4,100 yards to a par of 65. At first glance it appears much tamer than the venerable old links, but when I talked about various courses with the young assistant pro at Ardglass, just a few miles away, he said it is a deceptive little course. "You have to think about every shot," he said. And when I noted its length he added, "It's a shotmaker's course."

The old white two-story clubhouse is a wonderful place to share a pint and recall this marvelous golf course when you've finished the round, and I will bet it is a round you will recall fondly—regardless of your score—for ages to come.

ROYAL COUNTY DOWN GOLF CLUB (Championship Course, links, par 71)
Location: In the Irish Sea resort town of Newcastle
Facilities: Practice green, pro shop, rental clubs, caddies usually available, bar, restaurant
Green fees: Very Expensive
Telephone: (0801) 3967-23314   Fax: (0801) 3967-26281

hole	par	yards	hole	par	yards
1	5	500	10	3	200
2	4	374	11	4	429
3	4	473	12	5	476
4	3	217	13	4	422
5	4	418	14	3	213
6	4	368	15	4	445
7	3	129	16	4	265
8	4	428	17	4	376
9	4	431	18	5	528
out	35	3,338	in	36	3,354
			TOTAL	71	6,692*

*white markers

CHAPTER 3

Other Courses of Note

It's an exaggeration to say that every little hamlet in Ireland has a golf course, but the exaggeration is only slight. Given the fact that in all of Ireland there are only about five and a half million people, the ratio of golf courses to people is only a little lower than the ratio of tenured full professors to students in some major U.S. universities. Almost every community with more than a thousand inhabitants has a golf course. In 1999, Damian Ryan, Bord Failte's golf executive, boasted that there were more than 375 golf courses in the Irish Republic and Northern Ireland, with more on the drawing board. Not quite a hundred are nine-hole layouts and many of them have expansion plans.

There are golf courses in Ireland to suit the abilities, limitations, and tastes of almost everybody who has ever picked up a club. There are shorter and easier courses that would not hold much interest for low handicappers but that are both interesting and challenging for mid- and high-handicap players. There are flatter and gentler courses that better meet the needs of those who simply cannot take the physical test of walking a course like Tralee or Wicklow.

If Old Head, The European Club, and the Dunluce Links at Royal Portrush require every bit of concentration and physical ability a good golfer or even a professional can muster, then there are courses on which an average to good player can relax and switch his or her brain to auto-pilot as well. I find a steady diet of grueling golf

161

too much to take sometimes, and so a little breather is in order. It is also a balm to the ego to be able to shoot two or three pars in a row, instead of walking away grateful for a card full of bogies.

In short, there is a golf course in Ireland for every golfer of every ability. There are also courses that have achieved lofty status more as a result of favorable publicity than of merit or genuine quality.

The following is a representative listing of some noteworthy courses that don't quite meet the level of difficulty or challenge outlined in the previous chapter. It also includes some famous courses that may well be included on other lists of the "best" or "greatest" golf courses in Ireland but that, to me, are weak imitations of American golf courses. A few are noted because of their celebrity status, although I have found them disappointing because of hype or underperformance. Some may have been on your itinerary and you may want to rethink them based upon what is written here. Or you may—as several people who have written to disagree with my profiles in the first edition of this book have done—want to play the courses and make up your own mind.

County Clare

DROMOLAND GOLF CLUB

The back nine at Dromoland Golf Club (they pronounce it "Druh-*mo*-land") was completed in 1985, and in the ensuing years it has developed into a very pleasant, mature layout. Its highlights include an abundance of hills and trees and a track that takes the player all the way around Dromoland Lough. Dromoland Castle, with its towering parapets of thick stone, has been refurbished and turned into a luxury hotel. The breathtaking castle, built in the sixteenth century, dominates the view from several holes and makes you think you've emerged from a time warp somewhere in medieval Ireland.

The long par-5 second hole plays down a gentle hill and around a dogleg right to a green 548 yards away. The temptation to cut the corner is mitigated by a dense forest of tall and unforgiving trees that is unlikely to give back your ball if you're dumb enough to hit it in there. The placement of the ladies' tee unfortunately eliminates much of the dogleg, and hence much of the interest of the hole.

The 440-yard, par-4 fourth hole is rated the toughest on the card, playing up a hill that then slopes down to the left and to a green that's well protected.

The short 140-yard, par-3 seventh hole—rated the second easiest on the course—must be rated first for the view. It offers the most spectacular panorama of the lough, castle, and grounds. Women get a huge advantage on this little hole. It measures only 98 yards from tee to green, all downhill.

The par-5 eleventh is a severe dogleg right with Dromoland Lough in play on a long drive or a second that seeks to cut the corner.

While there is a feeling of openness over much of the back nine, it is not so open that shots straying too far will go unpunished.

The approach to the eighteenth green at Dromoland Golf Club is like stepping back in time, with the sixteenth-century Dromoland Castle looming in the distance.

My favorite hole is not the most difficult but is the most unique. The par-5 eighteenth tees off across a ditch and some scrub to a shallow landing area. The tee shot probably will not require the services of a driver. Many golfers use a long iron. The hole's 476 yards would make almost anyone think it's reachable in two shots, but it's not. The tee is shielded by the dense foliage of Temple Wood on the left and presents an almost ninety-degree dogleg left.

The blind tee shot should land at the point where you look left, down a long, narrow, tubelike approach to the green. The fairway is lined all the way to the green on the left by Temple Wood and on the right by great old trees and parts of the lake. In the distance, directly behind the flag, is Dromoland Castle.

If I have a major objection to Dromoland Golf Club it is that it is sometimes made too easy for women. The par-4 eighth hole, for example, which plays up a moderate hill and which is guarded on the right by tall, dense trees, plays 363 yards for the men and brings a slight double dogleg into play. The hole is leveled into a slight dogleg right for women and plays only 241 yards. It could be made a much stronger hole.

On the back, there are three par 4s that play shorter than 320 yards for men. The designer dropped so much yardage from the forward markers that only one of those holes exceeds 250 yards and two play just over 200 yards for women. That's too short even for a high-handicap beginner.

The round will not leave men or women huffing and puffing, nor will it make anyone remark about the tremendous level of difficulty involved, but it's a generally pleasing golf course and worth a stop if you're in county Clare for a few days and aren't up to more than a day or two of intimidation on the masterpiece of the county, the venerable Lahinch links.

DROMOLAND GOLF CLUB (parkland, par 71)
Location: About ten miles north of Shannon Airport on the
    Galway Road (N18) on the grounds of Dromoland Castle
Facilities: Practice green, pro shop, rental clubs, a few riding carts,
    bar, restaurant
Green fees: Expensive
Telephone: (061) 368444   Fax: (061) 368498

ENNIS GOLF CLUB

Only one serious drawback prevents the Ennis Golf Club from being a championship-caliber golf course: it's short. It measures only 5,860 yards. Its greatest asset, on the other hand, is its changing faces and shifting moods. It's a temperamental, picturesque little track, with good greens. The length aside, it requires shot making and thought in order to score. If it is not an arduous challenge, it is an interesting and pleasing diversion.

In fact, playing Ennis is like playing a golf course within a golf course.

The first seven holes (and the eighteenth) play among large, mature stands of trees that tighten the fairways and guard the greens. It's flat and fairly straight, and looks like an easy test at first glance. But you are directed to cross a small road and suddenly you are on the side of a massive slope that opens the whole vista of county Clare to you with distant farmsteads, verdant fields separated by rock walls, and an intriguing layout of varied and challenging golf holes. It's an entirely new golf course dominated by precariously slippery fairways and well-protected greens. Errant tee shots can find deep rough or simply roll off the short grass into the thatch as dictated by gravity. The greens are smallish, difficult to read, and hard to putt. And approach shots place a premium on skill and accuracy.

The par-4 eighth tees off from the top of the hill to a green 377 yards away. You have the whole glorious rural panorama to drink in as you ponder your second shot.

The fourteenth, fifteenth, sixteenth, and seventeenth holes are as good and challenging as any parkland holes in the country, each playing progressively from the base of the slope up to the pinnacle and each requiring precise approach shots to undulating greens in order to avoid three-putting or worse. The holes comprise an intricate amalgam of doglegs, bunkers, hills, moguls, trees, and rocks.

Despite the fact that the 218-yard, par-3 sixteenth plays downhill, it's a tough hole to score on because holding the green with your tee shot is difficult.

That leads to the deceptive penultimate hole. It looks gentle and serene; it is pitched steeply uphill and severely to the right. If you're winded by the time you climb the 322 yards to the seventeenth green, it's hardly a surprise. A glance back down the hill will tell you your eyes lied to you back on the tee.

The straight-away par-5 eighteenth requires precise shots in order to avoid the out of bounds on the left and the big mature trees on the right. It plays a solid 502 yards to the pleasant clubhouse. The bar is adjacent to the practice green, and most of the eighteenth hole can be viewed while you sip a pint.

I have enjoyed the Ennis Golf Club every time I've played it. It is a course that will produce a lot of pars and a few unexpected bogies, but it will yield birdies sparingly. I have never left it without a good measure of enjoyment.

ENNIS GOLF CLUB (parkland, par 70)
Location: About a half-mile west of Ennis
Facilities: Practice green, pro shop, bar, restaurant
Green fees: Inexpensive
Telephone: (065) 24074   Fax: (065) 41848
E-mail: egc@tinet.ie

KILKEE GOLF CLUB

Kilkee Golf Club used to be one of the most magnificently set nine-hole golf courses in the world. It played down a slope to a rocky gulch, up a steep hill that leads to Chimney Cove, and then back down to the clubhouse. Kilkee sits near the southern tip of the same series of cliffs and dunes on which the legendary golf course at Lahinch is built. Those bluffs rise from the strand at Kilkee village and end to the north of Lahinch at the rugged Cliffs of Moher.

In 1994, a new and expanded eighteen-hole version of the Kilkee Golf Club opened for play, a 6,470-yard, par-71 track that generated great excitement and numerous news stories when the project was announced. The golf-course expansion was the result of an economic development plan for Ireland by the European Union—which simply poured money into various infrastructure and development projects around the Irish Republic. County Clare and Kilkee town were the beneficiaries of EU largesse and, given the brilliant nature of the original nine holes, expectations were heightened for what the new nine would offer.

But on completion, a project that held unusually bright promise failed to deliver. The golf-course expansion appeared to have been designed in haste and opened for play before the place had matured enough to avoid costly damage. The first time I experienced the expanded course, it was so fragile it verged on the unplayable. It turned out that some of the grass had to be resown. But that's a relatively easy repair. The lingering and irreparable flaw remains the design of the new nine holes. Fixing that is almost as expensive as building them in the first place. A few bunkers have been added since 1994, and the fairways are lush. But the design problems are fundamental.

The front nine is the original track, for the most part. The back nine plays into a wide-open, relatively flat, and thoroughly uninteresting bit of pastureland. Those new holes are laid out side by side, smooth and straight, up and down the field. You'd think that with all the EU money that was pumped in they might have at least put in a few strategically placed bumps, mounds, or rocks but they did not.

The greens on the back nine are relatively large, relatively flat, relatively unprotected by bunkers, water, plantings, or anything else. They are, in fact, relatively boring. Comparing the front nine to the back is like comparing a Porsche to a Ford Fiesta. The engineering, design, and performance are simply not in the same class.

The front nine, after some emergency care from the grass doctor, along with some CPR for the greens, remains the brilliant test it was as a nine-hole course. The 474-yard, par-5 second hole plays to a green protected by rocks and deep rough and while the long hitters may be tempted to go for it in two, the better birdie opportunity lies in a well-placed chip and one putt. The 422-yard, par-3 sixth hole—the only par 3 on the front side—is a charming little one-shot hole that takes full advantage of the natural topography.

The seventh, eighth, and ninth holes (back-to-back par 4s and a par 5) play along the side of a hill that guarantees your drive will end anywhere but where it first comes to land. They play to turtle-back greens that are undulating and difficult to approach. These three are the best stretch of holes on the entire course. The 461-yard, par-5 ninth can be reached in two, and it presents the greatest chance on the front side for an eagle or birdie. It plays steeply uphill and requires more muscle than the yardage would indicate.

The back nine—mostly the new holes—is a yawn and, compared to the interesting and challenging design of the original, it appears to have been drawn up by a student architect as a class project with little feel for or understanding of the game of golf. It's even possible the expansion was sketched by a computer with minimal human assistance. It has that impersonal and cold feel to it. Aside from the eighteenth tee, which reveals a pleasant view of the rocky coast and cliffs in the distance, the new holes at the Kilkee Golf Club leave me sad and dissatisfied, given their potential and the degree to which that potential is unmet.

For women, it's two strokes harder than the men's card (par 73) but the women's tees are simply stuck anywhere there was a flat bit of grass in front of the men's markers. Instead of making women carry over any kind of hazard on the par-5 ninth, for example, the designers just moved the women's tee ahead of all the trouble and made it a par 4—a poor choice. In general, women appear to have been an afterthought.

The clubhouse—a popular local wateringhole on a Sunday afternoon—offers a pleasant view of the North Atlantic and the people are generally friendly. But what used to be a worthy detour for the nine-hole course has not been improved by its expansion.

KILKEE GOLF CLUB (links, par 71)
Location: Just north of Kilkee village on the N67
Facilities: Practice green, bar, restaurant
Green fees: Inexpensive
Telephone: (065) 56048   Fax: (065) 56977

SPANISH POINT GOLF CLUB

If there is a rugged, windswept, awe-inspiring piece of Irish real estate on which golf is played, it is the rocky coast from the Cliffs of Moher to Kilkee. Less than ten miles down the coast road from the breathtaking and spectacular links at Lahinch is a little gem of a nine-hole golf course that is well worth playing, especially if you are spending several days in that area.

Spanish Point features the same weather conditions—especially the relentless wind—that cause so much grief to golfers at Lahinch, but the course is a little kinder, a little easier, and certainly shorter. But don't be misled. If you can play it in level par, 60 for eighteen holes, you might consider a career change.

It features six par 3s, but the wind can cause huge variations in club selection. A hole played with a wedge when the wind is at your back may well require a five iron when you are facing a gale blasting in from the ocean. Very few players record pars on all six holes and double bogies can sneak up on you with astonishing speed.

In addition, it's a lovely drive to get there and the scenery from the golf course is delightful.

SPANISH POINT GOLF CLUB (links, par 30)
Location: About fifteen miles south of Lahinch off the N67
Facilities: Bar, snacks
Green fees: Inexpensive
Telephone: (065) 84198

County Cork

DONERAILE GOLF CLUB

I found the Doneraile Golf Club quite by accident one day as I was driving the narrow and winding backroads of county Cork. I stopped to play it simply to loosen my muscles and to take a break from the wheel. Besides, as I recall, it was too early for cocktails and too late for lunch and I didn't have anything else very pressing to do.

It turned out to be a lucky break. At that time, on that day, the clubhouse bar wasn't open and the course operated on an honor system. In the vestibule, there were small envelopes, a box, and a sign: *Write name on envelope. Put five pounds in it. Put envelope in box. Thank you.*

It was not until later that I learned the unique history of that little corner of Ireland. Back in the mid-1800s a horse race was staged from the church in Doneraile to the church in the neighboring town of Buttevant. There were no rules except that the first horse and rider to get there in one piece won. It was the first steeplechase and legend has it that the starting post was at the site of the first tee of today's Doneraile Golf Club.

The golf course itself is designed in the manner of many smaller turn-of-the-century English and Scottish courses. The fairways crisscross each other. In fact, play is suspended on the third green while players tee across it to the par-3 fourth green 185 yards away with a schoolyard fence delineating a tight out of bounds on the right.

The second hole plays across the first fairway and the ninth tees off across the third. It can be a bit confusing, especially the fourth tees. Women exit the third green to the rear. Men walk halfway back down the hole to a tee box hidden by a copse of pines.

The most unique hole is the 364-yard, par-4 sixth. You drive across a small stream and a little valley of wild grass and weeds to a fairway on which the village cemetery creates an unusual hazard. The green is tucked behind the far wall of the graveyard. It's not life threatening, but it is a penalty stroke if you fail to clear the high walls of the burial ground.

When you finish nine holes, you go back to the first tee and play them all again to make eighteen. The local etiquette, I am told, is for players concluding nine to have the right of way. If there are groups waiting to tee off, they alternate with groups finishing nine.

Doneraile is far from a championship golf course, but I have enjoyed it every time I've played it, not only for its history and pleasant setting, but because it does my ego good to score well once in a while.

DONERAILE GOLF CLUB (parkland, par 34)
Location: North of Mallow, east of the Limerick-Cork Road on the
    R581; look for the steeple of the church
Facilities: Bar
Green fees: Inexpensive
Telephone: (022) 24137

MALLOW GOLF CLUB

The market and business center of Mallow has long been home to one of the finest parkland golf courses in Ireland. It has five par 5s, five par 3s, and only eight par 4s, a unique and enjoyable mix of holes. The undulating course was cut through a dense forest and sculpted from hilly pastures. Strategically placed stands of trees increase the difficulty of several holes and a redesign implemented in 1994 delivered subtle and pleasant improvements.

The short, 480-yard, par-5 third hole typifies the layout. Its length would tempt even moderate hitters to muse on getting there in two, but a line of towering old trees bisects the fairway, about 150 yards in front of the green, and renders that difficult. A drive too close to the trees makes it nearly impossible to get enough elevation on the shot to clear them and still have enough velocity to make the green.

The front nine—the longer of the two—plays out a substantial 3,346 yards from the white markers, only about a hundred yards short of the championship tees. Women get a generous break on the yardage, but the ladies' tees are, for the most part, positioned in such a way that approach shots to the greens are every bit as challenging as those facing men.

I have always enjoyed the three finishing holes at Mallow. The charming, little, par-3 sixteenth plays from an elevated tee, over a gulch filled with rocks and trees and scrub-brush that returns very few balls hit into it, to a long, narrow green. That's followed by the 481-yard, par-5 seventeenth that can be reached in two. The long par-3 eighteenth, however, is a deceptive little rascal. With the clubhouse looming in the background, the hole looks much shorter from the tee than it is. A picture window in the bar provides a vantage point from which other golfers will be assessing your shot.

If I have a major objection to the layout at Mallow, it is the relatively easy approaches to most greens, although the 1994 upgrade took pains to address that with several additional or expanded greenside bunkers.

In addition to golf, the facility offers such unusual amenities as tennis courts, squash, and a sauna. The locker rooms are a bit Spartan, by U.S. standards, but they do provide shower facilities if you desire. (Bring your own towel!)

MALLOW GOLF CLUB (parkland, par 72)
Location: On the southeast side of Mallow off the Kilavullen Road
Facilities: Practice green, pro shop, rental clubs, tennis, squash, sauna, bar, snacks
Green fees: Moderate
Telephone: (022) 21145   Fax: (022) 42501

County Donegal

BUNDORAN GOLF CLUB

The legendary golf-course architect Harry Vardon designed this venerable old links by the shores of Donegal Bay. The club was established in 1894 as a nine-hole adjunct to the neighboring hotel. Vardon reworked it into its present eighteen-hole design in the 1920s. The golf course has not only hosted some of Ireland's biggest tournaments; it was once the home course of the island's most famous professional, Christy O'Conner.

The track itself is relatively open and short—less than 6,200 yards, playing to a par 69—but it's a fine test of the game. Keeping the ball in play will yield pars and birdies, but the rough is manageable and even a stray shot will not be punished beyond recovery. The greens are not kept particularly fast.

The first and tenth holes play away from the Great Northern Hotel, around which the course is built.

Two of the par 3s are simply monstrous, among the toughest scoring holes on the links. The fifth and thirteenth both play well in excess of 200 yards and require strength and pinpoint accuracy. The long, par-4 seventeenth will test the backbone of anybody, especially if the wind is howling off the bay.

The golf course, however, gets an enormous amount of play, which may account for the fact that the greens were in need of some maintenance work the last time I was there. Advance booking is essential, and then be prepared to deal with large groups and "golfing societies" with which Bundoran is a popular venue. In fact, the biggest drawback to Bundoran Golf Club is the great number of players and the often slow pace of play.

BUNDORAN GOLF CLUB (links, par 69)
Location: Between Bundoran and Ballyshannon, just off the N15
Facilities: Practice green, pro shop, bar (in the hotel)
Green fees: Moderate
Telephone: (072) 41302

NORTH WEST GOLF CLUB

In 1891, the year the North West Golf Club was established, the extreme north of county Donegal was a wild and rugged part of the world, isolated from the rest of Ireland by mountains and accessible only by horse, foot, or boat. The village of Buncrana, at the foot of the Mouldy Mountains on the banks of Lough Swilly, was a remote and largely unknown outpost in those days. Today it is a busy and popular beach resort.

The North West links is about a mile south of the town and offers both a good test of golf and some picturesque scenery. From almost every hole, players glimpse the lough with the Killalla Hills in the background. The golf course itself looks fairly flat and placid at first glance, but it takes no time at all to realize that what you don't see can derail your game in a heartbeat. There are concealed creek beds and pot bunkers, sandy mounds, ridges, deep indentations, and gnarly rough that imprisons any ball straying from the fairway.

There is virtually no warm up. The long par-4 opening hole foreshadows what is to come, although the back nine is the tougher of the two. The well-manicured greens are generous in size with both overt and covert contours and undulations. As with most links courses, a bump-and-run approach game will generally reap greater rewards than aggressive attacks on the flag.

The modern clubhouse overlooks the lough and distant hills, and at sunset the view is wonderful.

NORTH WEST GOLF CLUB (links, par 70)
Location: About a mile south of Buncrana and about twenty miles
    northwest of Derry
Facilities: Practice green, pro shop, bar, restaurant
Green fees: Moderate
Telephone: (077) 61715   Fax: (077) 63284

County Galway

GALWAY GOLF CLUB

Some golf guides actually list the Galway Golf Club as a seaside course, implying it is a links. It is true that the first four holes play alongside Galway Bay, but this is not a links golf course. It is a good, solid course, although I have found the greens a bit inconsistent. While they are true and can be cut very fast for tournaments, they have often been slow and not particularly well cut at other times. In addition they are not very arduously trapped or protected, with a few notable exceptions—such as the ninth and fourteenth.

That is not to suggest that the Galway Golf Club is a sure bet to lower your handicap or salve your ego. When the European PGA played the Celtic International there in 1984, eight under for three rounds walked off with all the marbles, and the three pros tied for second could only manage five under.

The course underwent an early-1990s redesign. The starter said the par-4 fourth hole's direction was reversed because too many people were slicing balls out onto the main road that edges the hole and causing havoc with the traffic.

There are some interesting and imaginative holes. The 439-yard, par-4 fifth—guarded by trees along the left side of the fairway—requires a substantial drive if you're going to be in scoring position. Too far left and your approach is blocked by trees.

The lengthy one-shot ninth hole will test the long-iron abilities of even the best players, and short hitters will use a fairway wood to find the green in regulation. The par-5 twelfth gives the big hitters a good chance of being on in two shots. This is a good par opportunity for everybody. Women will need two solid wood shots, leaving a mid- to short-iron approach for a run at a birdie. The dogleg right, uphill par-4 finishing hole is a very pleasant way to end the round.

The Galway Golf Club is an especially good test for women, and if this were solely a book for female golfers, there is no question that it would be ranked among the best courses in the land. In fact, if you are planning a women's golf getaway to Ireland, this is a course you should go out of your way to play. While there are only two par 5s for the men, there are five for women and all require three good shots to reach the greens. In addition, the women's tees are well positioned, requiring drives that carry scrub-brush, gorse and heather bowers, and all manner of other troubles. Even more so for women than for men, there is little latitude for an errant tee shot on a majority of the holes.

For example, the seventh hole is a 439-yard par 5 on the women's card and plays every inch of it. And the par-3 ninth requires a 130-yard carry to reach the green 145 yards away.

The clubhouse is a most pleasant haven after the round, sitting atop a hill that overlooks much of the golf course.

GALWAY GOLF CLUB (parkland, par 70)
Location: About two miles from the center of Galway city on the
   road to the resort village of Salthill
Facilities: Practice green, pro shop, bar, restaurant
Green fees: Moderate
Telephone: (091) 522033   Fax: (091) 522169

County Kerry

CASTLEGREGORY GOLF & FISHING CLUB

There is a narrow strip of land southwest of Tralee, sandwiched
between Brandon Bay and Lough Gill (not the one in county Sligo),
where lives one of the best nine-hole links golf courses in Ireland.
"You wouldn't think it, but it's a fine little test," said Morris Switzer,
an avid golfer from Killarney. "People kind of turn their nose up at
nine holers. But this one's a find." The Castlegregory Golf & Fishing
Club is quiet, largely undiscovered, and well worth a visit.

It is an especially valuable course to know about if you find yourself unable to get a tee time at the great nearby links, such as
Ballybunion or Tralee. And it is a lovely way to sample Irish links if
you are a new golfer, a high handicapper, or a bit timid about playing the big-name courses.

Castlegregory opens with a long but gentle par 5, bounded by the
lake along its right length, followed by a par 3. From there you head into
a stretch of holes that is a fine and challenging example of links golf.
The short par-4 third hole, which measures only 265 yards from the
championship tees, is a classic. The temptation to drive the hole is mitigated by the tiny elevated green with a steep drop to the left and high
dunes to the right. Trouble lurks on both sides of the razor-thin fairway.

The par-3 fifth—in excess of 200 yards from the back markers—
plays uphill to a well-protected rolling green with the bay as a backdrop. That is followed by a pair of tight, testing par 4s that offer a
quick trip out of bounds to the beach for shots that drift too far left
and that will snag your golf ball with deep, unfriendly rough and
precarious hills if you stray to the right. When the seventh is playing
into the wind, its 434 yards make bogie a very respectable score.

*Descending from the elevated and contoured eighth green at Castlegregory Golf &
Fishing Club with a par 4 or better is most satisfying.*

The ninth is a short par 3 that requires your tee shot to clear a small pond, but the flat putting surface makes par or birdie a distinct possibility for the turn or to finish the round. The course is played twice to make eighteen holes and while it is short, it is hardly a pushover.

As this edition goes to press, ambitious plans are on the drawing board to expand Castlegregory to eighteen holes. If that happens and the new nine are akin to the original, county Kerry will have yet another championship links for visiting golfers and locals alike to sample.

CASTLEGREGORY GOLF & FISHING CLUB (links, par 34)
Location: Off the Tralee-Dingle Road, just outside the village of
    Castlegregory
Facilities: Practice green, snacks
Green fees: Inexpensive
Telephone: (066) 7139444

KENMARE GOLF CLUB

The lovely town of Kenmare resides at the south end of Killarney National Park at the head of Kenmare Bay. The original nine-hole golf club was founded in 1903, largely as an amusement for tourists and for the benefit of local players. It was expanded to eighteen challenging holes in a glorious, picturesque setting in 1994. It plays to a sporting par 71 and features some breathtaking parkland scenery at the same time.

After six pleasant but fairly easy holes that play on gentle hills among stands of verdant old trees, the course crosses the Kilgarvan Road to the new nine, which will test both your stamina and shot-making ability. The new holes play up and down a steep valley in which a flat lie is the exception and shots that stray from the fairway can be driven deeply into the woods and rough by seemingly innocuous mounds and rocks. A treacherous little stream, pleasant to the eye but devastating to imprecise shots, meanders through the wooded vale, making its presence felt on most of the new holes. All nine of the valley holes demand accuracy and a good measure of length to score. The course favors straight hitters.

Back across the road, the finishing three holes will feel like flat ground after the hilly roller-coaster ride of the valley holes. The par-3 seventeenth is charming. It plays across a small pond to a shallow little green nestled in the shade of towering ancient trees. The short par-4 eighteenth is a good birdie hole and provides the opportunity for a strong finish.

As a rule, the greens at Kenmare are relatively level, not severely bunkered, and by Irish standards they tend to hold better than average, certainly better than any of the fabled links courses. Unfortunately, they tend to be kept a little long and furry, which produces a slow pace and sometimes less than true putts. The rough on the old nine holes tends to be more forgiving and golfer friendly than what you'll find on the new holes in the valley. Nonetheless, the Kenmare Golf Club is enjoyable and aesthetically pleasing. It is an especially good test for most women and high-handicap men.

KENMARE GOLF CLUB (parkland, par 71)
Location: On the Kilgarvan Road at the east edge of Kenmare town
Facilities: Practice green, bar, restaurant
Green fees: Inexpensive
Telephone: (064) 41291   Fax: (064) 42061

County Kildare

THE CURRAGH GOLF CLUB

The Curragh Golf Club proclaims itself to be the oldest golf club in Ireland, established in 1883. Golf was played there as early as 1857. It calls itself a "heathland" golf course. *Webster's New World Dictionary* defines *heath* as a tract of open wasteland. I am not sure The Curragh qualifies as wasteland, but it does sport a huge population of sheep, who graze on the fairways, tees, and greens at will. Horses, I am told, are also given the right of way.

The course is laid out on a hillside among stands of pines. It presents a panorama that heightens expectations. But for all of its history and lore, the golf course is disappointing, especially the greens, which are in desperate need of life support and trauma treatment from a grass doctor. The fairways, too, are in woeful shape in places.

If The Curragh—in its unhappy condition—is not worth a long

detour, it is worth a stop if you're passing that way. The long, par-5 opening hole offers a lovely view. It tees off from the top of the hill and looks out over the whole course. It plays to a smallish green almost 520 yards away. The second and third holes—a pair of par 4s—play back up the hill.

For my money, the back nine is the better of the two. The fourteenth and fifteenth holes are back-to-back par 5s. The fifteenth is a doozy. It is 495 yards long. The elevated tee presents a blind shot that must be kept to the right side of the fairway. Big old pines line the right side of the fairway, protecting the green.

The cute par-3 sixteenth is followed by the best hole on the course. The seventeenth is a long dogleg-left par 4 that measures 447 yards from tee to green. The hole requires two solid golf shots that avoid the trees. A big drive will make it reachable with a long iron; a short drive will bring in the services of a fairway wood. (Seventeen is rated the toughest hole on the course for women and plays 351 challenging yards from the red markers.)

With all of the course's history and its wonderful location—right in the heart of Ireland's thoroughbred racing country—I regret that it is not in better shape. Those sheep add character, but unfortunately they do not enhance playability and often leave you with nasty lies.

It does have a lovely new clubhouse, with a well-stocked pro shop and extraordinarily friendly members. Reserve your tee time well in advance, especially on weekends, as most weekend days are reserved for members' competitions.

THE CURRAGH GOLF CLUB (heathland, par 72)
Location: N7 to Newbridge, then follow the signposts south about three miles
Facilities: Practice green, practice tee, pro shop, bar, restaurant
Green fees: Moderate
Telephone: (045) 441238

THE K CLUB

The K Club could just as easily be in Maryland, Maine, or Montana as in county Kildare; there is virtually nothing to tell you it is Irish. Since it opened, its reputation has been built on its meticulous course maintenance, flawless greens, American-style amenities, and prohibitively expensive green fees. The European pros fell in love with it instantly and it has been the venue for scores of major tournaments. From the championship tees it plays just over 7,000 yards, among ancient woods and natural ponds.

Designed by Arnold Palmer, it is a startling contrast to his masterpiece of golf-course architecture, Tralee Golf Club at Barrow. If Tralee is quintessentially Irish in its character and temperament, The K Club is quintessentially American, although certainly not as difficult as Pinehurst No. 2, Doral's Blue Monster, or Pebble Beach. It is perfectly suited to the big-hitting European PGA players and there is little mystery about why the scores there are so low when it hosts pro tournaments. It is almost impossible to lose a golf ball unless, of course, you chunk one into a lake.

The visual effect of the place is extremely pleasant, enhanced by plantings of flowers, and the tees feature American-style markers telling you the name of the hole (yes, all the holes have names, which is fine at Royal County Down but a little precious at this place).

I am not suggesting there is anything wrong with the golf course. It is a demanding test of the game. The toughest hole on the course—the 429-yard, par-4 ninth—will get the attention of anybody. It is a double dogleg with strategically placed bunkers on the left designed to catch drives that try to cut the corner a little too much. The green is protected by big bunkers on both sides. Two long, accurate shots are required to score. (It is a far less daunting test for women, playing only 287 yards with a slight dogleg right.) And the picturesque eighteenth, on which a lovely little lake guards the big, rolling green and comes into play along much of the left side of the hole, is a marvelous finisher with the magnificent white clubhouse as a backdrop. But the course is just not Irish.

If you want to brag that you have played the track that has been a regular host to the European Open, have a nice time. To me, it is not worth the stiff tariff they demand to play the kind of golf course I belong to back home.

THE K CLUB (parkland, par 72)
Location: Follow the signposts north off the N7 to the village of
    Straffan

Facilities: Practice green, practice tee, golf school, pro shop, rental
   clubs, riding carts, bar, restaurant
Green fees: Very Expensive
Telephone: (01) 601-7300   Fax: (01) 601-7395
E-mail: golf@kclub.ie

County Kilkenny

MOUNT JULIET GOLF CLUB

When I first heard that Jack Nicklaus was designing a golf course
in county Kilkenny, I was thrilled. I knew of the area known as
Mount Juliet and expected Nicklaus to produce a course that would
be a cross between the magnificent Eagle-Vail layout in Colorado
and the legendary and venerable mountain track in Banff, Alberta,
Canada, only with an Irish accent. When I read the rave reviews of
the course after the 1993 Irish Open at Mount Juliet, I couldn't wait
to play it.

In my mind's eye, I envisioned an arduous test consistent with the
rolling Kilkenny landscape, honed from nature by one of the greatest
golfers ever to pick up a club. The outcroppings, ancient trees, and
river Nore all provide an unsurpassed backdrop. The potential is
limitless. Frankly, I expected to see the finest parkland golf course
in the entire country, a world-class experience.

But when I finally got there, my eagerness was supplanted with
disillusionment and my lofty expectations were left largely unful-
filled.

Mount Juliet is not a bad golf course. In fact, it's a fine golf
course. It's got lovely undulating greens, protected by strategically
placed and difficult bunkers and manmade water hazards that are
the signature of Jack Nicklaus-designed golf courses.

It has some picturesque and extremely challenging holes that
require both skilled shot making and good course management.
Most notable are the 185-yard, par-3 third hole (with water and trees
galore), the 550-yard, par-5 tenth hole (which has a split fairway that
can be approached from two different directions), and the 440-
yard, par-4 thirteenth hole (which requires two long, accurate shots
to carry the pond that guards the green). The eighteenth green is

tucked next to a big manmade lake and demands precision to score, as does the tight 400-plus-yard, par-4 fourth hole, also protected by a little pond.

The problem is that Mount Juliet Golf Club could be anywhere in the United States. It may be a rarity in Ireland, but to the visiting American, it is standard fare. The topography has been carved, caressed, manipulated, processed, and homogenized into looking and feeling like an American golf course.

There is nothing to suggest Ireland. Nothing reminds the golfer with each shot that the Kilkenny Mountains are a unique bit of real estate in a unique part of the world. The course appears to have been constructed in spite of the glorious mountains and valleys and gullies and copses instead of in conjunction with them. It is coerced from the landscape.

Despite the Nicklaus trademarks and a handful of interesting holes, Mount Juliet is relatively flat, open, and forgiving. In a word, it is ordinary. It aspires to greatness but manages to achieve only a cut above mediocrity.

The golf course is meticulously maintained and manicured. It may be, as its own voluminous, slickly produced publicity suggests, "the best maintained golf course in Ireland." It is certainly one of them. But the battalion of maintenance workers with its armored division of imported Toro-brand mowers, tractors, trimmers, and the like have proved only that it can grow extremely good grass. Raking, combing, brushing, and shaving the place within an inch of its life have failed to produce a golf course with any real Irish character.

As one looks over the course, it often appears there are more maintenance workers than golfers. And for a course that purports to be so special, I regret to report that some of those workers need to be told that women—who are charged the same hefty green fee as men—are entitled to the same exact courtesy, a detail that seems to have been overlooked. A fellow mowing the fringe on the par-3 sixth hole politely stopped and waited at the back of the green while I hit my tee shot. He proceeded to mow away while my wife hit hers.

Mount Juliet's own promotional literature says it is the "Augusta of Ireland." That's precisely what's wrong. Augusta is in Georgia. Why would anybody want to move it?

"The pros and the good amateurs are in love with this course," said the amiable and highly efficient starter just before we teed off for the first time. This is not surprising. Why wouldn't a tournament player love it? It has almost no trouble off the tees. The fairways are generous. And the rough is so well groomed that a tough lie is almost impossible. With a nasty little slice, I found the trees to the right on the par-5 tenth hole and expected disaster. It turned out, however, that my lie was so good and the trees were so far apart that even a ten handicapper like me could get back into play and into scoring position with little difficulty.

If Mount Juliet were a golf club anywhere in the U.S. it would be considered a good, average golf course. Its self-generated publicity leads the golfer visiting Ireland to believe it is so much more. Alas, it is not.

MOUNT JULIET GOLF CLUB (parkland, par 72)
Location: On the outskirts of Thomastown, about ten miles south
    of Kilkenny town
Facilities: Driving range, practice green, golf school, pro shop,
    rental clubs, a few riding carts, bar, restaurant
Green fees: Very Expensive
Telephone: (056) 73000   Fax: (056) 73019
E-mail: info@mountjuliet.ie

County Limerick

ADARE MANOR GOLF CLUB

For several years, there were two Adare Manor Golf Clubs, and the village of Adare, long the home of the earls of Dunraven, was the site of a titanic clash between the new (represented by the developers of the swank and ultra-expensive Adare Manor hotel and golf complex) and the old (represented by a quaint little golf course that has been a part of the village for more than a century).

The hotel developers, as the story was related by several local citizens, took it for granted that they could subsume the name Adare Manor Golf Club when they opened the hotel. After all, they had commissioned Robert Trent Jones, Sr., to build a par-72

championship parkland golf course that charges nonresidents a
hefty tariff to tee it up. It is all American. It's a manicured, mas-
saged, immaculate parkland course that's just like the courses
Americans play at home all the time.

Like some of its glitzy American-style cousins—The K Club, Mount
Juliet, Druids Glen—it would be a respectable course in the U.S.,
although it would not be comparable to, say, Oakmont, Firestone, or
the west course at Winged Foot. There's nothing particularly wrong
with it; it's just not Irish. It's not what I travel to Ireland to play.

The controversy about the name, and the attendant confusion
among those golfers trying to make sense out of things, was resolved

*The charming par-3 first hole at Adare Manor Golf Club plays up to the walls of a
fifteenth-century castle.*

in 1996 when the hotel owners agreed to call their slick new course
the Adare Golf Club. "If they wanted the name, they should bloody
well have paid for it," snipped one local resident over his glass of
Guinness.

This profile, then, is about the old Adare Manor Golf Club, the
one established in 1900, the one that is relatively short, easy, cheap,
and absolutely, totally charming. In stark contrast to its new, high-
priced neighbor, the old Adare Manor Golf Club is profoundly, distinctly, and completely Irish. It plays a little less than 5,800 yards to
a par 69 (about 5,100 yards for women, with a par of 70). It is lush
and weaves its way among the ruins of a Franciscan friary, founded
by the seventh earl of Kildare in 1464. It simply oozes character—
from those historic ruins to its old-fashioned layout. Yes, it is a parkland course, but it's a gem, from the par-3 first hole, with the ruins
of the old earl's castle as a backdrop, to the eighteenth, where a bad
slice will rattle the bones in the friary's cemetery.

In fact, if you hit a little long and to the left on the par-3 fourteenth hole, you'll find yourself chipping back from within the
stone walls of what was once a magnificent abbey. Don't hook your
approach on the par-4 sixteenth—the most difficult hole on the
course for men—or pull your drive on seventeen. Either can result
in a close encounter with the abbey walls.

All of the fairways on this splendid little track are narrow, lined
with huge, magnificent ancient trees that provide shade and shelter
and that reach out like a claw to catch the occasional errant golf
ball. Some of the holes are fairly easy. The par-5 ninth, for example,
a gentle dogleg left that plays only 476 yards, is reachable in two and
offers good chance for eagle or birdie. On the other hand, there are
some demanding golf holes. The par-4 fifth—a 376-yard dogleg left
that arcs around the cemetery and is rated the hardest hole on the
course for women—requires that you split the tight, narrow fairway
in order to score. And the testing 215-yard, par-3 eighth, which plays
to a long narrow green, requires a precise tee shot to have a birdie
putt. (For women, my wife tells me it is tougher than the number-
one stroke hole because of its length. It measures 191 yards but
remains a par 3.)

The Adare Manor Golf Club is lovely, peaceful, and good for the
ego. It is a personal favorite, less for the golf than for the aesthetics

of the place. If your option is to play Lahinch or Royal Portrush or if you're on a tight schedule, it's not worth a detour. On the other hand, it is worth a stop if you're passing through Adare or if you just want a breather from the likes of Old Head or Ballybunion.

ADARE MANOR GOLF CLUB (parkland, par 69)
Location: On the Limerick-city side of the village of Adare
Facilities: Practice green, pro shop, bar, restaurant
Green fees: Inexpensive
Telephone: (061) 396204   Fax: (061) 396800

County Meath

LAYTOWN & BETTYSTOWN GOLF CLUB

When you drive by the Laytown & Bettystown Golf Club on the Coast Road, it looks fairly tame and uninspired, but this pleasant and challenging links is the home of champions. "This is a player's course," said European PGA pro Sean Browne. "It's a great test and it's a lot of fun." He ought to know. His father, Bobby Browne, has been the pro there for as long as anybody can remember. "It's a course you keep coming back to." It's also a course that has produced world-class golfers, such as tour champion Des Smyth. And it is renowned for training youngsters to play the game.

L & B (as it is often written) is a narrow strip of linksland sandwiched between the Irish Sea and the Coast Road, just north of the coastal resort of Bettystown. The club was established in 1909, and it has long been a favorite of vacationers. In the late 1990s the course underwent a few design improvements that both made it more challenging and improved its playability.

The par-4 ninth, called "Lighthouse" after a local landmark and which takes you as far from the clubhouse as you will get, is a fine golf hole. The three finishers, especially the short par-5 eighteenth, offer good scoring opportunities, save for when the wind kicks up from the sea, making the green a difficult target.

The fairways are tight and demand accurate tee shots. The greens are fairly fast and true and present an assortment of designs to negotiate—plateau greens, turtleback greens, devilishly well protected greens. They are hard to hit and even harder to hold, which makes scoring a measure of how well you manage your short game.

LAYTOWN & BETTYSTOWN GOLF CLUB (links, par 71)
Location: Immediately north of Bettystown off the Coast Road
Facilities: Practice green, pro shop, bar, restaurant
Green fees: Moderate
Telephone: (041) 27170   Fax: (041) 28506

County Wexford

COURTOWN GOLF CLUB

Courtown Golf Club is an ideal taste of Irish golf if you are a mid- to high handicapper, a soupçon of flavor without what may seem like the overpowering nature of a coastal links. The well-treed layout is pleasant, but not particularly challenging to a single-digit or scratch player. The majority of the holes that make up its nearly 6,500 yards tend to be straight, relatively open, and forgiving. The greens are ample and well maintained but not particularly difficult to putt or approach. An imprecise shot will invariably leave a recovery shot that can salvage the hole. From a couple of tees and fairways you can glimpse the Irish Sea, but this is a parkland course in every sense of the word.

For the better players it is the par 3s on Courtown that hold the greatest interest. All four of them are sporting, if not hugely long. The 150-yard eighteenth, for example, requires a lengthy carry over a cute little lake that has swallowed more than its share of golf balls over the years.

The 516-yard, par-5 ninth hole with its graceful dogleg may be the best single hole on the course for men and women. It's long enough and designed in such a way that only the pros or abnormally long hitting players are likely to think about going for it in two. Heading into the back nine with a par here is fully satisfactory.

In an effort to make the course a little more difficult, plantings of trees and shrubs were added in several places in the mid-1980s and have grown and matured with each passing year. They now force players to hit with slightly more accuracy. Nonetheless, Courtown remains a wide, open, and golfer-friendly course.

Its principal attractions are its convenient location and its playability for less-than-expert golfers who might find such other courses in the area as The European Club and Wicklow simply beyond their abilities to play and enjoy. The biggest drawback to Courtown Golf Club is the enormous amount of play it receives.

COURTOWN GOLF CLUB (parkland, par 71)
Location: About four miles east of Gorey from the N11 and about
    a mile from the coastal resort of Courtown
Facilities: Practice green, pro shop, bar, snacks
Green fees: Moderate
Telephone: (055) 25166   Fax: (055) 25553

ROSSLARE GOLF CLUB

Rosslare Harbor (the Irish, like the British, actually spell it *Harbour*) is the gateway to Ireland from much of Europe. Ferries sail into the port daily from several ports in Britain as well as from Cherbourg and Le Havre in France. It is a bustling area replete with the feel of a seaside resort that has more than a touch of Coney Island to it.

Just a few miles from where the ferries dock is the Rosslare Golf Club, the first introduction to links golf that many visiting Europeans get. It is far from the most grueling or demanding links test you'll face, but it has some challenging holes, including the long par-5 third hole. It is a gentle dogleg left that requires two precise shots to set up a chip and a birdie putt. The par-4 fifth features a grassy gulch in front of the green that creates an optical illusion of the green being closer on the second shot than it is.

One of my biggest problems with Rosslare Golf Club is that it gets an enormous amount of play and the course policy seems to be to keep the greens a bit long and furry. As a result they are slow and sometimes less than true. In almost every case, there is less break than the eye perceives.

The par-4 sixth hole is an exceptionally good test for women. While it plays only 250 yards from the red markers, it demands a solid drive of about 175 yards or more to a small landing area in order to be in scoring position.

The best par 3 on the golf course is the fourteenth. It is protected by a gaping bunker in front, making a runup impossible, while a shot that's too bold can skitter right off the green and out onto the strand. The three finishers—a pair of par 4s and a par 5 that's reachable in two—make for a solid conclusion to the round.

Rosslare Golf Club was established in 1905 and a new nine was added in 1992.

ROSSLARE GOLF CLUB (links, par 72)
Location: In the town of Rosslare, about six miles from the harbor and about ten miles south of Wexford town
Facilities: Practice green, practice ground, pro shop, bar, lunch, dinner
Green fees: Moderate
Telephone: (053) 32203

The view across the front nine at Rosslare Golf Club.

ST. HELEN'S BAY GOLF & COUNTRY CLUB

The golf course at St. Helen's Bay is a hybrid—part links, part parkland. There are more parkland holes than links holes. The problem is that you have to play fourteen parkland holes in order to get to those that are of real interest and challenge. Opened in the mid-1990s, the course took some time to mature and suffered for what seemed to be a rush to allow players onto it. The fairways have become lush, the rough is generally well cared for, and the greens are respectable, though slow. The greens lend themselves to runup approach shots, even though that is not the optimal way to play most parkland courses. One of my biggest objections to architect Philip Walton's design at St. Helen's Bay is the largely unprotected nature of the greens. An errant shot rarely finds a bunker or dune that renders recovery difficult.

The best four holes on the course are the four finishers, which are pure links, with the water of Rosslare Harbor plashing onto the boulder-strewn beach. The fifteenth is a long, narrow par 5 that plays to nearly 530 yards from the white markers and rewards precision more than muscle. Men must strike two solid long shots to set up a chip and a birdie putt. (It is a 498-yard par 5 for women and requires three well-placed shots—often all three with woods—to be in scoring position. It is appropriately rated the most difficult hole on the course on the ladies' card.)

The par-3, 204-yard seventeenth is a fine test, tucked next to the harbor, with cargo ships and passenger ferries visible in the distance on clear days. It may be the best hole on the golf course. The long, undulating green is heavily protected on the left by dunes and high rough.

My initial impression of St. Helen's Bay was of a golf course with unmet potential because of the immature stage at which it was opened and the generally poor quality of the greens. It has now realized some of its possibilities and is a far better golf course than when it opened. The course has benefited from some well-planned and expertly executed maintenance and the greens have received substantial repair work. The result is a good, if not great, golf course on a spectacular piece of seaside real estate.

Since it opened, St. Helen's Bay has become a popular venue for European and Irish vacationers who flock to the beaches and seaside resorts in the area during the summer months. Advance booking, especially on weekends in July and August, is a must.

ST. HELEN'S BAY GOLF & COUNTRY CLUB (parkland/links, par 72)
Location: About a mile from Rosslare Ferryport off the N25 in the village of Kilrane
Facilities: Practice green, pro shop, bar, snacks
Green fees: Moderate
Telephone: (053) 33234 or 33669   Fax: (053) 33803

County Wicklow

DRUIDS GLEN GOLF CLUB

What would it take to build a spectacular, championship parkland golf course within easy driving distance of Dublin? A consortium of investors put that question to architects Tom Craddock and Pat Ruddy (the same man who designed the extraordinarily brilliant European Club links just a few miles south). Twelve million Irish punts, or not quite twenty million U.S. dollars later, they came up with an answer.

The architects have come up with a multiflavored golf course that purports to offer a smorgasbord of golfing delicacies. It serves up a soupçon of Old Tom Morris (the second hole, a par 4, was designed to emulate the famous "Road Hole" at St. Andrews), a slice of Dr. Alister MacKenzie (the par-3 eighth hole is supposed to feel like the sixteenth at Augusta), and a portion of Pete Dye's TPC Stadium Course at Sawgrass in Florida (the seventeenth is a par 3 that plays to an island green). As you might expect, with the kind of money that was lavished on the place, the fairways are lush. The greens are like a fine carpet. The setting is beautiful. The European pros who flock to tournaments there adore it.

But beyond the pros, beyond the wealthy European and American visitors, there is something about unrestrained conspicuous consumption that nettles the basically frugal Irish soul. Druids Glen has sparked an animated debate among golfers in Ireland. Some predict a brilliant future for the course, saying the owners are on the cutting edge of Irish golf; others predict dire consequences and economic failure. The expense of construction alone has raised eyebrows and set tongues to wagging.

The tariff to walk in the door is stiff and if you want to join, they'll sell you a membership for the equivalent of about forty thousand U.S. dollars, after you've served your time on the waiting list. It is allegedly the most expensive golf-club membership in Ireland.

"They won't see many local players," said my golfing partner over a postround pint at Blainroe Golf Club, a few miles south of Druids Glen. "That's just too much money for a round of golf."

"It's pretty clear they don't want to see much of the likes of us," chimed in a woman who had overheard our conversation. "They want to cater to the Germans and the Swiss and the Americans and the Japanese," sniffed another woman, joining the debate.

It is an argument that is unlikely to be resolved, but as the millennium dawned the course enjoyed financial success. While it attracts few locals as regular players, the club boasts a tee sheet that is often full through the summer months, with golfing visitors from around the world booking tee times months in advance.

DRUIDS GLEN GOLF CLUB (parkland, par 72)
Location: Newtownmountkennedy, about halfway between Bray
    and Wicklow town just off the N11
Facilities: Practice green, practice ground, pro shop, caddies (with
    advance notice), bar, restaurant
Green fees: Very Expensive
Telephone: (01) 287-3600   Fax: (01) 287-3699
E-mail: druids@indigo.ie

CHAPTER 4

Golf Resorts and Castles

If you do not want to restrict your golfing trip to Ireland's fabled links courses, there are other options. A growing number of Europeans and some Americans are eager to try the rapidly expanding collection of full-service Irish golf resorts or castles that have golf courses.

I have used the same approximate price scale employed in chapter 5 on hotels, restaurants, and the like. Note that many of these establishments offer discounts on green fees to hotel or castle guests, but few provide them free, as a benefit of staying there. As we go to press, some castles and resorts are experimenting with American-style packages that include golf in the price (such as three nights, breakfast, dinner, and golf for a certain set amount) but they are still a rarity. The following hotel ratings are based on double occupancy, and in most cases—as is traditional in Ireland—the price includes room and a full Irish breakfast. The restaurant ratings are based on the price of dinner for two (appetizer, entree, and dessert) excluding wine, beer, or cocktails.

The U.S. dollar values are an approximation based on the exchange rates of the Irish punt, British pound, and euro as we go to press. Travelers should be aware that foreign currency exchange rates change daily and over time are affected by such factors as macro- and microeconomics, global inflation, interest rates, and the like. When the U.S. dollar is strong, that usually means American travelers in Ireland will get a bargain; conversely when the dollar is weak, U.S. travelers will pay a premium.

Hotels

Very Expensive   above $250
Expensive $175-$250
Moderate $125-$175
Inexpensive   under $125

Restaurants

Very Expensive   above $135
Expensive $90-$135
Moderate $60-$90
Inexpensive   under $60

Golf Resorts

Golf resorts—self-contained venues for the traveling golfer, including excellent accommodations, good golf, and fine restaurants—have long been a staple in the United States. The first, and some of the most famous, golf resorts date to the 1920s and 1930s and were playgrounds for the rich. Today, from Hawaii to Florida, golf resorts are commonplace and encompass a wide range of price and quality. They are less prevalent in Ireland, and were all but unknown until the mid-1980s. But several noteworthy resorts have opened in the past few years, and more are on the drawing board.

For the most part I am not a big fan of golf resorts in Ireland. It's too much like staying at home. I do not travel to wonderful, rural, friendly Ireland in order to get the same exact thing I can get in a thousand different places back in the States. Nonetheless, in the interest of providing a full range of information for golfers considering a trip to Ireland, I include the following.

The Irish Republic

County Cavan

SLIEVE RUSSELL HOTEL, GOLF AND COUNTRY CLUB

Location: Ballyconnell
Rooms: Expensive   Restaurant: Moderate/Expensive
Telephone: (049) 952-6444   Fax: (049) 952-6474
E-mail: slieverussell@sqgroup.com

Slieve Russell has matured and benefited from skilled management and some design changes since it opened. The hotel boasts 151 well-appointed guest rooms along with elegant public rooms and a restaurant that enjoys a fine reputation. The resort is part of a 300-acre estate that includes parkland, gardens, and lakes in the north-central part of Ireland, about a two-hour drive from Dublin or Belfast. The par-72 championship golf course plays more than 7,000 yards from the back tees among trees and lakes and has been the site of professional and amateur tournaments since it opened in 1992. The resort also has a nine-hole executive course and a lighted driving range. There is also a heated indoor swimming pool, four tennis courts, a fitness center, and a steam room. Golf packages are available.

County Cork

FERNHILL GOLF & COUNTRY CLUB

Location: Carrigaline
Rooms: Inexpensive   Restaurant: Inexpensive
Telephone: (021) 372226   Fax: (021) 371011
E-mail: fernhill@iol.ie

Fernhill Golf & Country Club bills itself as a full service resort with an emphasis on sports. In addition to its own eighteen-hole golf course, there's tennis, an indoor swimming pool, sauna, and health club facilities. The hotel is small, with only seventeen guest rooms. Prices are extremely modest. The location just south of Cork city in the village of Carrigaline is convenient to the Cork airport and passenger ferry port. Golf packages are available.

County Donegal

BUNDORAN GOLF CLUB AND GREAT NORTHERN HOTEL

Location: Bundoran
Rooms: Moderate   Restaurant: Moderate
Telephone: (072) 41204   Fax: (072) 41114

This large, beach-resort hotel has long been a family and tour-bus favorite. The Atlantic coast, from Rosses Point up to Donegal town, is dotted with resorts of various quality. This is one of the better ones, but be warned that it gets booked up well in advance from early June through September and even into October. The hotel is surrounded by the 6,150-yard, par-69 Bundoran Golf Club—a good, if short, links course. (See chapter 3.) The facility is situated between Donegal Golf Club, about ten miles to the north, and County Sligo Golf Course, about a half-hour south on the N15.

ROSAPENNA GOLF CLUB AND HOTEL

Location: Downings
Rooms: Expensive   Restaurant: Moderate
Telephone: (074) 55301   Fax: (074) 55128
E-mail: rosapenna@tinet.ie

Old Tom Morris—the legendary architect of such brilliant tests of the game as Lahinch and Royal County Down—built the Rosapenna links for the third earl of Leitrim in 1893. It plays a little over 6,200 yards to a par 70 and is about as far north as you can go, at the northernmost tip of Donegal. Friends who have played it say the course is worth the trip, but not for low handicappers or big hitters. The forty-six-room hotel, which sits almost at the center of the golf course, is loaded with golfing memorabilia. A new nine-hole course opened in the summer of 1995.

County Dublin

DEER PARK HOTEL AND GOLF COURSES

Location: Howth
Rooms: Moderate/Expensive   Restaurants: Expensive
Telephone: (01) 832-2624   Fax: (01) 839-2405
E-mail: sales@deerpark.iol.ie

Deer Park immodestly bills itself as Ireland's largest golf complex, with a fifty-room hotel; eighteen-hole, par-72 golf course; 3,130-yard nine-hole course; and twelve-hole, par-36 executive course. The facility sits on the grounds of Howth Castle, on a hillside overlooking Dublin Bay, and offers some excellent scenery. Golf packages are available for hotel guests.

PORTMARNOCK HOTEL & GOLF LINKS

Location: Portmarnock
Rooms: Very Expensive   Restaurants: Expensive/Very Expensive
Telephone: (01) 846-0611   Fax: (01) 846-2442

This modern, luxury hotel is set on what was once the estate of the John Jameson family, makers of the Irish whiskey of the same name. The original manor house has been converted into the public rooms of the hotel, including a cozy bar and two highly acclaimed restaurants. A guest-room wing, designed very much in the image of the Jamesons' magnificent country house, offers more than one hundred well-appointed rooms.

PGA pro and European Ryder Cup star Bernhard Langer was commissioned to design a world-class links golf course. It was opened in 1995, plays to a par 72, and features myriad pot bunkers, natural water hazards, and turtleback greens.

County Galway

GALWAY BAY GOLF AND COUNTRY CLUB HOTEL

Location: Oranmore
Rooms: Expensive   Restaurant: Moderate
Telephone: (091) 790500   Fax: (091) 792510
E-mail: gbaygolf@iol.ie

The imposing hotel features views of the golf course—designed by Irish touring pro Christy O'Connor, Jr.—and of Galway Bay, and offers golf packages for hotel guests both at the local course and at other courses in county Galway and county Clare. The facility is conveniently located within a ten-minute drive of Galway city center, with its restaurants and nightlife.

County Kildare

THE KILDARE HOTEL & COUNTRY CLUB

Location: Straffan
Rooms: Very Expensive   Restaurant: Very Expensive
Telephone: (01) 601-7200   Fax: (01) 601-7299
E-mail: hotel@kclub.ie

Arnold Palmer—in his second venture into Irish golf-course design—is the architect of record for the 7,150-yard, par-72 parkland golf course called "The K Club." (See chapter 3.) The luxury facility also offers fishing, tennis, swimming, exercise room, and a croquet field.

The resort's literature describes the French restaurant as "sublime elegance." The hotel itself was constructed out of the nineteenth-century mansion known as Straffan House, which overlooks a mile stretch of the river Liffey, the fabled river that flows through Dublin. The place is superbly appointed and the service is exceptional. It is one of the most expensive resorts in Ireland, with room prices to rival the Arizona Biltmore or the Greenbrier and green fees in the range of Doral or Pebble Beach in the United States.

County Kilkenny

MOUNT JULIET

Location: Thomastown
Rooms: Very Expensive   Restaurant: Very Expensive
Telephone: (056) 73000   Fax: (056) 73019
Toll free: 1-800-447-7462
E-mail: info@mountjuliet.ie

Mount Juliet's guest house and golf course are about ten miles south of Kilkenny town on the outskirts of the village of Thomastown. The manor house was built in the mid-1700s as a country estate for Irish nobility on the banks of the river Nore. The accommodations are well appointed and extremely comfortable.

The Lady Helen McCalmont dining room offers up some incredibly delicious dishes prepared with a combination of classical French and innovative Irish touches, and the baking-done in the hotel kitchen-is nothing short of magnificent. The complex also offers tennis, a gym, and squash courts, as well as fishing. Jack Nicklaus designed the golf course. (See chapter 3.)

County Limerick

ADARE MANOR

Location: Adare
Rooms: Very Expensive   Restaurant: Very Expensive

Telephone: (061) 396566   Fax: (061) 396124
Toll free: 1-800-462-3273
E-mail: reservations@adaremanor.com

Adare Manor, a Gothic mansion built in the middle of the 1800s, sits on the outskirts of the village of Adare, about ten miles from Limerick city. The town is quaint and charming with thatched-roof houses painted in bright colors. For those into blood sport, Adare is the headquarters of several major Irish hunt clubs—the people who chase after dogs on horseback as the dogs run some poor fox to death. ("The unspeakable in full pursuit of the uneatable," said Oscar Wilde.)

The manor itself is highly regarded for its amenities and service. The restored mansion is furnished with antiques, Waterford crystal chandeliers, and ornate fireplaces. The guest rooms are richly appointed and the bathrooms are generous and verge on the spectacular.

The parkland, par-72 golf course on the grounds of the estate opened in the summer of 1995. It was the design of Robert Trent Jones, Sr. In addition, for the serious golfer in search of a golf resort, Adare Manor is centrally located and convenient to other courses. It is less than an hour from Shannon Airport and within easy driving distance of Ballybunion, Shannon Golf Club, and Lahinch.

County Monaghan

NUREMORE HOTEL AND COUNTRY CLUB

Location: Carrickmacross
Rooms: Expensive   Restaurant: Expensive
Telephone: (042) 966-1438   Fax: (042) 966-1853
E-mail: nuremore@tinet.ie

This large, well-equipped hotel is in the Irish heartland on the shores of a pleasant little lake, around which the golf course is designed. The hotel offers big modern rooms and features an indoor swimming pool, steam room, and gym. The golf course has been home to the PGA Ulster Open since 1992 and plays nearly 6,500 yards to a par 72.

County Tipperary

DUNDRUM HOUSE HOTEL
AND COUNTY TIPPERARY GOLF CLUB

Location: Dundrum
Rooms: Very Expensive   Restaurant: Expensive
Telephone: (062) 71116   Fax: (062) 71366

The imposing manor house was built in 1730 as the stronghold of the Irish chieftains who ruled that part of the world. Today's sixty-room hotel sits on 170 acres on the banks of the Multeen River. The Georgian-style guest rooms are spacious. The public rooms feature large, welcoming fireplaces and stained-glass windows. The par-72 golf course is long enough to give virtually all golfers a challenge. It plays some 6,700 yards through woods and along the river.

County Waterford

GOLD COAST GOLF HOTEL
AND LEISURE CENTRE

Location: Dungarvan
Rooms: Moderate   Restaurants: Moderate
Telephone: (058) 42249   Fax: (058) 43378
E-mail: cionea@indigo.ie

This modern, thirty-seven-room resort's literature says it "specializes in golf holidays," offering golf packages, first-class accommodations, two restaurants, and a pleasant bar. It also touts its other athletic facilities, including a large heated swimming pool, gym, and Jacuzzi. The hotel is located just a short chip away from Dungarvan Bay, and the eighteenth hole on the par-72 golf course plays along the sea.

County Wicklow

CHARLESLAND GOLF AND
COUNTRY CLUB HOTEL

Location: Greystones
Rooms: Moderate/Expensive   Restaurant: Expensive

Telephone: (01) 287-6764   Fax: (01) 287-3882
E-mail: charlesland@tinet.ie

This facility near the Irish Sea coast is south of Dublin in the shadow of Sugarloaf Mountain. The golf course was designed by Eddie Hackett, one of my favorite Irish golf-course architects, who designed the magnificent Ring of Kerry course in county Kerry. The signature hole, the thirteenth, features spectacular views from the highest point on the golf course. The hotel is small and has only a dozen rooms. The restaurant offers Irish and continental cuisine.

RATHSALLAGH HOUSE AND GOLF CLUB

Location: Dunlavin
Rooms: Expensive   Restaurant: Very Expensive
Telephone: (045) 403112   Fax: (045) 403343

Rathsallagh House—which was a stable back in the late 1700s—sits on more than five hundred wooded acres, which include ponds, streams, and lovely gardens. This seventeen-room small hotel is known for its personal service and its kitchen, which boasts a wall-full of awards. Dishes using fresh, organically grown vegetables, fish, and seasonal game are the specialties of the chef and the breakfasts are a fine way to prepare for a day of golf.

The par-72 parkland golf course was designed by Irish pro Christy O'Connor, Jr., and amateur champion Peter McEvoy. The holes are laid out on the rolling terrain among mature trees and natural water hazards.

TULFARRIS GOLF CLUB

Location: Blessington Lakes
Rooms: Moderate   Restaurant: Moderate
Telephone: (045) 867555   Fax: (045) 867561

Tulfarris House Hotel has long been a comfortable location from which golfers could sample the courses of county Wicklow, county Kildare, and those west of Dublin city. The twenty guest rooms are comfortable and the food is good. The serene location at the foot of the Wicklow Mountains overlooks Poulaphuca and Blessington

Lakes. In fact, there are no less than fifteen ponds and lakes that come into play on the golf course. The course itself was opened in spring 1999 and plays to a demanding 7,194 yards from the back tees.

Northern Ireland

County Armagh

SILVERWOOD GOLF HOTEL & COUNTRY CLUB

Location: Lurgan
Rooms: Inexpensive   Restaurant: Moderate
Telephone: (0801) 762-327722   Fax: (0801) 762-325290

This small, modern hotel is under the Best Western umbrella and enjoys a reputation for comfort and convenience (it's only a couple of minutes from the M1 highway out of Belfast). It offers a variety of golf packages and features its own eighteen-hole parkland golf course, a nine-hole executive-length track, and a lighted driving range.

County Derry

BROWN TROUT GOLF & COUNTRY INN

Location: Aghadowey
Rooms: Inexpensive/Moderate
Telephone: (0801) 265-868209

This hostelry sits on the banks of the Agivey River and boasts an impressive list of hospitality awards, including the 1993 British Airways Tourism Award. Its seventeen bedrooms have all been refurbished and visitors are welcomed with cozy peat fires. The nine-hole golf course plays through some very pleasant, treelined parkland.

RADISSON ROE PARK HOTEL & GOLF RESORT

Location: Limavady
Rooms: Expensive   Restaurants: Moderate/Expensive
Telephone: (0801) 5047-22222   Fax: (0801) 5047-22313
E-mail: reservations@radisson.nireland.com

Of all the golf resorts in Ireland, this one has the most American look and feel to it. It is part of the Radisson group, which cut its teeth on golf resorts in the United States, and this transplant features everything you would expect at any upscale golf resort from Portland, Maine, to Portland, Oregon. In addition to more than sixty first-class rooms, it advertises a comfortable bar; two restaurants; rec center with pool, sauna, gym, steam room, and Jacuzzi; beauty salon; and children's playroom. The golf course is a par-70 parkland track that meanders through what used to be a Georgian estate. In addition, there's a pro shop, practice green, and driving range.

Castles with Golf Courses

The castles of Ireland have been the subject of many books and magazine articles over the years. Since the 1950s, many of Ireland's fabled castles have been turned into magnificent hotels. A few of these castles have their own golf courses. If you have a special interest in sampling a bit of Irish history along with your golf, the following notes are for you.

Be advised that the castle hotels with golf courses are very close to the top of the price scale. The golf, on the other hand, covers a broad spectrum, ranging from championship caliber to barely a cut above unplayable.

County Clare

DROMOLAND CASTLE

Location: Newmarket-on-Fergus
Rooms: Very Expensive   Restaurant: Very Expensive
Telephone: (061) 368144   Fax: (061) 363355
Toll free: 1-800-346-7007

The luxurious and elegant seventy-five rooms of Dromoland Castle are only outdone by the magnificent setting. It's just ten minutes from Shannon Airport, but you'll think you've passed through a time warp into another century. The public rooms are decorated with medieval suits of armor, woodcarvings, tapestries, and ornately framed oil paintings. The golf course (see chapter 3) is a fine test that plays to a par 71. Green fees are discounted for hotel residents and preferential tee times are available.

The restaurant overlooks Dromoland Lough and the eighteenth green and serves very respectable French cuisine. For the accommodations, food, service, and golf, Dromoland Castle is one of the best in this class and its proximity to the airport makes it an ideal place to start or end your Irish golfing vacation. In addition, it is an easy drive from Lahinch if you opt to dine and sleep in medieval splendor but prefer something more challenging in the way of golf.

County Kildare

KILKEA CASTLE

Location: Castledermot
Rooms: Very Expensive   Restaurant: Expensive
Telephone: (0503) 45156   Fax: (0503) 45187

Kilkea Castle bills itself as the oldest inhabited castle in Ireland, dating to 1180. It is reputed to be haunted by the ghost of the eleventh earl of Kildare. The new eighteen-hole parkland golf course, which plays to a par 71, was opened in 1994. It surrounds the castle and offers some spectacular views along with an abundance of water—the river Greese flows in and around it and there are two manmade lakes.

The bar features stained-glass windows, a huge fireplace, and the original twelfth-century stone walls. The restaurant boasts innovative Irish cuisine. There is also a heated swimming pool and gym. (No, they don't make you exercise with maces, pikes, and battle axes.)

County Mayo

ASHFORD CASTLE

Location: Cong
Rooms: Very Expensive   Restaurants: Very Expensive
Telephone: (092) 46003   Fax: (092) 46260
Toll free: 1-800-346-7007
E mail: ashford@ashford.ie

Many Americans became familiar with the thirteenth-century Ashford Castle in 1984, when President Reagan took a trip to his ancestral home in the village of Ballyporeen and then went up to Cong for the night. It was a made-for-TV stop. The drawbridge and battlements made their way onto all the U.S. television newscasts. Ashford Castle is big and luxurious, with prices to match.

It's been a hotel since before World War II. It boasts two fine restaurants—one Irish and the other French. The golf isn't much to write home about. There is a nine-hole golf course—a pleasant little patch of grass in an equally pleasant little forest—with one of the bunkers cut into the shape of a shamrock.

County Waterford

WATERFORD CASTLE

Location: Ballinakill
Rooms: Very Expensive   Restaurant: Very Expensive
Telephone: (051) 871633   Fax: (051) 871634
Toll free: 1-800-221-1074

Waterford Castle is about as secluded as you can get. It sits on a 300-acre island in the river Suir, southeast of Waterford city, and is reachable only by a private car ferry. The castle is upscale, richly appointed, and regal. The golf course is a par-72 parkland course opened in 1992, designed by Des Smyth, a well-known Irish golf pro and course designer.

CHAPTER 5

Where to Stay, Where to Eat, and What to Do When You're Not Golfing

Ireland is one of the most user-friendly places in the world for visitors. Much of the Irish economy is dependent on tourism and the whole island is pleasant and welcoming. Northern Ireland has moved quickly to recapture that spirit after years of sectarian strife kept many tourists away. But it's more than business. The Irish are genuinely hospitable. What is lacking in climatic warmth is more than amply recompensed by the warmth of the people. It is an especially welcoming place for Americans. There is hardly a family in Ireland that doesn't have a relative—or a whole branch of the clan, for that matter—living in the United States or Canada.

The booming popularity of Ireland as a destination for European and American tourists, and golfers in particular, resulted in a corresponding price increase for hotels and meals. It also resulted in a late 1990s bull market for hotels and restaurants, both in the construction of new facilities and the expansion or refurbishing of existing ones. I am pleased to report for this second edition that Ireland remains a comparative bargain when measured against golf destinations in Europe and North America. The service and value that have been Irish traditions have not been appreciably compromised by the expanded tourist market, and in many cases the scale of luxury has actually increased.

The types of accommodations range from richly refurbished castles and elegant country houses to inexpensive private homes that

bear B&B (bed and breakfast) signs and offer thoroughly acceptable lodging.

In both the Irish Republic and Northern Ireland, all public
accommodations are subject to regular government inspection to
ensure certain minimum standards are met. Throughout this chapter, I have attempted to point out hotels and restaurants that are
especially convenient to the best golfing venues or that cater particularly to golfers. There are several new entries in this edition, most
of which are completely new or newly remodeled since publication
of the first edition. Alas, some old favorites no longer measure up
and have been removed.

A charming benefit in most, but not all, hotels and guest houses
in Ireland is that breakfast is included in the cost of the room. (It's
not universal, so it's always a good idea to check this at the time you
make your reservations.)

What they call "a full Irish breakfast" is something to behold. It is
a serious meal. It is not a retreat for weight watchers. So try not to
think too much about fat and cholesterol. Irish breakfast is off the
charts. Unfortunately, I find it wholly irresistible. In most cases it
consists of fruit and fruit juice, cereal (hot or cold), breads of all
varieties (from white toast to hearty Irish brown bread to soda bread
to croissants), eggs, bacon, sausage, grilled tomatoes, mushrooms,
black pudding (an Irish blood sausage that requires a developed
taste and which is optional), white pudding (a kind of warm liver-
wurst that also takes some getting used to), and sometimes fresh or
smoked fish.

I have found that a full Irish breakfast will almost always get me
through eighteen holes and all the way to dinner without any difficulty. (Some people have a light midday snack. I haven't encoun-
tered anyone—possibly excepting someone in Olympic training or
who has the metabolism of a hummingbird—who can eat three full
meals a day in Ireland and not balloon up like a dirigible.)

You've probably read or heard about European taxes, but this is
where the rubber meets the road. Get ready to come face to face with
"VAT"—the Value Added Tax. The price of a room will include your
contribution to the national treasuries and the general welfare of the
governments that run the island. In the Irish Republic the VAT is

12.5 percent; in Northern Ireland, it's a whopping 17.5 percent, the same as in Britain. Most, but not all, hotels will also add on a service charge—ranging from 10 to 15 percent. The average is 12.5 percent in both the North and the Republic.

The VAT will also be a part of your meals in restaurants, with some establishments including an additional service charge in the price. All of them will say somewhere on the menu what that service charge is. If the service is good and the service charge is less than 15 percent I usually leave a little extra for the waiter or waitress. When there is no service charge, tip as you would at home.

At many older Irish restaurants, you may not be shown immediately to your table on entering. The host or hostess will give you menus and invite you to be seated in a lounge area for a cocktail. The server or maitre d' will then take your order while you drink and you'll be shown to your table when the first course is about to be delivered. The practice is less widespread than it used to be, but where you encounter it, it is not an effort to induce you to spend money in the bar that you don't want to spend.

In addition to hotels and restaurants, all of your shopping will include the VAT, but documents can be obtained through which the VAT on merchandise to be taken out of the European Union can be refunded when you get to the airport to head home. Always ask about the VAT refund when you're shopping.

Prices in this chapter are based on the rough equivalent of the U.S. dollar's value against the Irish punt, British pound, and euro as we go to press. Most major newspapers will give you a current exchange rate as you get closer to your departure date. It is good to remember when traveling abroad that when the dollar is strong against other currencies, American travelers get something of a bargain, and conversely when the dollar is weak, things cost more overseas.

Hotels and restaurants are rated here on a scale from *Very Expensive* to *Inexpensive* based on the following two charts. As with hotels and restaurants in the U.S., prices can be changed arbitrarily. The hotel ratings are based on double occupancy, including a full Irish breakfast in most cases. The restaurant ratings are based on the price of dinner for two—appetizer, entree, and dessert—excluding wine, beer, or cocktails.

Hotels

Very Expensive	above $250
Expensive	$175-$250
Moderate	$125-$175
Inexpensive	under $125

Restaurants

Very Expensive	above $135
Expensive	$90-$135
Moderate	$60-$90
Inexpensive	under $60

Where to Stay

COUNTRY HOUSES

Without a doubt, my favorite way to travel in Ireland is to stay in the magnificent, charming, and elegant country house hotels that dot the country. While they are not a bargain, they are not the most expensive way to travel either, although some of Ireland's country house hotels do fall into the superluxury category.

A small group of Irish merchants, seafarers, and farmers grew wealthy and powerful in the years after the potato famine of 1847 and the mass migration that ensued until 1855. These affluent men commissioned construction of some of the world's finest private homes, structures to match their fortunes and position. This building boom left Ireland a legacy of country estates and grand manor houses, from Dublin to Dingle, from Dungarvan to Donegal.

But as the age of the clipper ship and farm-based wealth was supplanted by the industrial revolution, the fortunes of some of those moneyed families dwindled and many of the great manor houses fell into disrepair.

The late twentieth century, however, produced a remarkable and dedicated group of Irish entrepreneurs who set about resurrecting numerous wonderful country estates with an eye toward turning a profit from them. What has happened is that many of the greatest manor houses in Ireland have been converted into delightful, cordial, and comfortable small hotels, a bounty for modern visitors from the scrap heap of Irish history.

These are not castles. These are private "homes" where people have raised families, worried over bills, and done all the things that separate residences from the sterile glass-and-steel hostelries that are too often the last refuge for tired travelers. Irish country houses range from elegant family-owned small hotels to cozy places that leave the visitor with a feeling that he or she has been a guest in somebody's magnificent house.

Some of the country estates that are particularly attractive to golfers will be highlighted individually later in this chapter. But for more general information, the Irish Country House and Restaurant Association—which sets demanding and impeccable standards for its members—publishes its own guide every year, known to most users as *The Blue Book*. For the years I have been going to Ireland (since the mid-1980s) it has been the best, most consistently reliable guide around and remains so as this edition goes to press. In the United States, you can get a copy or make reservations at one of the member houses through

Josephine Barr, Hotel Representative
Telephone: 1-800-323-5463   Fax: 1-847-251-6845

Or you can write or call the Irish Country House and Restaurant Association directly:

Hilary Finlay, Ireland's *Blue Book*
Ardbraccan Glebe, Navan, County Meath
Republic of Ireland
Telephone: (046) 23416   Fax: (046) 23292
E-mail: bluebook@iol.ie

GROUPS AND CHAINS

The big American hotel chains are beginning to make inroads into the Irish market. Radisson is involved in several ventures, including a golf resort in county Derry. Holiday Inns, Best Western, and Choice Hotels are all active. Other projects are in various stages of planning and development as we go to press.

There are several noteworthy hotel chains in the Republic, including the Tower Group, Great Southern, and Jury's. Tower hotels cover a wide range of prices and appointments, from the modest Castlerosse Hotel in Killarney to the splendid Faithlegg

House Hotel, once an elegant country mansion, in county Waterford. I've had decent experiences over many years with both Great Southern and Jury's Hotels.

The Great Southern Hotels are generally large and well maintained. It's a firmly established group with a good reputation. The Great Southern in Killarney, for example, is extremely popular with organized tour groups there to travel the Ring of Kerry Road. The Great Southern on Eyre Square in Galway is one of that city's grandest, venerable landmarks.

Jury's Hotels cover a broad spectrum and, in fact, will occasionally have more than one hotel of different price and quality levels in the bigger cities, such as Cork. Some Jury's Hotels tend to be more akin to U.S. motels than what we think of as hotels, although that is certainly not the case with the huge Jury's Hotel in Dublin's fashionable Ballsbridge section. Even the smaller, more motel-like, and more inexpensive Jury's are usually clean and comfortable.

The Hastings Hotel Group is an active and expanding family of hotels in Northern Ireland. Its facilities are upscale and extremely well run with a friendly staff.

Reservations can be made at many major hotels in Ireland through UTELL International Resorts, at 1-800-223-6510. Bord Failte and the Northern Ireland Tourist Board endorse a reservation service run by a company called Gulliver, reachable at 1-800-398-4376. You will need your credit card for either to guarantee your room.

BED AND BREAKFASTS

They are simply known as B&Bs. Virtually nobody calls them anything else. There must be 5,000 private homes all over Ireland on which *B&B* signs are hung. You'll be driving on some wilderness trail in Connemara or up in Macgillicuddy's Reeks and, sure enough, there will be a B&B. For the most part they are clean, comfortable, and extremely friendly.

They range from very Spartan to cozy. The problem is you never quite know what you're getting when you drive up and knock on the door. Nonetheless, if you are on a tight budget, B&Bs are an inexpensive and often pleasant way to golf in Ireland. They are also an extremely good way to get a flavor of the land and people. For an extra charge, a few offer an "evening meal" as well as breakfast, but their number has diminished as the number of full-service restaurants in small towns has increased.

In both the Republic and Northern Ireland, B&Bs are inspected regularly and must maintain certain minimum standards, but quality can (and does) vary enormously. Exercise caution.

Hotels

The following list of hotels makes no pretense of being exhaustive or unbiased. It does offer a broad range of facilities that are in convenient proximity to the best golf courses in Ireland and that provide comfortable accommodations to traveling golfers. The list is alphabetical by county and starts with the Republic of Ireland and then addresses Northern Ireland.

The Irish Republic

County Clare

ABERDEEN ARMS

Location: Lahinch
Rooms: Moderate
Nearby golf courses: Lahinch, Kilkee,
Spanish Point
Telephone: (065) 81100   Fax: (065) 81228
E-mail: aberdeenarms@websters.ie

The hotel is nearly a century and a half old and bills itself as the oldest golf-links hotel in Ireland. Its fifty-five guest rooms were completely refurbished in 1989. The rooms are modern and utilitarian. Its most endearing feature is that it sits just down the road and around the corner from the fabled Lahinch links. (See chapter 2.)

OLD GROUND HOTEL

Location: Ennis
Rooms: Expensive
Nearby golf courses: Ennis, Lahinch, Dromoland,
Kilkee, Spanish Point, Shannon

Telephone: (065) 28127   Fax: (065) 28112
E-mail: oghotel@iol.ie

The Old Ground is in the heart of Ennis, convenient to every-thing in the seat of county Clare. The two-story, ivy-covered ancient building dates to the mid-1700s and a part of it was once the city hall and county jail. Another part of it was an inn used by people bring-ing their goods to what was once a bustling market town. The rooms are generally large and cozy with well-appointed bathrooms. This hotel has improved in every way since the first edition was pub-lished. The bar is always busy, and the bar meals are hearty and well prepared. The bar also often has traditional Irish music. The formal dining room is a popular local spot as well for wedding receptions and other special occasions. The service is very good.

County Cork

ARBUTUS LODGE

Location: Cork city
Rooms: Expensive
Nearby golf courses: Old Head, Cork, Mallow, Doneraile
Telephone: (021) 501237   Fax: (021) 502893

There are few better views of the pleasant university city of Cork and the river Lee than from Arbutus Lodge, which was once the home of the lord mayor of Cork. It's a short walk down the hill to the center of the city with its shopping and restaurants.

The lodge itself—with its broad, ornate central staircase and beautifully restored Victorian decor in what was once the main drawing room of the mansion—is an inviting place to stay and has one of the best kitchens in Ireland. It offers traditional French and new Irish cooking and has one of the finest wine cellars in the land. While Arbutus Lodge is in the heart of Cork city, it is only about an hour's drive from some mighty fine golf. The food and accommo-dations make it worth it.

LONGUEVILLE HOUSE

Location: Mallow
Rooms: Very Expensive

Nearby golf courses: Mallow, Doneraile, Old Head, Cork
Telephone: (022) 47156   Fax: (022) 47459
Toll free: 1-800-223-6510
E-mail: longuevillehouse.ie

Longueville House is about as far from hectic urban American life as you can get. It sits on a gentle hill overlooking the Blackwater River and the rolling countryside, about three miles from the Mallow traffic circle just off the Killarney Road (N72). Sheep graze and cattle low in the majestic pasture just across the driveway from the main house. On the western side of this elegant Georgian mansion, built in 1720, is Ireland's only vineyard, which produces a pleasant white wine when growing conditions are right. Unfortunately, growing grapes in Ireland is a tricky business and there is often less wine than conversation about the vineyard.

From the time Longueville House opened as a comfortable sixteen-room country house hotel, the bulk of the inside work was the province of Jane O'Callaghan. Husband Michael was in charge of the farm, the grounds, the livestock, and the vineyard. But as the years passed, son William assumed many of the day-to-day duties of running the place, including the demanding job of presiding over one of the best kitchens in Ireland.

The guest rooms are spacious and airy, furnished with unusual antiques and family heirlooms, and graced with fresh flowers and lace. No detail was too small to escape the critical eye of Jane O'Callaghan. "Face flannels!" she once declared, referring to face cloths. "Americans just love their face flannels."

Dublin City
(See chapter 6.)

County Donegal

INISHOWEN GATEWAY HOTEL

Location: Buncrana
Rooms: Moderate
Nearby golf courses: North West, Ballyliffin
Telephone: (077) 61144   Fax: (077) 62278
E-mail: inigatho@iol.ie

The view of Lough Swilly and the Killalla Hills from the dining room at the Inishowen Gateway Hotel.

Virtually every room in this big, modern hotel offers spectacular views of Lough Swilly and the Killalla Hills and sunset is nothing short of breathtaking. The rooms are ample, efficiently appointed, and very comfortable. The views are also lovely in the Peninsula Bar and Restaurant. Golf packages are available, including access to the marvelous links at Ballyliffin.

County Galway

CASHEL HOUSE HOTEL

Location: Cashel Bay
Rooms: Very Expensive
Nearby golf courses: Connemara, Galway
Telephone: (095) 31001   Fax: (095) 31077
Toll free: 1-800-223-6510
E-mail: cashelhh@iol.ie

The Cashel House Hotel is still trading on the fact that Charles de Gaulle slept there. In fact, General and Madame de Gaulle spent a fortnight there in 1969, the year after the hotel opened. It's a pleasant place, all white against the surrounding green hills, located up a curving driveway behind a well-flowered and -shrubbed front yard. The last time I was there, the house had a pair of enormous Irish Wolfhounds who would romp across the front lawn with reckless abandon.

The kitchen has won numerous awards and the service is exceptional.

OYSTER MANOR HOTEL

Location: Clarinbridge
Rooms: Expensive
Nearby golf courses: Galway, Connemara, Ennis
Telephone: (091) 796777   Fax: (091) 796770

Pull off the N18 south of Galway city in the village of Clarinbridge, into the parking lot of this lovely pink building with welcoming flowers all around the entrance, and you think you are taking a step back in time. The fact is it's a wonderful illusion.

Oyster Manor is completely modern, made to feel antique. The service is splendid. The new rooms are large and tastefully decorated. The restaurant serves up very good food with an emphasis on local Galway Bay seafood, including the famous Galway oysters. One of the two hotel bars frequently has live music. (If you are planning your trip in late July when the Galway races are run, book well in advance.)

VICTORIA HOTEL

Location: Galway city
Rooms: Moderate
Nearby golf courses: Connemara, Galway
Telephone: (091) 567433　Fax: (091) 565880

This pleasant and efficient new hotel a block from Eyre Square, in the heart of Galway city, offers comfortable, modern rooms with outstanding large bathrooms. While not quite reaching elegant, the decor is very tasteful and satisfactory. The staff is extremely gracious and helpful. The bar is welcoming and the kitchen manages to turn out a very acceptable menu in thoroughly pleasing surroundings. This is a fine hotel at which you get your money's worth and more.

ZETLAND HOUSE HOTEL

Location: Cashel Bay
Rooms: Very Expensive
Nearby golf courses: Connemara, Galway
Telephone: (095) 31111　Fax: (095) 31117
Toll free: 1-800-447-7462

This charming, beautifully refurbished sporting lodge, established in the mid-1800s, was once one of the favorite haunts of the earl of Zetland, for whom it is named. It is now a cheerful and welcoming small hotel in the heart of Connemara. Most of the guest rooms are large, airy, and comfortable and feature glorious views of the bay. Sunset at Zetland House is nothing short of remarkable.

The kitchen favors local seafood and fresh vegetables, dressed with herbs from the hotel's own impressive garden, all wrapped up with a French flair.

If you have a yen to do a little fishing—in addition to playing golf—this is an ideal place to do it. The hotel owns one of Ireland's premier commercial fisheries and the staff caters to anglers from all over the world.

County Kerry

BALLYSEEDE CASTLE HOTEL

Location: Tralee
Rooms: Expensive
Nearby golf courses: Tralee, Ceann Sibéal,
Ballybunion, Castlegregory
Telephone: (066) 35799   Fax: (066) 25287
Toll free: 1-800-223-5695

This fifteenth-century castle with its turrets and stone walls was a private home until the mid-1980s, when it was converted into a hotel. The goal was to make guests feel as though they were visiting royalty from another age. It had been the military headquarters of the earls of Desmond, one of whose ghosts allegedly roams the halls still.

BUTLER ARMS HOTEL

Location: Waterville
Rooms: Moderate
Nearby golf courses: Waterville, Dooks, Ring of Kerry
Telephone: (066) 74144   Fax: (066) 74520
Toll free: 1-800-447-7462

The magnificent ocean views from this western tip of the Ring of Kerry have drawn visitors for much of the twentieth century. On any given day you can watch brooding, slate-gray clouds roll in from the North Atlantic, the sun burn off the fog to reveal the majestic coastline, or the frequent squalls that buffet the village and its multicolored cottages and buildings. Butler Arms was once the favorite vacation retreat of Charlie Chaplin and has been extensively modernized. The restaurant enjoys a fine local reputation for its fresh seafood. Hotels guests can obtain discounted green fees at the nearby Waterville links.

HOTEL ARD-NA-SIDHE

Location: Carragh Lake
Rooms: Expensive
Nearby golf courses: Killarney, Dooks, Tralee, Ceann Sibéal,
Waterville, Ballybunion, Castlegregory, Ring of Kerry
Telephone: (066) 69105   Fax: (066) 69282
Toll free: 1-800-221-1074
E-mail: khl@iol.ie

Hotel Ard-Na-Sidhe is one of the group of hotels owned by the same people who own Hotel Europe. The hotel, whose name means "hill of the fairies" in Irish Gaelic, is on the banks of Carragh Lake, one of the lakes of Kerry into which the towering mountains seem to fall. The twenty-room Victorian-style mansion offers charming, antique-filled rooms, delightful views, and quiet surroundings.

HOTEL EUROPE

Location: Killarney
Rooms: Expensive
Nearby golf courses: Killarney, Dooks, Tralee, Ceann Sibéal,
Waterville, Ballybunion, Castlegregory, Ring of Kerry
Telephone: (064) 31900   Fax: (064) 32118
Toll free: 1-800-221-1074
E-mail: khl@iol.ie

One of the world's great hotels is perched on the shore of Lough Leane—one of three magnificent lakes by which the town of Killarney is built. The views from almost every room are spectacular. Directly across the lake from Hotel Europe is the spot where Macgillicuddy's Reeks, the country's tallest mountains, finally descend from the clouds and meet the water.

The hotel sets an impeccable standard, from the splendid and inviting public rooms, all of which are walled with glass through which Lough Leane and the mountains show their ever-changing personality, to the guest rooms, which are modern, furnished with country pine, and enormously comfortable. Many of the bathrooms feature both a huge bathtub and a separate shower and are fitted with such amenities as heated towel racks.

Almost all of the deluxe guest rooms have private balconies that overlook the lake and mountains and provide a panorama of the rich farmland that rings Lough Leane to the north. A keen eye will catch a glimpse of the Killarney golf courses less than two miles to the south. Discount vouchers are available to hotel guests for green fees at Killarney, Dooks, Tralee, and Waterville.

While the hotel's restaurant has occasionally disappointed at dinner, the kitchen serves up the best breakfast buffet in the whole country, from sausages and bacon and eggs (cooked to your order while you watch) to fresh breads and rolls to smoked salmon. It is the kind of feast that will nourish you as you tackle Tralee or Ballybunion.

KATHLEEN'S COUNTRY HOUSE

Location: Killarney
Rooms: Moderate
Nearby golf courses: Killarney, Dooks, Tralee, Ceann Sibéal,
Waterville, Ballybunion, Castlegregory, Ring of Kerry
Telephone: (064) 32810   Fax: (064) 32340

Kathleen O'Regan-Sheppard is a charming, intelligent woman whose boundless energy and graciousness fill her house with warmth and personality. Personal attention is her hallmark and people return year after year to be treated to her special brand of hospitality. The modern house sits above the main Limerick-Tralee road, about a mile from the center of Killarney. The rooms are tastefully appointed and the bathrooms are large and comfortable.

Few details escape the watchful eye of the owner, yet every guest is made to feel as though he or she is an old friend spending the night in a splendid private home. She's only got sixteen rooms, so book early because she's almost always filled to capacity, especially in July, August, and September.

THE 19TH GREEN

Location: Killarney
Rooms: Inexpensive
Nearby golf courses: Killarney, Dooks, Tralee, Ceann Sibéal,
Waterville, Ballybunion, Castlegregory, Ring of Kerry

Telephone: (064) 32868   Fax: (064) 32637
E-mail: 19thgreen@tinet.ie

The 19th Green is a small family-run guest house that is located almost across the Killorglin Road from the entrance to the Killarney Golf & Fishing Club, only a short distance from the center of the town. Only eight of the ten rooms have their own showers, so check what you're getting when you book. The place is friendly and convenient.

PARK HOTEL

Location: Kenmare
Rooms: Very Expensive
Nearby golf courses: Kenmare, Ring of Kerry,
Waterville, Killarney
Telephone: (064) 41200   Fax: (064) 41402
Toll free: 1-800-233-6764
E-mail: phkenmare@iol.ie

A good number of people argue passionately that the Park Hotel in Kenmare is the best hotel in Ireland. Some rank it among the world's best. Perched on a hill overlooking the mountains of Kerry, this Victorian chateau is as majestic as it is charming and friendly. The panorama is breathtaking. The rooms are decorated with Georgian and Victorian antiques and the hotel has one of the best kitchens in Ireland, having earned one of those coveted Michelin stars.

Don't be surprised to see the palm trees and other tropical-looking plants in the gardens around the hotel. While far from steamy, the warm ocean currents that bathe the Kerry coast keep the temperature from ever falling much below forty degrees Fahrenheit even in the dead of winter. The Kenmare Golf Club is thirty feet away.

County Kildare

MOYGLARE MANOR

Location: Maynooth
Rooms: Very Expensive

Nearby golf courses: The Curragh, Portmarnock, Mount Juliet,
The K Club, County Louth, Laytown & Bettystown
Telephone: (01) 628-6351   Fax: (01) 628-5405
Toll free: 1-800-223-6510
E-mail: moyglare@iol.ie

In the heart of Ireland's horse country, just off the Dublin-Sligo Road (N4), surrounded by towering ancient trees and fields where thoroughbreds graze is the fully and delightfully refurbished Georgian mansion, Moyglare Manor. After a day of golf, it's a friendly and welcoming little hotel that offers comfortable rooms decorated with antiques and abundant Irish lace. A pleasant, airy lounge with a tiny bar at one end features an open fire around which to have cocktails before dinner. It has a lovely dining room that serves up extremely well prepared meals, with an accent on local produce.

County Limerick

DUNRAVEN ARMS

Location: Adare
Rooms: Moderate/Expensive
Nearby golf courses: Adare Manor, Shannon, Ballybunion,
Dromoland, Ennis, Lahinch
Telephone: (061) 396633   Fax: (061) 396541
E-mail: dunraven@iol.ie

Dunraven Arms has been a favorite for as long as I have been going to Ireland. I have often used this delightful, recently refurbished and modernized hotel as my last stop. It's less than an hour from Shannon Airport and leaves the visitor with an unforgettable image of another time, when life was slow and things were simple. The main street of the village of Adare is lined with brightly painted, thatched-roof cottages that could well have been lifted from another century.

Dunraven Arms' rooms are spacious and modern—about half in the original house and the rest in a new wing that overlooks the excellent restaurant's vegetable and herb garden. Among the daily offerings is what the Irish call a "carvery." A roast of some kind—

lamb, beef, or even venison in season—is carved and served at table-side. It's a wonderful traditional kind of Irish dining.

Dunraven Arms is also a hunting hotel (fox hunting, that is) but that's primarily a winter activity. The manager, Brian Murphy, is a renowned horse lover, and if you're up to a canter around the countryside after your round of golf, he's the guy to talk to.

The bar is a pleasant place that often features live music.

County Meath

NEPTUNE BEACH HOTEL

Location: Bettystown
Rooms: Expensive
Nearby golf courses: Laytown& Bettystown, County Louth
Telephone: (041) 27107   Fax: (041) 27412

I found the Neptune Beach Hotel quite by accident while looking for a place to stay near the wonderful County Louth Golf Club (see chapter 2) a few miles away across the fabled river Boyne. I had heard there was a great new hotel in Bettystown, and as I rounded the corner into town on the Coast Road, there it was. I had booked it two days earlier, not knowing quite what to expect. What I got was a marvelous complex that includes beautiful, tastefully decorated rooms (pay the extra fee to get one with a view of the Irish Sea and let the sound of the waves lull you to sleep), two friendly bars, a health club, and fine formal restaurant. The menu features local seafood and well-prepared Wicklow lamb; the pub serves a fine steak.

County Sligo

BALLINCAR HOUSE HOTEL

Location: Rosses Point Road
Rooms: Moderate
Nearby golf courses: County Sligo, Donegal,
Enniscrone, Bundoran
Telephone: (071) 45361   Fax: (071) 44198

This attractive, small hotel is about a mile from the County Sligo Golf Club at Rosses Point (see chapter 2) and convenient to Sligo town. The rooms are small but comfortable and pleasantly decorated with vibrant colors complementing rich woods. The dining room looks out on the well-landscaped estate and produces above-average Irish cuisine with continental overtones. It also offers a solid wine list. Book well in advance, especially in the summer months.

COOPERSHILL HOUSE

Location: Riverstown
Rooms: Expensive
Nearby golf courses: County Sligo, Donegal,
Enniscrone, Bundoran
Telephone: (071) 65108   Fax: (071) 65466
Toll free: 1-800-223-6510
E-mail: ohara@coopershill.com

This wonderful place just keeps getting better and better. Coopershill House—home to seven generations of the O'Hara family—was going strong long before William Butler Yeats immortalized such county Sligo landmarks as Lough Gill and Ben Bulben. The stately Georgian mansion, about eleven miles southeast of Sligo town just off the Dublin road (N4), is an inviting and charming stop for golfers making the pilgrimage to play the wonderful northwestern golf courses, including Enniscrone, Donegal, and County Sligo Golf Club. (See chapter 2.)

After winding up the long driveway from the main road, you can usually count on being met by at least one of the family's friendly old dogs and by Brian or Lindy O'Hara, as if you are an eagerly awaited guest in the O'Haras' home. A massive central staircase leads to the second level, where the guest rooms are located. There are only six, each one different, each one charming, each one decorated with antiques and family heirlooms. There are no locks on the doors. They aren't needed. Predinner cocktails are served around a cozy fire in the marvelous drawing room.

Lindy runs the kitchen and makes sure everything else inside is top notch. Brian cultivates the magnificent vegetable garden (from which a fair amount of the evening's meal will be plucked). Dinner

The stately Georgian mansion that is Coopershill House is the author's favorite country house hotel in Ireland.

is whatever strikes Lindy's fancy, usually a choice of two appetizers and two entrees. The meal also includes a wonderful homemade soup, cheese course, and dessert. In years of repeat visits, I've never had a bad meal at Coopershill. In fact, some of what Lindy O'Hara has presented has verged on culinary brilliance, Irish home cooking at its very best. Brian's wine cellar is remarkably good and he cheerfully shares his personal knowledge of the inventory.

TOWER HOTEL SLIGO

Location: Sligo town
Rooms: Moderate
Nearby golf courses: County Sligo, Donegal,
Enniscrone, Bundoran

Telephone: (071) 44000   Fax: (071) 46888
E-mail: towers@iol.ie

This big, modern, stone and red brick hotel with a clock tower is in the heart of Sligo town. It's part of the Tower Group and offers more than fifty high-quality rooms in the Euro-modern tradition. What it lacks in the kind of personal warmth you get at the upscale Irish country houses, the Tower Hotel makes up for in professional management and efficiency. It's a good bet if you're a little tardy in making reservations and you find everything else full, although it accommodates a large number of tour groups. The place is unbeatable for convenience to the town itself, with restaurants, pubs, and shopping all in easy walking distance.

County Wexford

MARLFIELD HOUSE

Location: Gorey
Rooms: Very Expensive
Nearby golf courses: Courtown, The European Club,
Rosslare, St. Helen's Bay
Telephone: (055) 21124   Fax: (055) 21572
Toll free: 1-800-223-6510
E-mail: marlf@iol.ie

With its abundance of chintz and prints and fresh flowers and antiques, Mary Bowe's Marlfield House has won just about every award for hospitality and cuisine. It is the quintessence of what you'd imagine a superior country house ought to be—canopied beds, luxurious sheets and towels, lace curtains. The ornate Victorian glass-and-steel solarium is a wonderful spot to enjoy a hearty Irish breakfast and look out on the bountiful garden. This superior country house is worth a special detour.

County Wicklow

THE GRAND HOTEL

Location: Wicklow town
Rooms: Moderate

Nearby golf courses: Wicklow, Blainroe,
The European Club, Druids Glen
Telephone: (0404) 67337   Fax: (0404) 69607
E-mail: grandhotel@tinet.ie

This old landmark in the heart of Wicklow town has recently been remodeled from head to toe. The rooms are decorated in Euro-modern style—heavy on built-ins and pastels—and are a bit Spartan, though thoroughly acceptable. The bathrooms are claustrophobic. Those rooms that front on the main street can pick up a bit of noise, especially in the summer. The restaurant offers Irish fare in pleasant surroundings, though service can suffer occasional lapses.

HUNTER'S HOTEL

Location: Rathnew
Rooms: Expensive
Nearby golf courses: Wicklow, Blainroe,
The European Club, Druids Glen
Telephone: (0404) 40106   Fax: (0404) 40338
Toll free: 1-800-223-6510
E-mail: hunters@indigo.ie

This place has been catering to visitors since long before the automobile first appeared on the roads of county Wicklow. It is one of the oldest coaching hotels in the country. From the road, it appears a modest little place, but once you get inside and see the wonderfully renovated rooms filled with antiques, the splendid flower-laden formal garden, the cozy lounge, and the lovely dining room, you'll know how misleading the facade really is. The restaurant specializes in local fare, including various preparations of Wicklow lamb, brill, and salmon.

TINAKILLY HOUSE

Location: Rathnew
Rooms: Very Expensive
Nearby golf courses: Wicklow, Blainroe,
The European Club, Druids Glen
Telephone: (0404) 69274   Fax: (0404) 67806

Rooms at Hunter's Hotel look out on an inviting formal garden.

Toll free: 1-800-223-6510
E-mail: wpower@tinakilly.ie

In the winter of 1876 Capt. Robert Halpin bought the 300 acres along the Irish Sea coast and commissioned construction of Tinakilly House, a land base for his family while he was at sea. Halpin started amassing his fortune by outrunning Yankee ships and taking cargoes to Southern ports during the American Civil War. He became internationally famous, commanding the biggest ship of the day, *The Great Eastern,* which laid the first telegraph cable from North America to Europe. This imposing house is about thirty miles south of Dublin (just off the N11) and not much more than a driver and five iron from the Wicklow town line.

Tinakilly House was occupied by members of the captain's family until 1962, when his last daughter died. It was subsequently converted into a guest house. But its great success did not begin until it was bought by William and Bee Power, two decades later. Together, they lovingly and painstakingly restored it to its nineteenth-century elegance, after rescuing it from a case of dry rot that almost claimed the old building. In 1991, the Powers expanded the house—from thirteen rooms to twenty-six rooms and three suites.

Guests enter through a massive double doorway, into the original vestibule and what was once the front parlor, decorated in rich red brocades with heavy exposed beams and a huge fireplace that glows warm and inviting on chilly days. It's a lovely spot to gather near for afternoon tea or evening cocktails. A wide, two-tiered staircase leads to the guest rooms in the "old" section of the house, rooms delightfully furnished with period antiques.

While Bee Power no longer personally runs the kitchen, her penchant for fresh vegetables, extraordinary Wicklow lamb, wildfowl, and fresh local fish prevails, and her famous brown bread graces every meal. William Power remains a constant presence and no detail is too small to escape his skilled eye.

While there are scores of magnificent places to stay in Ireland, Tinakilly House, over the years, has grown to be my favorite small hotel anywhere. It is well worth a special detour.

Northern Ireland

County Antrim

BUSHMILLS INN

Location: Bushmills
Rooms: Moderate
Nearby golf courses: Royal Portrush,
Portstewart, Castlerock
Telephone: (0801) 2657-32339
Fax: (0801) 2657-32048

There are other places to stay when you're up on the Antrim coast, but I am hard pressed to name a better one. Richard Wilson and his partner, Roy Bolton, have established one of Northern Ireland's finest small hotels, creating an atmosphere of bygone days with all the modern conveniences.

This seventeenth-century inn is almost as old as the famous Bushmills Distillery, just down the road, which was first licensed to make whiskey in 1608 and is the world's oldest such enterprise. Guests are greeted by cozy fires in ancient hearths and a warm, congenial atmosphere that carries right into the cheerful and pleasant guest rooms. Bushmills Inn was fully modernized in the late 1980s and features a wonderful, quaint sitting room and an agreeable little bar in which to sip a cocktail or a cup of tea.

The kitchen produces high-quality dishes, many featuring innovative uses of Bushmills whiskey. The cuisine is Irish, but draws inspiration from all over. One night I had a marvelous, spicy (unusual in Ireland) rendition of Cajun fish and chips. The local, whiskey-smoked salmon is not to be missed, and the young, enthusiastic kitchen staff has a talent for preparing the region's fish. Wisely, the owners encourage experimentation.

This is an extremely popular place, and justifiably so. It is advisable to book as early as possible because even in the "off season" it's difficult to get a room at the inn.

County Derry

EVERGLADES HOTEL

Location: outskirts of Derry
Rooms: Moderate/Expensive
Nearby golf courses: Castlerock, Royal Portrush,
Portstewart, North West, Ballyliffin
Telephone: (0801) 504-346722   Fax: (0801) 504-349200
E-mail: res.egh@hastingshotels.com

This hotel is not deep in the heart of golf country, but it's one of the better places to stay in the area and it's worth a little trip to play. It's about an hour's drive to Castlerock, Portstewart, Portrush, or Ballyliffin for a round of golf. The Everglades is a cheerful, modern, well-run hotel (part of the Hastings Group). It offers extremely pleasant rooms, a good restaurant, and a friendly bar for the traveling golfer. If you should find everything booked solid up in the Portrush-Portstewart area, this is a good fallback.

It's just across the river Foyle from the old walled city of Derry and provides easy access to that city's shopping, restaurants, pubs, and night life. Its Florida theme sounds bizarre in the heart of Ulster, but they don't overdo it and it works very well.

County Down

SLIEVE DONARD

Location: Newcastle
Rooms: Very Expensive
Nearby golf courses: Royal County Down, Ardglass
Telephone: (0801) 3967-23681   Fax: (0801) 3967-24830
E-mail: res.sdh@hastingshotels.com

I am very fond of the hotels that are part of the Hastings Group in general, and this one in particular. The Hastings hotels are all a cut above good. They are run smoothly and very professionally. As the crown jewel of the group, the Slieve Donard is just what you'd expect—a well-managed, luxury hotel.

This lovely old place by the sea has been greeting visitors to the beach resort of Newcastle for more than a century. The magnificent red-brick structure, with its landmark tower, is only a wedge—or nine iron, at most—from the clubhouse of the legendary Royal County Down links. (See chapter 2.)

The smell of salt air greets you whenever you step out the front door, and from many of the guest rooms there is a wonderful panorama of both the Irish Sea and the Mountains of Mourne. On a fine, sunny day, it's spectacular; when the rain and chill come in off the sea, it's a cozy refuge. The rooms are modern and comfortable and in the winter of 1995 many of them underwent a substantial facelift. The cavernous old hotel dining room has hosted some of the most famous names in golf for much of the past century and produces Irish cuisine with a French accent. About a hundred yards away, but still part of the Slieve Donard complex, is the Percy French Bar and Grille, a lively and enjoyable place that serves up hearty fare with an emphasis on steaks and ale—just the thing you need after a day on the golf course.

Where to Eat

There was once a time when the phrase "Irish cuisine" would bring a smirk to the lips of anybody with a sophisticated palate. Irish cuisine was exemplified by corned beef and cabbage, boiled potatoes, and vegetables cooked into submission. Those days are deader than Elvis.

Today, kitchens all over Ireland—from small hotels and guest houses to castles and resorts to freestanding restaurants—have been heavily influenced by the great chefs of France, Germany, Italy, and Spain. Young Irish chefs have learned from the rest of Europe, and to a lesser degree from developments in the United States. They have created a new and innovative version of Irish cuisine that relies on the bounty of the land and the wonderful flavors of local seafood, lamb, and beef. From the coast of Cork to the coast of Antrim, from the Mountains of Mourne to Macgillicuddy's Reeks, it is possible to eat as well in Ireland as anywhere in the world.

In most cases, the hotels, guest houses, resorts, and castles mentioned previously in this chapter have restaurants that are very good to superior. Unless there is special reason to mention them for a second time in the section below, such as the fact that the kitchen is worth a special detour even if you're not staying there, I have not duplicated the listing. In one or two cases, a restaurant listed below has accommodations with it, and as with the food criteria I have not duplicated the entry unless the lodging is so outstanding that it merits two mentions.

The following is a selective list of reliable favorites, listed alphabetically by county.

The Irish Republic

County Clare

DROMOLAND CASTLE
(EARL OF THURMOND RESTAURANT)

Location: Newmarket-on-Fergus
Dinner: Very Expensive   Reservations: Suggested
Telephone: (061) 368144

This elegant room features award-winning French/Irish cuisine served in pleasant, if formal, surroundings. Fresh local salmon is often on the menu, which changes seasonally, and is always a good choice. Dressy.

BROGAN'S

Location: 24 O'Connell St., Ennis
Dinner: Inexpensive/Moderate   Reservations: Suggested
Telephone: (065) 29859

This bustling, popular restaurant and pub serves hearty, appetizing fare that is a cut above your average pub-style food. In fact, Brogan's is just what the doctor ordered after a day on the links. Dishes are innovative and well prepared, ranging from Irish stew to a delectable curried chicken to traditional grilled salmon. You can't go wrong with the steaks. The service is friendly. Nice atmosphere. Casual.

County Cork

BLUE HAVEN HOTEL & RESTAURANT

Location: Kinsale
Dinner: Expensive   Reservations: Required

Telephone: (021) 722209   Fax: (021) 774268
E-mail: bluhaven@iol.ie

The Blue Haven Hotel & Restaurant occupies the space that used to be the Old Fish Market in the port town of Kinsale, just south of Cork city. The hotel is quaint and cozy, with small but nicely appointed rooms and big modern bathrooms with extralong bathtubs, just what you'll need for a soak after you've played Old Head (see chapter 2) a few miles away. The biggest problem at the Blue Haven is there is no parking lot, so you're stuck with street parking or a public lot a few blocks away.

The kitchen is the main reason for a stop here. As its history implies, the seafood is the star of the show at the Blue Haven, although the nonseafood costars are fine as well. The house special is hot smoked salmon napped with a creamy, herbed sauce. It is a most unusual and absolutely delicious culinary treat. My wife fell in love with an appetizer of kidney and liver in a wine sauce. The restaurant features an airy dining room with a high, glass-ceilinged atrium at one end. Moderately dressy.

LONGUEVILLE HOUSE
(PRESIDENT'S RESTAURANT)

Location: Mallow
Dinner: Very Expensive   Reservations: Required
Telephone: (022) 47156

It's well worth the detour for dinner, even if you're not staying at Longueville House. The innovative Irish cuisine gives local vegetables a starring role, many from the O'Callaghans' own garden. There is often game in season, along with wonderful seafood. Drinks are served beside a comforting fire, where orders are taken. You are shown to your table just before your first course is served. The saucing often verges on the inspired. The preparation and presentation are outstanding. Dressy.

County Galway

DRIMCONG HOUSE

Location: Moycullen

Dinner: Expensive   Reservations: Required
Telephone: (091) 85115

This lovely lakeside restaurant is in a seventeenth-century cottage, just north of the village of Moycullen on the N59. Your cocktails are served in a room that is reminiscent of a library, with an open fireplace. The kitchen features game (in season), Galway oysters, and a changing roster of international dishes. Moderately dressy.

County Kerry

BRICIN

Location: 26 High St., Killarney
Dinner: Moderate   Reservations: Required
Telephone: (064) 34902

This splendid, airy, cheerful restaurant resides above one of Killarney's most unique crafts shops. Bricin (pronounced "Bri-keen") is a small trout or a bridge in Irish Gaelic. The kitchen specializes in modern Irish cuisine, although one of its best presentations is an Irish classic known as boxty. Boxty are potato pancakes with various fillings. The curried-lamb boxty are wonderful and the seafood and vegetarian fillings are appetizing. The changing and eclectic menu offers wonderful seasonal specialties such as chicken with Irish Cashel blue cheese and bacon or crispy roast duck. Bricin's success is the result of the boundless energy and enthusiasm of owner Johnny McGuire. Beer and wine only. Casual.

DINGLES

Location: 40 New St., Killarney
Dinner: Expensive   Reservations: Required
Telephone: (064) 31079

Down two steps from the street, this charming little restaurant furnished with heavy country-pine tables and chairs serves superbly prepared and delicious food. Since the days when "new Irish cuisine" was the exception, it has exemplified modern Irish cooking at its best, with a heavy emphasis on local fish, meat, and vegetables. It's hearty. It's tasty. And the place is, simply, a gem, one of the most consistent, solid restaurants in southwestern Ireland.

The seafood crepe is one of the best, most original appetizers anywhere and the steaks and local salmon are tops. The atmosphere is relaxed and cozy. The service is efficient and friendly, always with the personal attention of owners Gerry and Marion Cunningham and their daughters. Dingles has been a personal favorite since I first dined there in the late 1980s, and as this edition goes to press it remains as good as ever, conjuring up memories of simply marvelous food and making me eager for my annual return visit. Casual.

DOYLE'S SEAFOOD BAR

Location: John St., Dingle
Dinner: Expensive   Reservations: Required
Telephone: (066) 51174

An award-winning restaurant that's well worth a detour. If you want to stay the night, Doyle's also has eight rooms to let. The rates are moderate. But the reason to visit is the food. The menu consists of what was brought in that day by Dingle fishermen. Soups, lobster, grilled fresh fish, and a delectable seafood mornay that caresses your nose even before it caresses your taste buds are house specialties. The atmosphere is cozy. Casual.

NICK'S

Location: Lower Bridge St., Killorglin
Dinner: Moderate   Reservations: Required
Telephone: (066) 61219

This well-known establishment is an old stone house with a cozy interior that draws locals and travelers alike for hearty and satisfying Irish fare, leaning heavily on regional seafood and steaks. Game is featured in season. Casual.

ROBERTINO'S

Location: 9 High St., Killarney
Dinner: Moderate   Reservations: Suggested
Telephone: (064) 34966

There's a mouthwatering hint of basil, garlic, and oregano in the air as you stroll along High Street. When Robertino's opened in the early 1990s, the jury was out as to whether it would survive. Well the jury is in and Robertino's is here to stay. This terrific restaurant in the heart of Killarney serves up some of the best Italian food in Ireland. From hearty, garlicky bruschetta to rib-sticking pizzas in the zesty tradition of Naples to saltimbocca alla Romana, the menu is a delight. The pasta is soul satisfying. Homemade ravioli napped in a robust marinara sauce is a winner, as is the fettuccini con panna— fresh pasta with wild mushrooms, ham, and cream sauce. My wife's favorite is a wonderful Irish-Italian creation, Italian penne pasta with local Irish salmon and tomato-cream sauce.

The staff is efficient and eager to please. The Mediterranean decor is unusual and relaxing. And as far as I know, it's the only place in Killarney where you can accompany an espresso with a glass of grappa. Casual.

County Limerick

THE WILD GEESE

Location: Adare
Dinner: Expensive   Reservations: Required
Telephone: (061) 396451

Located in one of the thatched-roof cottages along Main Street in this wonderful little village, the restaurant offers a delightful variety of innovative dishes. Chef Serge Coustrain, born in Toulon, France, and trained in Strasbourg and Monte Carlo, brings the influence of French culinary tradition to fresh local ingredients. He does simply wonderful things with game birds and fish and has a magical touch with sauces. The desserts are spectacular. This is not a place to count calories. Moderately dressy.

County Sligo

AUSTIE'S

Location: Rosses Point
Dinner: Moderate   Reservations: Suggested
Telephone: (071) 77111

This unpretentious restaurant with a seafaring decor is as popular with the locals as it is with the tourists. It overlooks Sligo Bay, and

The Wild Geese, a marvelous, innovative restaurant, sits in a row of thatched-roof cottages in the village of Adare.

while it is often billed as a pub and even looks barlike from the outside, the food far exceeds standard pub fare. The emphasis is on fresh seafood prepared in a variety of simple yet mouthwatering ways, including a memorable pan-fried Dover sole. Casual.

CROMLEACH LODGE

Location: Ballindoon, Castlebaldwin
Dinner: Very Expensive   Reservations: Required
Telephone: (071) 65155

This marvelous country house is about twenty miles south of Sligo town just off the N4, and it's well worth the drive. Beware that it's so popular, however, that last-minute booking—especially on summer weekends—is often impossible. The menu is an Irish concerto with continental overtones and harmonies. Roast quail in port wine and local lamb flavored with Irish Mist are among the haunting preparations, all served with panache on fine china and Irish linen. The wine list is noteworthy. Dressy.

Northern Ireland

County Antrim

RAMORE

Location: Ramore St., Portrush
Dinner: Moderate/Expensive   Reservations: Required
Telephone: (0801) 265-824313

This marvelous, bustling restaurant overlooks Portrush Harbor and is securing a place as one of the best restaurants in Ireland. The Irish cuisine with a distinctly Italian accent is superbly prepared and delightfully presented. The gleaming, modern decor is more Italian than Irish and serves as a wonderful setting in which to dine. A delicious and innovative creation featuring roast pork with bacon on a bed of kale will live in my memory for many years. Ramore has a fine wine list and the desserts are worth your saving a little extra room. Dressy.

(*Note:* On the lower level there is a friendly, busy pub that serves up thoroughly acceptable pub grub from an unusually long menu.

It's serve yourself, no reservations, and bring a hearty appetite. Very casual.)

County Down

THE PERCY FRENCH BAR AND GRILLE

Location: Newcastle
Dinner: Moderate   Reservations: Not required
Telephone: (0801) 3967-23681

I have a great fondness for this pub and restaurant, located across the parking lot from the landmark Slieve Donard hotel, of which it is a part. From the outside it looks like a chain restaurant in a U.S. suburb, the kind of place I generally avoid. But inside it is instantly addicting, more so when you discover just how good the kitchen really is. The Percy French is big. It's noisy. It's festive. It's just pure fun. The food is hearty, after-golf fare with an emphasis on steaks, chops, grilled fish, potatoes, and fresh vegetables, washed down with pints of ale. There's just nothing very much like it elsewhere in Ireland. It has the feel of something a Londoner might open in Los Angeles. Casual.

What to Do When You're Not Golfing

Even if you plan to play golf from the moment you step off the plane until the day you depart, you may want to do a few things, other than eat, drink, sleep, and golf. The following is far from an exhaustive list, but it hits some of the highlights in most of the areas you'll visit to play the golf courses in this book. The general categories and notes speak for themselves.

Pubs

There is no shortage of pubs in Ireland. Some sage once estimated that there is one bar for every 300 people on the island. The pub is the center of social activity in many villages. Pubs are also a wonderful way to meet people and to sample some infectious Irish traditional music. Many serve food, although the quality covers a broad spectrum. The following are personal favorites.

The Irish Republic

County Clare

DURTY NELLY'S

Location: Bunratty
Telephone: (061) 364861

Convivial, crowded, and carefree. This used to be the place where the guards at Bunratty Castle went for a pint when they got done soldiering. Some readers of the first edition of this book suggested it's too touristy. I side with the late Speaker of the House, Tip O'Neill, who never went to Ireland without stopping for a pint or two at Durty Nelly's. Traditional music sessions or ballad singing take place most nights.

GUS O'CONNOR'S

Location: Doolin
Telephone: (065) 74168

Tin whistles, fiddles, and bodhrans (Irish drums) can be heard most evenings at this legendary pub on the Atlantic coast. Some of Ireland's most famous traditional musicians have been there at one time or another to play. Not only do the locals gather there, people drive from miles around for a tot and a song.

County Kerry

THE LAURELS

Location Killarney
Telephone: (064) 31149

This landmark graces the point where New Street bisects Main Street. Tourists pack into the basement every night to hear music, but the small, dark upstairs pub—where the locals gather after work for a beer or a bowl of soup—is my favorite bar in Ireland, my local pub when I'm in Killarney. What it lacks in interior design it makes up for in local flavor and friendliness. Con (the owner), Christy, Liz, and Seamus go out of their way to make visitors welcome, even if the

The Laurels, in the heart of Killarney, is the author's favorite pub in a country that has thousands from which to choose.

resident Jack Russell terriers will only growl a greeting as they saunter through. It also serves up a thoroughly satisfactory pub meal if you're in the mood for a quick bite to eat. Try the traditional Irish potato cakes, a wonderful, flavorful dish infused with ham, smoked chicken, and spinach, napped with a mushroom sauce.

THE DANNY MANN

Location: 97 New St., Killarney
Telephone: (064) 31640

Traditional music—and sometimes some traditional slip dancing to go with it (a Celtic step dance popular in Kerry)—is the mainstay of this noisy, cavernous, and friendly bar. It's a favorite evening wateringhole for both residents and tourists. The place is always busy and can be absolutely jammed if the musicians are hot.

THE GRAND HOTEL

Location: Main Street, Killarney
Telephone: (064) 31159

Ignore all the tourists, get yourself a pint of Guinness or Smithwicks, try to find a stool, and get ready for some of the best traditional Irish music around. This hotel bar has entertainment nightly in the summer months featuring a broad spectrum of local performers. It can be as simple as a guitar, bodhran, and concertina or as elaborate as fiddles, whistles, a banjo, guitar, and uilleann pipes (small bagpipes). It's always shoulder to shoulder and it's always great fun.

County Sligo

HARGADON'S

Location: 4 O'Connell St., Sligo town
No telephone

For more than a century this has been a favorite gathering place in Sligo town, and at one time it also served as a grocery store. Some of the shelves are still in evidence, as are cozy snugs and lots of memorabilia of the area.

County Wicklow

BRIDGE TAVERN

Location: Bridge Street, Wicklow town
Telephone: (0404) 67718

The Bridge Tavern—which also houses a popular B&B—is a local hangout that draws only a smattering of tourists, and this is a big part of its attraction. It is cozy and friendly. It's not unusual to find yourself engaged in a conversation about almost any old subject, including golf. Every now and then you'll find traditional music, sometimes on a scheduled basis and sometimes just as an impromptu set.

Northern Ireland

County Derry

GWEEDORE BAR

Location: 61 Waterloo St., Derry
Telephone: (0801) 504-263513

Some locals say this is the best pub for traditional music, but there are many bars in Derry that have either scheduled or unscheduled Irish music. In fact, there are two other very popular pubs in the same block of Waterloo Street so an old-fashioned pub crawl won't require too much stamina.

Shopping

The Irish Republic

County Cork

BLARNEY WOOLLEN MILLS

Location: Blarney
Telephone: (021) 385280

This huge, world-famous shop is always jam-packed with people. The parking lot is loaded with buses. Nonetheless, it is worth an after-golf visit. Despite the name, the place is noted for more than just woollens, although the selection of sweaters, jackets, skirts, slacks, and the like is reason enough for going. There are rows and rows of cashmere, local knitwear, Donegal tweeds, and Aran Island sweaters. There are also glass, china, linens, lace, music, art, and other Irish gifts.

The original shop—the flagship of a chain that is in several other locations, including Killarney and Dublin—is located in the shadow of Blarney castle, about six miles north of Cork city. You might as well take a look around the castle while you're there, but avoid kissing the Blarney stone at all costs, unless you enjoy hanging upside down and backward from a battlement and touching your lips to a rock on which half the Western World has slobbered.

County Galway

CLARINBRIDGE CRYSTAL SHOP

Location: Clarinbridge
Telephone: (091) 796178

Don't blink as you drive through the village of Clarinbridge or you'll miss the turn. This excellent little venture seems to pop up out of nowhere. The village is immediately south of Galway city on the Limerick Road. In addition to a wonderful selection of Irish crystal—from Waterford to Kerry glass—the shop features a fine assortment of Belleek china, tweeds, and other top-of-the-line Irish products.

MILLAR'S CONNEMARA TWEEDS, LTD.

Location: Clifden
Telephone: (095) 21038

This is one of the most unique little shops in the whole country. It specializes in hats. Not any old hat, mind you. But the hat that is widely known as the Irish Walking Hat. Some people call it the Irish Fishing Hat. If you want one, and you happen to be playing the Connemara Golf Club a few miles down the road toward Ballyconneely, stop in on your way to or from the golf course. The locals say it's entirely proper to wear these hats anywhere but in bed or church.

County Kerry

KERRY GLASS STUDIO AND VISITOR CENTER

Location: Killorglin Rd., just outside Killarney
Telephone: (064) 44666

Kerry glass is unique and original. Each piece of bright, multi-colored glass is hand-blown and hand-crafted. This is not fine crystal like Waterford. These artistically designed glass pieces are unlike anything else in the field. Not only can you watch the craftspeople work, there's a shop connected to the studio. (Kerry glass is available at gift and specialty shops throughout Ireland, but this is where you can watch the artisans at work.)

QUILL'S WOOLLEN MARKET

Location: 1 High St., Killarney
Telephone: (064) 32277

There are sweater boutiques all over Ireland. The population lives in sweaters and the variety and styles are enough to boggle the mind. This store, to me, is one of the best such shops in the entire country in terms of variety, sizes, styles, and quality for both men and women.

County Wicklow

ARKLOW POTTERY

Location: South Quay, Arklow
Telephone: (0402) 32401

Fishermen clean their boats and gulls keen over the water just a stone's throw away from this cavernous complex, the biggest pottery factory in Ireland. It produces all manner of pottery, from rustic earthenware to fine bone-china tableware. You don't have to worry about how to get your table settings back on Aer Lingus. Arklow Pottery will gladly ship for you.

AVOCA HANDWEAVERS

Location: Avoca
Telephone: (0402) 35105

Up in the Wicklow Mountains, not far from the town of Arklow, is the tiny hamlet of Avoca. They've been weaving fine woollens there since the early 1700s. Today, the little cluster of whitewashed cottages houses a sheep-to-shawl operation at which visitors can watch yarn spun from the wool of local lambs and then woven into rare fabrics.

Across the parking lot is one of Ireland's best knitwear shops. It ain't cheap, but you'll pay a lot less than you would for the same products in the U.S., if you can find them at all. The selection of high-quality knits covers a broad spectrum, including men's and women's jackets and sweaters, slacks, hats, scarves, and neckties. Avoca Handweavers is worth a trip out of the way. The trip into the Wicklow Mountains is made all the easier by the pleasant scenery.

Business is booming for this quality operation. There are Avoca Woolen outlets in Bray (also in county Wicklow), at Bunratty in county Clare, and at several other locations.

Northern Ireland

County Derry

DERRY CRAFT VILLAGE

Location: Shipquay St., Derry
Telephone: (0504) 260329

This unusual shopping center has combined buildings constructed from the 1500s to the 1800s into one complex that mirrors the history of the old, walled city of Derry. The area now boasts more than thirty specialty shops and craft workshops.

Buildings, Monuments, and Sights

For the most part the places included in this subsection are in reasonable proximity to major golf courses or locations where you may decide to spend the night. The list is highly idiosyncratic and does not purport to be a complete listing of sights to see. After all, if you wanted a book on sightseeing, you'd have grabbed a different one than this.

The Irish Republic

County Clare

BUNRATTY CASTLE AND FOLK PARK

Location: Bunratty

It's crowded and it's touristy and those are things I usually avoid like the plague, but the castle is worth a look and the workshops and craft shops offer some interesting goods for sale. It doesn't merit a detour, but it's conveniently located between Shannon Airport and Limerick and is easily visited before or after golf at any of the nearby courses—Shannon, Dromoland, Ennis, Lahinch—or even on the road to Ballybunion.

CLIFFS OF MOHER

When you've finished playing the treacherous and testing links at Lahinch, drive about five miles to the north along the scenic coastal road and stop at the Cliffs of Moher. It is one of the finest views in Ireland. On a clear day you can see all the way to the Aran Islands. On a stormy day the angry Atlantic lashes the rocks with the fierceness of a hurricane. The cliffs are free; if you want to go into the nineteenth-century O'Brien's Tower at the north end, there is a nominal charge.

County Galway

KYLEMORE ABBEY

Location: Kylemore

The Benedictine nuns opened Kylemore Abbey to the public shortly after they took it over in 1920. It remains their home and a popular tourist attraction today. The abbey includes a working farm and a pottery studio along with a shop where pots and souvenirs can be purchased. They ring the abbey bell at 6 P.M. for vespers and it tolls across the rugged hills of Connemara like something out of a Cecil B. de Mille movie. The sisters ask for a small donation for the privilege of touring their home.

County Kerry

DINGLE PENINSULA

If you have a little time when you've finished playing Ceann Sibéal, there are fascinating historic sites nearby. The most notable is the Gallarus Oratory, a thousand-year-old church that looks like an upside-down stone boat. The stones are held together by gravity alone, no mortar, and for a millennium they have kept water out of the sanctuary. In various locations on the peninsula are Ogham Stones, pillars into which the oldest known examples of the written Irish Gaelic language are chiseled, and beehive huts, stone dwellings named for their appearance in which the earliest Druid settlers and later Christian monks once lived.

The Dingle Peninsula was home to a hundred or more hermit monks from the fifth century on. It was in that century that Christianity made its way to Ireland and from there that Christianity became infused with Druid and Celtic mysticism and legend.

MUCKROSS HOUSE AND GARDENS

Location: South of Killarney
Telephone: (064) 31440   Fax: (064)33926

This is a magnificent mansion set in the heart of Killarney National Park, a short way out of Killarney town on the Kenmare Road. The house was built in the mid-1800s and is now a museum of Kerry folk life. What used to be the main drawing room looks across a grassy expanse, about a driver and a six iron from Muckross Lake, the middle of the three Lakes of Killarney. The gardens that surround the mansion are worth some time themselves, especially if the weather is clement. Muckross House is not to be missed. If you have children with you, Muckross Traditional Farm, a working example of rural Irish life in the 1930s, is a fascinating way to spend a few hours. The gardens are free; it will cost you a nominal entrance fee to get into the mansion and farm.

THE RING OF KERRY

This is worth a special trip, even though it will take you about four hours. The magnificent scenery—the spires and peaks of Macgillicuddy's Reeks on one side and the sparkling Atlantic on the other—is simply unsurpassed. The narrow, winding road from Moll's Gap to Killarney (with its unequaled views of the Upper Lake and the valley that leads from the mountains to the town and forms a large part of Killarney National Park) is awesome.

One way to do it is to drive part of the way, stop and play the links at Waterville, and then take the other half of the drive. Another approach is to take the drive clockwise in the morning and stop at Dooks for lunch and to play a round of golf after the lengthy car ride.

County Sligo

LOUGH GILL AND PARKE'S CASTLE

The twenty-six-mile drive around Lough Gill, made famous in the Yeats poem "Lake Isle of Innisfree," has clear signs to direct you and is one of the prettiest parts of the country. The lake itself fills the landscape and the eye as you crest the hills just outside of Sligo town. The drive then takes you from the flat farmland at the east end of the lake to the foot of the mountain Ben Bulben, crossing from county Sligo into county Leitrim and back.

On the Ben Bulben side of the lake, almost on the county line in county Leitrim, Parke's Castle has been fully restored and is open to visitors. From various vantage points from the lake, Parke's Castle seems to rise from the mists like a ghost of the past, the only man-made structure visible for miles in any direction. There is a small admission charge. The castle has a tearoom where you can get a soft drink or snack.

County Wicklow

GLENDALOUGH

In Irish Gaelic, Glendalough means "valley of the two lakes." It is pronounced "*Glen*-du-lokh" and was the site of a large sixth-century monastery. What started as a tranquil retreat for the hermitlike Saint Kevin—who picked that spot for its natural beauty and peacefulness—evolved into a major center of learning in Europe three centuries later. But, as with many of Ireland's treasures, Glendalough was plundered, at first by the Vikings and then the English. Today, visitors can see the skeletal remains of much of the monastery, including Saint Kevin's chapel and a 100-foot round tower that is in almost perfect condition. The director of the movie *Braveheart* fell in love with the magnificent scenery and used it as part of the backdrop for the film. Admission to the ruins is free; the visitors' center charges admittance.

Northern Ireland

County Antrim

BUSHMILLS DISTILLERY

Location: Main St., Bushmills
Telephone: (0801) 2657-31521

In a land where whiskey is near and dear to the hearts of the people, the place where it all began is nothing less than a shrine. Bushmills is the oldest distillery in Ireland, first licensed in 1608 and in existence more than three centuries before that. Visitors can view the entire process, from where the water is drawn from the adjacent river Bush to where the labels are plastered on the distinctive square bottles. They'll charge you a nominal fee for the half-hour tour, and it's a good idea to call up and reserve a place, because they limit the number of people they can accommodate.

DUNLUCE CASTLE

The ruins of Dunluce Castle are about halfway between Royal Portrush Golf Club and the Giant's Causeway. On a nice day it provides some wonderful views of the Northern Ireland coast. On a blustery or stormy day it gives you a good indication of what life was once like in that isolated part of the world. The castle dates to the fourteenth century. It served as the base for local warlords and nobles for four centuries. There is a small charge to stroll around. The visitors' center shows a video on the history of the place.

THE GIANT'S CAUSEWAY

This natural wonder runs along a three-mile stretch of the coast just outside the village of Bushmills. Some forty thousand, mostly hexagonal, basalt columns that look as if they were the work of master craftsmen lead from a cliff right into the ocean.

Geologists will tell you that the Giant's Causeway is the result of a volcanic eruption in the Cenozoic era.

Irish mythology will tell you that the causeway was built by the giant Finn MacCool to facilitate a challenge to fight a Scottish giant. The lore has it that as the enormous Scottish giant lumbered across the causeway, Finn MacCool got nervous and asked his wife to help him out. She dressed Finn up in infant's clothing and laid him in bed, and when the Scottish giant appeared she said, "Here's the baby. You should see what his father looks like!" The Scottish giant fled back to Scotland across the causeway, knocking the steps into the sea as he went. I find the legend more impressive than the rocks themselves.

The causeway's free, but there is a charge to park your car at the visitors' center.

County Derry

GUILDHALL AND THE WALLED CITY OF DERRY

The Guildhall sits across a small cobblestone square from Shipquay Gate, one of the four huge old gates to the ancient walled city. The Gothic structure resembles the building of the same name in London and features a giant four-faced clock and stained-glass windows that depict major events in Ulster history in the past century.

The walled city, built on the banks of the river Foyle, has withstood sieges and attacks since Viking days. In the early seventeenth century, more than a mile of eighteen-foot-thick walls was constructed to protect the residents. The gates—Shipquay, Ferryquay, Bishop's, and Butcher's—were shut to keep out attackers. Bishop's Gate was later redesigned to accommodate a soaring Tudor arch. Right by Bishop's Gate is the imposing Gothic structure, the Cathedral of St. Columb.

Today, the shopping and social hub of the city is within those imposing walls. A stroll around the area is a most enjoyable way to spend a few hours. Parking is always a challenge. I generally use one of the big public parking garages outside the walls.

CHAPTER 6

Dublin

Other than the fact that it's the capital and the city of James Joyce and Sean O'Casey, I have never found a compelling reason for golfers to go to Dublin at all. Dublin is a city that is best left to the imagination of those who have never been there or to those who knew her when she was younger.

It once had a certain perverse charm, despite the fact that it was a nasty little industrial town. Singers and poets doted fondly on the river Liffey (which runs through the heart of it and has never smelled particularly good) and its bridges (which, frankly, have never done much for me). Now, however, Dublin has been Eurofied almost beyond recognition. Grafton Street—a fine little shopping street—has been turned into a cutesy pedestrian mall; a glass-and-steel monstrosity of a shopping arcade now scars a corner across from St. Stephen's Green; even the Book of Kells has been moved into a special, sterile viewing room, removed from its former resting place in "the long room" of the library at Trinity College.

Indeed, the foggy, grimy Dublin that once had almost as many pubs as longshoremen, the Dublin that inspired playwrights and poets and songwriters for generations, exists no more. Dublin today is a hustling, bustling center of industry and trade. If the core of activity was once the harbor, it's now the plush offices in modern downtown buildings. If deals were once made in back alleys and pubs, they are now made in trendy restaurants and cafes.

Unfortunately, Dublin's building boom and modernization have not extended to its streets and highways. There is no major artery through the city. The divided highways end where the western suburbs begin and there is no easy way to get from north to south, save for the narrow, zigzagging city streets and those small, ancient bridges across the river Liffey.

If you feel that you absolutely cannot, or will not, visit Ireland without stopping in the city once walked by Leopold Bloom, here are a few notes and guides.

Hotels

THE SHELBOURNE

Location: 25 St. Stephen's Green
Rooms: Very Expensive
Telephone: (01) 676-6471   Toll free: 1-800-CALL-THF

As far as I'm concerned, there's only one hotel in Dublin—the Shelbourne. This red stone landmark is a magnificent, charming, and outrageously expensive hostelry centrally located on St. Stephen's Green. The Irish Constitution was signed in one of the guest rooms in 1921. The rooms are plush and superbly furnished and the bathrooms are among the most elegant in Europe. The service is first rate. The Horseshoe Bar has been written about by every writer—fiction and nonfiction—who ever put Dublin in a book, story, or play. The upper crust of Dublin book their tables days, if not weeks, in advance for dinner on Friday and Saturday night.

BELGRAVE GUESTHOUSE

Location: 8-10 Belgrave Square
Rooms: Moderate
Telephone: (01) 496-3760   Fax: (01) 497-9243

If the Shelbourne is booked, south of central Dublin in a fashionable residential neighborhood is a pair of adjoining Victorian buildings that have been crafted into a charming and comfortable twenty-four-room hotel. Many of the rooms overlook the lovely old well-treed square.

Restaurants

PATRICK GUILBAUD

Location: 46 James Pl.
Dinner: Very Expensive   Reservations: Required
Telephone: (01) 676-4192

As you might expect in any city the size of Dublin, you can get a very good meal for a variety of prices. From the Tex-Mex joint on Nassau Street near the entrance to Trinity College to pizza parlors to haute cuisine, Dublin will offer something to satisfy your palate.

If you have only one night and you want a truly special meal, however, Patrick Guilbaud is one of the city's finest restaurants. It is hidden behind a bank building in what looks like a dark alley off lower Baggot Street. The inventive and incredibly appetizing menu features French preparations of wonderfully fresh Irish ingredients. A rack of lamb with garlic and fresh herbs transcended almost any other similar dishes I've had anywhere. Sea bass with saffron butter is a remarkable creation.

If there is a complaint about the place, it is that too many people seem to go there to worship the food rather than to eat it. Conversations tend to be muted, even reverential. Maybe there is an assumption that if you're paying an arm and a leg, you should keep quiet about it, a theory I've never subscribed to.

Pubs

There are more than one thousand pubs in Dublin. You'll have no difficulty finding one.

O'DONOGHUE'S

Location: 15 Merrion Row
Telephone: (01) 661-4303

O'Donoghue's—hidden between St. Stephen's Green and Merrion Street—is the godfather of all so-called singing pubs, bars that feature traditional Irish music and ballads. It's always noisy, smoky, crowded, and fun. Be prepared to stand and be jostled.

Impromptu sets of Irish music can erupt into hand-clapping, foot-stomping revelry at almost any hour of night or day.

DAVY BYRNES

Location: 21 Duke St.
Telephone: (01) 677-5217

Davy Byrnes has been in the same location just off Grafton Street since the 1870s and has long drawn poets, writers, and artists, although almost every time I've been there the main occupation has been drinking. James Joyce mentioned it in *Ulysses.*

Shopping

GRAFTON STREET

Dublin's version of Rodeo Drive, Grafton Street, is now a three-block-long pedestrian mall that features all manner of specialty shops, as well as street musicians, sidewalk art shows, and assorted other distractions.

BROWN THOMAS

Location: 15-20 Grafton St.
Telephone: (01) 679-5666

The city's most famous department store, Brown Thomas, is well worth browsing in for everything from lace to Waterford crystal, Belleek china, all kinds of woollens, tweeds, and designer clothing.

POWERSCOURT CENTRE

Location: 59 S. William St.
Telephone: (01) 679-4144

Only a few blocks from Grafton Street, the Powerscourt Centre houses more than sixty boutiques, art galleries, and craft shops. It's located in a restored four-story townhouse, featuring a skylit central atrium that often has live music during shopping hours.

H. JOHNSTON

Location: 11 Wicklow St.
Telephone: (01) 677-1249

One of the most unique and unusual little shops in a city that's loaded with such places, H. Johnston specializes in umbrellas, canes, walking sticks, and the like.

HERALDIC ARTISTS

Location: 3 Nassau St.
Telephone: (01) 679-7020

If you'd like a little background on your surname, especially if it's Celtic, drop into Heraldic Artists.

Sightseeing

It seems that just about everybody's list of top attractions in Dublin includes Trinity College and the famous eighth-century illuminated manuscript of the four gospels known as the Book of Kells. You can forget the Book of Kells, as far as I'm concerned, unless you have an unquenchable thirst to stand in a long line with every other tourist in the city only to be told by a bored young guard to "move along, please; you can't stand there forever." There is a nominal charge to hurry past the Book of Kells.

The famous "long room" in the library is worth a peek, and the campus of Trinity College, itself, makes for a delightful stroll, especially on a nice day. They haven't started charging for either yet. Trinity College is the oldest university in Ireland, founded by England's Queen Elizabeth I exactly a century after Columbus set sail for the New World.

The National Gallery is a pleasant little museum, located at Merrion Square West, telephone (01) 661-5133. This isn't the

Louvre or the Uffizi, but it boasts more than two thousand paintings along with prints, drawings, sculpture, and objets d'art. Admission is free.

Christ Church Cathedral is one of the oldest buildings in Dublin. It dates to 1038. The king of Dublin—whose name was Sitric and who happened to be Danish—built the first wooden house of worship on that spot. They ask for a small donation. Telephone: (01) 677-8099.

Of all the disappointments connected with Dublin, the greatest tragedy is the abolition of tours of the Guinness Brewery. There is a charge to visit the Hop Store and watch a movie (whoopee!) but it just won't replace going into the brewery and smelling that dark, rich Guinness Stout being made.

CHAPTER 7

Superlatives and Favorites

Golf and Facilities

THE AUTHOR'S TEN BEST GOLF COURSES IN IRELAND

1. Old Head
2. Lahinch
3. Royal County Down
4. Royal Portrush
5. Ballybunion
    (Old Course)
6. County Louth
7. Ballyliffin (Old Links)
8. The European Club
9. Cork Golf Club
10. Tralee

THE AUTHOR'S FAVORITE GOLF COURSES

1. Dooks
2. Old Head
3. Cork Golf Club
4. Lahinch
5. Ceann Sibéal
6. Ballybunion (Cashen Course)
7. The European Club
8. Ring of Kerry
9. County Sligo
10. Ballyliffin (Old Links)

THE AUTHOR'S EIGHTEEN DREAM HOLES

The Four Best Par 3s

1. Royal Portrush, fourteenth hole ("Calamity")
2. Lahinch, sixth hole ("the Dell")

3. Ring of Kerry, eighteenth hole
4. Killarney (Mahoney's Point), eighteenth hole

The Four Best Par 5s

1. Old Head, twelfth hole
2. Waterville, eleventh hole
3. Lahinch, fifth hole
4. Ceann Sibéal, thirteenth hole

The Ten Best Par 4s

1. Royal County Down, ninth hole
2. County Sligo, seventeenth hole
3. The European Club, eighth hole
4. Ballybunion (Old Course), eleventh hole
5. Portstewart, second hole
6. Tralee, twelfth hole
7. Royal Portrush, seventh hole
8. County Louth, fourteenth hole
9. Ballyliffin (Old Links), fifteenth hole
10. Ballybunion (Cashen Course), thirteenth hole

THE FIVE MOST DIFFICULT COURSES FOR MEN TO SCORE ON

1. Ballybunion (Cashen Course)
2. Tralee
3. Donegal
4. Ballyliffin (Old Links)
5. The European Club

THE FIVE MOST DIFFICULT COURSES FOR WOMEN TO SCORE ON

1. The European Club
2. County Louth
3. Ballybunion (Cashen Course)
4. Ballyliffin (Old Links)
5. Wicklow

THE BEST, FAIREST GOLFING TESTS FOR WOMEN

1. Portstewart
2. Dooks
3. Ceann Sibéal
4. Old Head
5. Ballybunion
   (Old Course)
6. Cork Golf Club
7. Blainroe
8. Ardglass
9. Castlerock
10. Ring of Kerry

THE BEST GREENS

1. Old Head
2. Royal Portrush
3. Royal County Down
4. Cork Golf Club
5. Ballybunion
   (Old Course)
6. County Louth
7. Enniscrone
8. Ballybunion (Cashen Course)
9. Portstewart
10. Ballyliffin (Old Links)

THE TOUGHEST GREENS TO APPROACH

1. Ballybunion (Cashen Course)
2. Tralee
3. The European Club
4. County Louth
5. Waterville

THE TOUGHEST BUNKERS

1. The European Club
2. Lahinch
3. Tralee
4. Ballybunion (Cashen Course)
5. Old Head

THE FIVE BEST PRO SHOPS

1. Old Head
2. Druids Glen
3. The K Club
4. Mount Juliet
5. Ballybunion

THE TEN BEST CLUBHOUSES

1. Old Head
2. The K Club
3. Mount Juliet
4. Druids Glen
5. Killarney
6. Ballybunion
7. Waterville
8. Ballyliffin
9. Tralee
10. Ring of Kerry

IRELAND'S MOST SCENIC GOLF COURSES

1. Old Head
2. Ring of Kerry
3. Tralee
4. Royal County Down
5. Ballyliffin
6. Blainroe
7. Killarney (Mahoney's Point)
8. Ceann Sibéal
9. County Sligo
10. Waterville

Nongolf Superlatives

THE BEST BIG HOTEL

Park Hotel, Kenmare, county Kerry

THE BEST LITTLE HOTEL

Tinakilly House, Rathnew, county Wicklow

FAVORITE COUNTRY HOUSE

Coopershill House, Riverstown, county Sligo

THE BEST PLACE TO BUY WOOLLENS

Avoca Handweavers, Avoca, county Wicklow

THE BEST PLACE TO BUY GIFTS

Clarinbridge Crystal Shop, Clarinbridge, county Galway

THE BEST TRADITIONAL IRISH BREAKFAST

Hotel Europe, Killarney, county Kerry

FAVORITE RESTAURANTS

1. Dingles, Killarney, county Kerry
2. The Wild Geese, Adare, county Limerick
3. The President's Restaurant (Longueville House), Mallow, county Cork
4. Ramore, Portrush, county Antrim
5. Tinakilly House, Rathnew, county Wicklow
6. Bricin, Killarney, county Kerry
7. The Percy French Grille, Newcastle, county Down
8. Blue Haven, Kinsale, county Cork
9. Cromleach Lodge, Castlebaldwin, county Sligo
10. Robertino's, Killarney, county Kerry

FAVORITE PUBS

1. The Laurels, Killarney, county Kerry
2. The Grand Hotel, Killarney, county Kerry
3. Bridge Tavern, Wicklow, county Wicklow
4. O'Donoghue's, Dublin, county Dublin
5. Durty Nelly's, Bunratty, county Clare

Ireland's Eighteen-Hole Golf Courses

Green fees (per person)

Very Expensive	above $75
Expensive	$50-75
Moderate	$30-50
Inexpensive	under $30

The Irish Republic

County Carlow

CARLOW GOLF CLUB (parkland, par 70)
Location: Two miles north of Carlow town on the N9
Green fees: Moderate
Telephone: (0503) 31695   Fax: (0503) 40065

MOUNT WOLSELEY GOLF & COUNTRY CLUB (parkland, par 72)
Location: Just outside the town of Tullow
Green fees: Moderate
Telephone: (0503) 51675   Fax: (0503) 52123
E-mail: wolseley@iol.ie

County Cavan

COUNTY CAVAN GOLF CLUB (parkland, par 70)
Location: One mile northwest of Cavan town

Green fees: Inexpensive
Telephone: (049) 31541

SLIEVE RUSSELL GOLF CLUB (parkland, par 72)
Location: Ballyconnell
Green fees: Expensive
Telephone: (049) 952-6444   Fax: (049) 952-6474
E-mail: slieverussell@sqgroup.com

County Clare

DROMOLAND GOLF CLUB (parkland, par 71)
Location: About ten miles north of Shannon Airport on the N18 on the
    grounds of Dromoland Castle
Green fees: Expensive
Telephone: (061) 368444   Fax: (061) 368498

EAST CLARE GOLF CLUB (parkland, par 71)
Location About twenty-five miles east of Ennis in the town of Bodyke on
    the R352
Green fees: Inexpensive
Telephone: (061) 921322   Fax: (061) 921717

ENNIS GOLF CLUB (parkland, par 70)
Location: About a half-mile west of Ennis
Green fees: Inexpensive
Telephone: (065) 24074   Fax: (065) 41848
E-mail: egc@tinet.ie
NOTE: Wednesday is ladies' day; few or no visitors Sundays

KILKEE GOLF CLUB (links, par 71)
Location: On the coast road immediately north of Kilkee
Green fees: Inexpensive
Telephone: (065) 56048   Fax: (065) 56977

KILRUSH (parkland, par 70)
Location: In the town of Kilrush
Green fees: Inexpensive
Telephone: (065) 59005
E-mail: kelgolf@iol.ie

LAHINCH GOLF CLUB (Old Course, links, par 72; Castle Course, links,
    par 70)
Location: On the north edge of Lahinch
Green fees: Very Expensive
Telephone: (065) 81003   Fax: (065) 81592
E-mail: lgc@iol.ie
NOTE: Book well in advance for summer weekends

SHANNON GOLF CLUB (parkland, par 72)
Location: At Shannon Airport
Green fees: Moderate
Telephone: (061) 471849   Fax: (061) 471507
NOTE: Tuesday is ladies' day; few or no visitors Sundays

WOODSTOCK GOLF & COUNTRY CLUB (parkland, par 72)
Location: About two miles west of Ennis on the Lahinch Road
Green fees: Expensive
Telephone: (065) 29463   Fax: (065) 20304

County Cork

BANDON GOLF CLUB (parkland, par 70)
Location: About two miles southwest of Bandon off the N71
Green fees: Inexpensive
Telephone: (023) 41111   Fax: (023) 44690

CHARLEVILLE GOLF CLUB (parkland, par 72)
Location: On the outskirts of Charleville off the N20
Green fees: Inexpensive
Telephone: (063) 81257   Fax: (068) 81274
NOTE: Expanded to 27 holes; very popular with golfing societies; very busy
    on weekends

CORK GOLF CLUB (parkland, par 72)
Location: About five miles east of Cork city off the N25 in Little Island
Green fees: Expensive
Telephone: (021) 353451   Fax: (021) 353410

DOUGLAS GOLF CLUB (parkland, par 70)
Location: Southeast of Cork city center off the Ringaskiddy Road

Green fees: Moderate
Telephone: (021) 895297
NOTE: Tuesday is ladies' day; few or no visitors on weekends

EAST CORK GOLF CLUB (parkland, par 69)
Location: About a mile north of Midleton off the Fermoy Road
Green fees: Inexpensive
Telephone: (021) 631687   Fax: (021) 613695
NOTE: Member competitions most weekends

FERMOY GOLF CLUB (parkland, par 70)
Location: About three miles from Fermoy town just off the road to Corrin
    Cross
Green fees: Inexpensive
Telephone: (025) 31472   Fax: (025) 33072

FERNHILL GOLF & COUNTRY CLUB (parkland, par 70)
Location: South of Cork city and about four miles from Cork Airport in
    the village of Carrigaline
Green fees: Inexpensive
Telephone: (021) 372226   Fax: (021) 371011
E-mail: fernhill@iol.ie

FOTA ISLAND GOLF CLUB (parkland, par 72)
Location: In the village of Carrigtwohill, about nine miles east of Cork city
    off the N25
Green fees: Moderate
Telephone: (021) 883700   Fax: (021) 883713
E-mail: fotagolf@iol.ie

HARBOR POINT GOLF CLUB (parkland, par 72)
Location: About four miles east of Cork city at Little Island, off the N25
Green fees: Moderate
Telephone: (021) 353094   Fax: (021) 354408
E-mail: hpoint@iol.ie

KANTURK GOLF CLUB (parkland, par 70)
Location: About a mile from Kanturk town, three miles off the Mallow-
    Killarney road at Ballymaquirke Cross
Green fees: Inexpensive
Telephone: (029) 50534

KINSALE GOLF CLUB (Farrangalway Course, parkland, par 72;
  Ringenane Course, parkland, par 35)
Location: Just east of Kinsale
Green fees: Moderate
Telephone: (021) 777422   Fax: (021) 773114
E-mail: kinsaleg@indigo.ie

LEE VALLEY GOLF CLUB (parkland, par 72)
Location: Near the village of Ovens, about eight miles west of Cork city
Green fees: Moderate
Telephone: (021) 331721   Fax: (021) 331695

MACROOM GOLF CLUB (parkland, par 72)
Location: Through the arch of the castle in the center of Macroom in the
  area called Lackaduv
Green fees: Inexpensive
Telephone: (026) 41072   Fax: (026) 41391
E-mail: mcroomgc@iol.ie

MAHON GOLF CLUB (parkland, par 68)
Location: In Blackrock off the Douglas Road
Green fees: Inexpensive
Telephone: (021) 294280

MALLOW GOLF CLUB (parkland, par 72)
Location: Immediately southeast of Mallow off the Kilavullen Road
Green fees: Moderate
Telephone: (022) 21145   Fax: (022) 42501
NOTE: Few visitors on weekends because of member competitions

MONKSTOWN GOLF CLUB (parkland, par 70)
Location: About eight miles southeast of Cork city
Green fees: Moderate
Telephone: (021) 841376

MUSKERRY GOLF CLUB (parkland, par 71)
Location: About three miles from Blarney, northwest of Cork city
Green fees: Moderate
Telephone: (021) 385297

OLD HEAD GOLF LINKS (links, par 72)
Location: About seven miles south of Kinsale
Green fees: Very Expensive
Telephone: (021) 778444   Fax: (021) 778022
E-mail: info@oldheadgolf.ie
NOTE: Book well in advance for summer weekends

SKIBBEREEN GOLF CLUB (parkland, par 71)
Location: About a mile south of Skibbereen off the Baltimore Road
Green fees: Inexpensive
Telephone: (028) 21227

WATER ROCK GOLF COURSE (parkland, par 70)
Location: About eleven miles east of Cork city off the N25 near Midleton
Green fees: Inexpensive
Telephone: (021) 613499   Fax: (021) 633150

YOUGHAL GOLF CLUB (parkland, par 70)
Location: Just off the N25 overlooking the town of Youghal
Green fees: Inexpensive
Telephone: (024) 92787   Fax: (024) 92641
NOTE: It's pronounced "Yawl" and Wednesday is ladies' day

County Donegal

BALLYBOFEY AND STRANORLAR GOLF CLUB (parkland, par 68)
Location: Just outside Stranorlar on the Ballybofey-Lifford Road
Green fees: Inexpensive
Telephone: (074) 31093 or 31104   Fax: (074) 30158

BALLYLIFFIN GOLF CLUB (Old Course, links, par 71; Glashedy Links,
    links, par 72)
Location: About fifteen miles north of Buncrana in the village of Ballyliffin
Green fees: Expensive
Telephone: (077) 76119   Fax: (077) 76672
E-mail: ballyliffingolfclub@tinet.ie
NOTE: Few or no visitors on weekends; book well in advance for the sum-
    mer months

BUNDORAN GOLF CLUB (links, par 69)
Location: Between Bundoran and Ballyshannon, just off the N15

Green fees: Moderate
Telephone: (072) 41302

DONEGAL GOLF CLUB (links, par 73)
Location: South of Donegal town in the village of Murvagh
Green fees: Moderate
Telephone: (073) 34054   Fax: (073) 34377
NOTE: Monday is ladies' day

DUFANAGHY GOLF CLUB (links, par 68)
Location: North-northwest of Donegal town just outside the village of
    Dufanaghy, overlooking Sheephaven Bay
Green fees: Inexpensive
Telephone: (074) 36335

LETTERKENNY GOLF CLUB (parkland, par 70)
Location: About two miles north of Letterkenny, off the Ramelton Road
Green fees: Inexpensive
Telephone: (074) 21150
NOTE: Visitors must book in advance on weekends

NARIN AND PORTNOO GOLF CLUB (links, par 69)
Location: Northwest of Donegal town between the villages of Narin and
    Portnoo
Green fees: Inexpensive
Telephone: (075) 45107

NORTH WEST GOLF CLUB (links, par 70)
Location: About a mile south of Buncrana and about twenty miles north-
    west of Derry, Northern Ireland
Green fees: Moderate
Telephone: (077) 61715   Fax: (077) 63284

PORTSALON GOLF CLUB (links, par 69)
Location: About two miles north of Letterkenny
Green fees: Inexpensive
Telephone: (074) 59459

ROSAPENNA GOLF LINKS (links, par 70)
Location: About twenty-five miles north of Letterkenny in the village of
    Downings

Green fees: Moderate
Telephone: (074) 55301   Fax: (074) 55128
E-mail: rosapenna@tinet.ie

ST. PATRICK'S LINKS (two links courses, par 72 and par 74)
Location: In the northern part of the county, about two miles from the
   town of Carrigart on Sheephaven Bay
Green fees: Inexpensive
Telephone: (074) 55114   Fax: (074) 55250

County Dublin

BALBRIGGAN GOLF CLUB (parkland, par 71)
Location: Immediately south of Balbriggan off the N1
Green fees: Inexpensive
Telephone: (01) 841-2229   Fax: (01) 841-3927

BALCARRICK GOLF CLUB (parkland, par 72)
Location: North of Dublin Airport in Corballis, near the village of Donabate
Green fees: Inexpensive
Telephone: (01) 843-6957   Fax: (01) 843-6228

BEAVERSTOWN GOLF CLUB (parkland, par 71)
Location: North of Dublin Airport near the village of Donabate
Green fees: Moderate
Telephone: (01) 843-6721
E-mail: bgc@iol.ie

BEECH PARK GOLF CLUB (parkland, par 72)
Location: About two miles south of Rathcoole, off the N7
Green fees: Inexpensive
Telephone: (01) 458-0522   Fax: (01) 458-8365

BLACK BUSH GOLF CLUB (parkland, par 72)
Location: Just outside Dunshaughlin village off the N3
Green fees: Moderate
Telephone: (01) 825-0021

BLANCHARDSTOWN GOLF CENTER (parkland, par 54)
Location: About two miles from Blanchardstown Shopping Center adjacent to Mulhuddart Cemetery

Green fees: Inexpensive
Telephone: (01) 821-3206   Fax: (01) 821-7431

CASTLE GOLF CLUB (parkland, par 70)
Location: About five miles from Dublin city center in the village of
   Rathfarnham
Green fees: Expensive
Telephone: (01) 490-4207   Fax: (01) 492-0264
NOTE: Few or no visitors on weekends

CITYWEST GOLF RESORT (parkland, par 70)
Location: West of Dublin city at the Saggart exit off the N7
Green fees: Moderate
Telephone: (01) 458-8566   Fax: (01) 458-8565
E-mail: info@citywest-hotel.iol.ie
NOTE: Golf packages available for hotel guests

CLONTARF GOLF CLUB (parkland, par 69)
Location: Just north of Dublin city off the Malahide Road
Green fees: Moderate
Telephone: (01) 833-1892   Fax: (01) 833-1933
NOTE: Women face serious restrictions

CORBALLIS GOLF LINKS (links, par 65)
Location: Just outside the village of Donabate off the main Dublin-Belfast road
Green fees: Inexpensive
Telephone: (01) 843-6583   Fax: (01) 822-6668
E-mail: carrgolf@indigo.ie

CORRSTOWN GOLF CLUB (parkland, par 72)
Location: In the town of Kilsallaghan, north of Dublin city
Green fees: Inexpensive
Telephone: (01) 864-0533   Fax: (01) 864-0537

DEER PARK HOTEL AND GOLF COURSES (eighteen-hole parkland, par
   72; twelve-hole parkland, par 36; nine-hole parkland, par 35)
Location: Howth, on the grounds of Howth Castle
Green fees: Inexpensive
Telephone: (01) 832-2624   Fax: (01) 839-2405
E-mail: sales@deerpark.iol.ie
NOTE: Golf packages available for hotel guests

DONABATE GOLF CLUB (parkland, par 70)
Location: North of Dublin Airport in Donabate
Green fees: Moderate
Telephone: (01) 843-6346

DUN LAOGHAIRE GOLF CLUB (parkland, par 70)
Location: South of Dublin just outside Dun Laoghaire on the Tivoli Road
Green fees: Moderate
Telephone: (01) 280-3916   Fax: (01) 280-4863
NOTE: Few or no visitors on weekends

EDMONDSTOWN GOLF CLUB (parkland, par 70)
Location: About seven miles from Dublin city on the Edmondstown Road,
    near the village of Rathfarnham
Green fees: Moderate
Telephone: (01) 493-1082   Fax: (01) 493-3152

ELM PARK GOLF & SPORTS CLUB (parkland, par 69)
Location: Nutley Lane off the N11 or Merrion Road
Green fees: Expensive
Telephone: (01) 269-3438
NOTE: Visitors are asked to phone in advance

ELMGREEN GOLF CENTER (parkland, par 71)
Location: In Dublin city near Phoenix Park
Green fees: Inexpensive
Telephone: (01) 820-0797   Fax: (01) 822-6668
E-mail: carrgolf@indigo.ie

FORREST LITTTLE GOLF CLUB (parkland, par 70)
Location: Adjacent to Dublin Airport
Green fees: Inexpensive
Telephone: (01) 840-1183   Fax: (01) 840-1060
NOTE: Few or no visitors on weekends

GRANGE GOLF CLUB (parkland, par 68)
Location: About six miles south of Dublin city near the village of
    Rathfarnham
Green fees: Expensive
Telephone: (01) 493-2889

HERMITAGE GOLF CLUB (parkland, par 71)
Location: About two miles from Lucan off the N4
Green fees: Moderate
Telephone: (01) 626-4781
NOTE: Phone in advance for tee times

HOLLYSTOWN GOLF CLUB (parkland, par 72)
Location: On the Dublin-Ashbourne Road off the N2
Green fees: Inexpensive
Telephone: (01) 820-7444   Fax: (01) 820-7447

HOLYWOOD LAKES GOLF CLUB (parkland, par 72)
Location: North of Dublin Airport, off the N1 to Ballyboughal on the R129
Green fees: Moderate
Telephone: (01) 843-3407   Fax: (01) 843-3002

HOWTH GOLF CLUB (heathland, par 71)
Location: Outside Howth off Carrickbrack Road, about two miles from
    Sutton Cross
Green fees: Inexpensive
Telephone: (01) 832-3055   Fax: (01) 832-1793

ISLAND GOLF CLUB (links, par 71)
Location: About two miles east of Donabate on the Corballis Peninsula
Green fees: Very Expensive
Telephone: (01) 843-6205   Fax: (01) 843-6860
NOTE: Advance reservations recommended; few or no visitors on weekends

KILTERNAN GOLF CLUB (parkland, par 68)
Location: Kilternan, on Dublin Bay
Green fees: Inexpensive
Telephone: (01) 295-5559   Fax: (01) 295-5670

LUCAN GOLF CLUB (parkland, par 71)
Location: West of Dublin city center off Celbridge Road in Lucan village
Green fees: Inexpensive
Telephone: (01) 628-0246   Fax: (01) 628-2929

LUTTRELLSTOWN CASTLE GOLF CLUB (parkland, par 72)
Location: West of Dublin city in the village of Castleknock

Green fees: Expensive
Telephone: (01) 808-9988   Fax: (01) 808-9989
E-mail: golf@luttrellstown.ie

MALAHIDE GOLF CLUB (eighteen-hole parkland, par 71; nine-hole
    parkland, par 35)
Location: North of Dublin in an area of Malahide town called The Grange
Green fees: Expensive
Telephone: (01) 846-1611   Fax: (01) 846-1270
E-mail: malgc@club.ie
NOTE: Few or no visitors on weekends

MILLTOWN GOLF CLUB (parkland, par 71)
Location: South of Dublin city center off Churchtown Road in Milltown
Green fees: Expensive
Telephone: (01) 497-6090   Fax: (01) 497-6008
E-mail: millgolf@iol.ie

NEWLANDS GOLF CLUB (parkland, par 71)
Location: Between Dublin and Naas, off the N7 at Newlands Cross
Green fees: Moderate
Telephone: (01) 459-3157   Fax: (01) 459-3498

PORTMARNOCK GOLF CLUB (links, par 72)
Location: In Portmarnock village, north of Dublin city center off the
    Malahide Road
Green fees: Very Expensive
Telephone: (01) 846-2968   Fax: (01) 846-2601
E-mail: secretary@portmarnockgolfclub.ie
NOTE: Very busy in summer; few or no visitors on weekends; book well in
    advance

PORTMARNOCK HOTEL & GOLF LINKS (links, par 72)
Location: North of Dublin city center in the village of Portmarnock on the
    Strand Road
Green fees: Very Expensive
Telephone: (01) 846-0611   Fax: (01) 846-2442

ROYAL DUBLIN GOLF CLUB (links, par 72)
Location: Northeast of Dublin city center off the coast road to Howth at
    Bull Island

Green fees: Very Expensive
Telephone: (01) 833-6346   Fax: (01) 833-6504
NOTE: Limited visitors' tee times, especially on weekends; book in advance

ST. ANNE'S GOLF CLUB (links, par 70)
Location: Northeast of Dublin city center north of Bull Island
Green fees: Moderate
Telephone: (01) 833-6471   Fax: (01) 833-4618

ST. MARGARETS GOLF & COUNTRY CLUB (parkland, par 72)
Location: In the Dublin suburb of St. Margarets
Green fees: Very Expensive
Telephone: (01) 864-0400   Fax: (01) 864-0289
E-mail: stmarggc@indigo.ie

SKERRIES GOLF CLUB (parkland, par 73)
Location: On the outskirts of Skerries town, north of Dublin city
Green fees: Moderate
Telephone: (01) 849-1567   Fax: (01) 849-1591

SLADE VALLEY GOLF CLUB (parkland, par 69)
Location: Southwest of Dublin city near the mountain village of Brittas
Green fees: Inexpensive
Telephone: (01) 458-2739   Fax: (01) 458-2784

STACKSTOWN GOLF CLUB (parkland, par 72)
Location: South of Dublin city near the village of Rathfarnham, off the Kellystown Road
Green fees: Moderate
Telephone: (01) 494-2338
NOTE: Few or no visitors Saturdays

SWORDS OPEN GOLF CENTRE (parkland, par 71)
Location: On Balheary Avenue about two miles from the town of Swords
Green fees: Inexpensive
Telephone: (01) 840-9819

TURVEY GOLF & COUNTRY CLUB (parkland, par 71)
Location: Just off the Dublin-Belfast road on Turvey Avenue heading toward Donabate

Green fees: Inexpensive
Telephone: (01) 843-5169   Fax: (01) 843-5179

County Galway

ARDACONG GOLF CLUB (parkland, par 70)
Location: About a mile from the Tuam exit from the N17 on Miltown Road
Green fees: Inexpensive
Telephone: (093) 25525

ATHENRY GOLF CLUB (parkland, par 70)
Location: East of Galway in Oranmore, off the Athenry Road
Green fees: Inexpensive
Telephone: (091) 794466   Fax: (091) 794971
NOTE: Few or no visitors Sundays

BALLINASLOE GOLF CLUB (parkland, par 72)
Location: West of Ballinasloe, turn from the N6 onto the Portumna Road
Green fees: Inexpensive
Telephone: (0905) 42126   Fax: (0905) 42538

BEARNA GOLF & COUNTRY CLUB (heathland, par 72)
Location: West of Galway city on the coast road in the village of Bearna
Green fees: Moderate
Telephone: (091) 592677   Fax: (091) 592674
NOTE: Few or no visitors Sundays

CONNEMARA GOLF CLUB (links, par 72)
Location: About three miles west of Ballyconneely, roughly midway
    between Clifden and Cashel Bay
Green fees: Expensive
Telephone: (095) 23502   Fax: (095) 23662
E-mail: links@iol.ie

GALWAY BAY GOLF & COUNTRY CLUB (parkland, par 72)
Location: About seven miles southeast of Galway city, outside the village of
    Oranmore
Green fees: Expensive
Telephone: (091) 790500   Fax: (091) 792510
E-mail: gbaygolf@iol.ie
NOTE: Golf packages available for hotel guests

GALWAY GOLF CLUB (parkland, par 70)
Location: About two miles west of Galway city center off the Salthill Road
Green fees: Moderate
Telephone: (091) 522033   Fax: (091) 522169

GORT GOLF CLUB (parkland, par 71)
Location: Turn from the N18 at Gort onto the Kilmacdugh Road and go
    about two and a half miles
Green fees: Inexpensive
Telephone: (091) 632244
NOTE: Few or no visitors Sundays

OUGHTERARD GOLF CLUB (parkland, par 70)
Location: About fifteen miles northwest of Galway city off the N59
Green fees: Inexpensive
Telephone: (091) 82131   Fax: (091) 82733
NOTE: Visitors are discouraged on ladies' day, Wednesday

PORTUMNA GOLF CLUB (parkland, par 68)
Location: Just outside the town of Portumna
Green fees: Inexpensive
Telephone: (0509) 41059

TUAM GOLF CLUB (parkland, par 72)
Location: South of Tuam town off the Athenry Road
Green fees: Inexpensive
Telephone: (093) 28993   Fax: (093) 26003

County Kerry

BALLYBUNION GOLF CLUB (Old Course, links, par 71; Cashen Course,
    links, par 72)
Location: About a mile from the center of Ballybunion town
Green fees: Very Expensive
Telephone: (068) 27146   Fax: (068) 27387
E-mail: bbgolffc@iol.ie
NOTE: Book in advance, especially for summer weekends

BEAUFORT GOLF CLUB (parkland, par 71)
Location: West of Killarney off the Killorglin Road
Green fees: Moderate
Telephone: (064) 44440   Fax: (064) 44752

CEANN SIBEAL (links, par 72)
Location: As far west on the Dingle Peninsula as you can go and still be dry
Green fees: Moderate
Telephone: (066) 915-6255   Fax: (066) 915-6409

DOOKS GOLF CLUB (links, par 70)
Location: About four miles from Killorglin (toward Waterville), turn right
    off the Ring of Kerry Road just before the village of Glenbeigh
Green fees: Moderate
Telephone: (066) 976-8205   Fax: (066) 976-8476
NOTE: Few or no visitors on weekends; book in advance in summer

KENMARE GOLF CLUB (parkland, par 71)
Location: Just outside Kenmare off the Kilgarvan Road
Green fees: Inexpensive
Telephone: (064) 41291   Fax: (064) 42061

KILLARNEY GOLF & FISHING CLUB (Killeen Course, parkland, par 72;
    Mahoney's Point Course, parkland, par 72)
Location: Immediately outside Killarney on the Killorglin Road
Green fees: Expensive
Telephone: (064) 31034   Fax: (064) 33065
E-mail: kgc@iol.ie

KILLORGLIN GOLF CLUB (parkland, par 72)
Location: About one mile from the Killorglin town bridge off the Tralee Road
Green fees: Inexpensive
Telephone: (066) 61979   Fax: (066) 61437

PARKNASILLA (parkland, par 72)
Location: About fifteen miles west of Kenmare at the Great Southern
    Hotel in the village of Sneem
Green fees: Inexpensive
Telephone: (064) 45122   Fax: (064) 45323

RING OF KERRY GOLF & COUNTRY CLUB (mountain/parkland, par 72)
Location: About four miles west of Kenmare in Templenoe, just off the
    Ring of Kerry Road
Green fees: Expensive
Telephone: (064) 42000   Fax: (064) 42533
E-mail: ringofkerrygolf@tinet.ie

TRALEE GOLF CLUB (links, par 71)
Location: Off the Spa/Fenit Road about eight miles northwest of Tralee
Green fees: Very Expensive
Telephone: (066) 713-6379   Fax: (066) 713-6008
NOTE: Book well in advance, especially in summer

WATERVILLE GOLF CLUB (links, par 72)
Location: Immediately northwest of Waterville off the Ring of Kerry
    Road
Green fees: Very Expensive
Telephone: (066) 947-4102   Fax: (066) 947-4482
E-mail: wvgolf@iol.ie
NOTE: Book well in advance, especially in summer

County Kildare

BODENSTOWN GOLF CLUB (Old Course, parkland, par 72; Ladyhill
    Course, parkland, par 71)
Location: About five miles north of Naas just outside the village of Sallins
Green fees: Inexpensive
Telephone: (045) 897096
NOTE: Few or no visitors on Old Course on weekends

CASTLEWARDEN GOLF & COUNTRY CLUB (parkland, par 72)
Location: Off the N7 between Naas and Newlands Cross
Green fees: Moderate
Telephone: (01) 458-9254   Fax: (01) 458-8972
E-mail: castlewarden@club.ie

CRADDOCKSTOWN GOLF CLUB (parkland, par 72)
Location: About a mile and a half from Naas on the Blessington Road
Green fees: Inexpensive
Telephone: (045) 897610   Fax: (045) 896968

THE CURRAGH GOLF CLUB (heathland, par 72)
Location: Off the N7 just outside Newbridge
Green fees: Moderate
Telephone: (045) 441238
NOTE: Phone in advance; few or no visitors on weekends because of mem-
    ber competitions

HIGHFIELD GOLF CLUB (parkland, par 72)
Location: About two miles from Enfield and the N4, off the Edenderry
    Road
Green fees: Inexpensive
Telephone: (0405) 31021

THE K CLUB (parkland, par 72)
Location: Off the N7 in Straffan
Green fees: Very Expensive
Telephone: (01) 601-7300   Fax: (01) 601-7395
E-mail: golf@kclub.ie
NOTE: Advance booking is essential, especially on summer weekends

KILKEA CASTLE GOLF CLUB (parkland, par 71)
Location: About three miles from Castledermot
Green fees: Moderate
Telephone: (0503) 45555   Fax: (0503) 45505
E-mail: kilkeagolfclub@net.ie

KILLEEN GOLF CLUB (parkland, par 71)
Location: Between Naas and Dublin off the N7, just outside the village of Kill
Green fees: Inexpensive
Telephone: (045) 866003   Fax: (045) 875881

KNOCKANALLY GOLF & COUNTRY CLUB (parkland, par 72)
Location: Northwest of Naas, take the Donadea exit off the M4/N4
Green fees: Inexpensive
Telephone: (045) 869322   Fax: (045) 869322

NAAS GOLF CLUB (parkland, par 71)
Location: About three miles from Naas off the road between Sallins and
    Johnstown
Green fees: Inexpensive
Telephone: (045) 897509

County Kilkenny

CALLAN (parkland, par 72)
Location: About one mile from Callan town on the Knocktopher Road
Green fees: Inexpensive
Telephone: (056) 25136
NOTE: Few or no visitors Sundays

KILKENNY GOLF CLUB (parkland, par 71)
Location: Just north of Kilkenny city
Green fees: Moderate
Telephone: (056) 65400

MOUNT JULIET GOLF CLUB (parkland, par 72)
Location: On the western edge of Thomastown, about ten miles south of
　Kilkenny town
Green fees: Very Expensive
Telephone: (056) 73000　Fax: (056) 73019
E-mail: info@mountjuliet.ie
NOTE: Book in advance, especially for summer weekends

County Laois

THE HEATH GOLF CLUB (parkland, par 71)
Location: About five miles northeast of Portlaois off the N7
Green fees: Inexpensive
Telephone: (0502) 46533

County Limerick

ADARE GOLF CLUB (parkland, par 72)
Location: On the grounds of Adare Manor hotel
Green fees: Very Expensive
Telephone: (061) 395044　Fax: (061) 396124
NOTE: This luxury course was designed by Robert Trent Jones, Sr.

ADARE MANOR GOLF CLUB (parkland, par 69)
Location: On the Limerick-city side of the river Maigue on the edge of the
　village of Adare
Green fees: Inexpensive
Telephone: (061) 396204　Fax: (061) 396800
NOTE: The short old course that plays around an ancient monastery; few
　or no visitors on weekends

CASTLEROY GOLF CLUB (parkland, par 71)
Location: About three miles east of Limerick off the N7
Green fees: Moderate
Telephone: (061) 335753　Fax: (061) 335373
NOTE: Member competitions make it very hard for visitors to book tee
　times on weekends

KILLELINE PARK & LEISURE (parkland, par 72)
Location: In the town of Newcastle West
Green fees: Inexpensive
Telephone: (069) 61600   Fax: (069) 77428

LIMERICK COUNTY GOLF & COUNTRY CLUB (parkland, par 72)
Location: About five miles south of Limerick city
Green fees: Expensive
Telephone: (061) 351881   Fax: (061) 351384

LIMERICK GOLF CLUB (parkland, par 72)
Location: About three miles south of Limerick city off the Fedamore Road
Green fees: Moderate
Telephone: (061) 415146
NOTE: Few or no visitors on weekends unless with a member

NEWCASTLE WEST GOLF CLUB (parkland, par 71)
Location: About six miles from Newcastle West off the N21
Green fees: Inexpensive
Telephone: (069) 76500   Fax: (069) 76511

County Longford

COUNTY LONGFORD GOLF CLUB (parkland, par 70)
Location: Just outside Longford town off the N4
Green fees: Inexpensive
Telephone: (043) 46310

County Louth

ARDEE GOLF CLUB (parkland, par 69)
Location: Townspark, Ardee town
Green fees: Inexpensive
Telephone: (041) 53227

COUNTY LOUTH GOLF CLUB (links, par 73)
Location: About five miles northeast of Drogheda in the village of Baltray
Green fees: Expensive
Telephone: (041) 982-2329   Fax: (041) 982-2969
E-mail: baltray@indigo.ie
NOTE: Few or no visitors on Tuesdays and weekends; book well in ad-
    vance, especially in summer

DUNDALK GOLF CLUB (parkland, par 72)
Location: south of Dundalk just outside Blackrock
Green fees: Moderate
Telephone: (042) 21731   Fax: (042) 22022
NOTE: Few or no visitors on weekends

GREENORE GOLF CLUB (links, par 71)
Location: About sixteen miles northeast of Dundalk on Carlingford Lough
Green fees: Moderate
Telephone: (042) 73678

KILLIN PARK GOLF CLUB (parkland, par 69)
Location: About one mile from Dundalk off the Castleblaney road, turn
    right at the Claret Lounge for a mile
Green fees: Inexpensive
Telephone: (042) 39303

SEAPOINT GOLF CLUB (links, par 72)
Location: Northeast of Drogheda off the Clogher Head Road
Green fees: Moderate
Telephone: (041) 22333   Fax: (041) 22331
E-mail: golflinks@seapoint.ie

County Mayo

BALLINROBE GOLF CLUB (parkland, par 74)
Location: Outside Ballinrobe town at Clooncastle
Green fees: Inexpensive
Telephone: (092) 41118   Fax: (092) 41889
E-mail: bgcgolf@iol.ie

CARNE GOLF COURSE (links, par 72)
Location: About a mile southwest of Belmullet on the extreme west coast
    of county Mayo
Green fees: Inexpensive
Telephone: (097) 82292   Fax: (097) 81477

CASTLEBAR GOLF CLUB (parkland, par 71)
Location: Just outside Castlebar off the Belcarra Road
Green fees: Inexpensive
Telephone: (094) 21649
NOTE: Few or no visitors Sundays

CLAREMORRIS GOLF CLUB (parkland, par 73)
Location: In the village of Claremorris
Green fees: Inexpensive
Telephone: (094) 71527

WESTPORT GOLF CLUB (parkland, par 73)
Location: About three miles northwest of Westport in Carrowholly
Green fees: Moderate
Telephone: (098) 28262   Fax: (098) 27217

County Meath

ASHBOURNE
Location: Not quite a mile south of Ashbourne village off the N2
Green fees: Moderate
Telephone: (01) 835-2005

COUNTY MEATH (TRIM) GOLF CLUB (parkland, par 73)
Location: Just outside Trim off the Longwood Road
Green fees: Inexpensive
Telephone: (046) 31463   Fax: (046) 37554

GLASSON GOLF & COUNTRY CLUB (parkland, par 72)
Location: About six miles northeast of Athlone in Glasson
Green fees: Expensive
Telephone: (0902) 85120   Fax: (0902) 85444
E-mail: glasgolf@iol.ie
NOTE: Course features twenty-one holes

GLEBE GOLF COURSE (parkland, par 73)
Location: About one mile from Trim in Dunlever
Green fees: Inexpensive
Telephone: (046) 31926

HEADFORT GOLF CLUB (parkland, par 73)
Location: Immediately outside Navan off the Kells Road
Green fees: Inexpensive
Telephone: (046) 40857

LAYTOWN & BETTYSTOWN GOLF CLUB (links, par 71)
Location: Immediately north of Bettystown off the Coast Road

Green fees: Moderate
Telephone: (041) 27170   Fax: (041) 28506

MOORPARK GOLF CLUB (parkland, par 72)
Location: About three and a half miles from Navan in Kentstown, off the
   main Ashbourne road
Green fees: Inexpensive
Telephone: (046) 27661   Fax: (046) 27181

ROYAL TARA GOLF CLUB (parkland, par 72)
Location: About six miles south of Navan off the N3 near the Hill of
   Tara
Green fees: Moderate
Telephone: (046) 25508 or 25244
NOTE: Few or no visitors Tuesdays (ladies' day) or on weekends

County Monaghan

NUREMORE GOLF & COUNTRY CLUB (parkland, par 72)
Location: About a mile south of Carrickmacross off the N2
Green fees: Moderate
Telephone: (042) 966-1438   Fax: (042) 966-1853
E-mail: nuremore@tinet.ie

ROSSMORE GOLF CLUB (parkland, par 70)
Location: About two miles out of Monaghan city off the Cootehill Road
Green fees: Inexpensive
Telephone: (047) 81316

County Offaly

BIRR GOLF CLUB (parkland, par 70)
Location: About two miles west of Birr off the Banagher Road
Green fees: Inexpensive
Telephone: (0509) 20082   Fax: (0509) 22155

CASTLE BARNA GOLF CLUB (parkland, par 72)
Location: About nine miles east of Tullamore in the town of Daingean off
   the N6 at the Tyrellspass exit
Green fees: Inexpensive
Telephone: (0506) 53384

NOTE: The golf course is occasionally still listed with its Gaelic spelling, *Caslebarnagh*

EDENDERRY GOLF CLUB (parkland, par 72)
Location: Immediately outside the town of Edenderry
Green fees: Inexpensive
Telephone: (0405) 31072

ESKER HILLS GOLF & COUNTRY CLUB (parkland, par 71)
Location: In the town of Tullamore
Green fees: Inexpensive
Telephone: (0506) 55999   Fax: (0506) 55021

PORTARLINGTON GOLF CLUB (parkland, par 72)
Location: Just outside Portarlington off the Mountmellick Road
Green fees: Inexpensive
Telephone: (0502) 23115   Fax: (0502) 23044
NOTE: Few or no visitors Tuesdays (ladies' day) or on weekends

TULLAMORE GOLF CLUB (parkland, par 71)
Location: About two and a half miles south of Tullamore off the Kinnity
    Road
Green fees: Moderate
Telephone: (0506) 21439
NOTE: Advance booking advised, especially on weekends

County Roscommon

ATHLONE GOLF CLUB (parkland, par 71)
Location: About three miles northwest of Athlone off the Roscommon
    road
Green fees: Inexpensive
Telephone: (0902) 92073   Fax: (0902) 94080

County Sligo

COUNTY SLIGO GOLF CLUB (links, par 71)
Location: About five miles northwest of Sligo town, toward Donegal off the
    N15, and left at the sign to Rosses Point
Green fees: Expensive
Telephone: (071) 77186 or 77134   Fax: (071) 77460
E-mail: cosligo@iol.ie

ENNISCRONE GOLF CLUB (links, par 72)
Location: About ten miles north of Ballina in the village of Enniscrone
Green fees: Expensive
Telephone: (096) 36297   Fax: (096) 36657
E-mail: enniscronegolf@linet.ie
NOTE: Very popular course with golfing societies; book in advance in summer

STRANDHILL GOLF CLUB (links, par 69)
Location: About five miles west of Sligo city off the Strandhill Road
Green fees: Inexpensive
Telephone: (071) 68188   Fax: (071) 68811

County Tipperary

BALLYKISTEEN GOLF CLUB (parkland, par 72)
Location: About two miles from the town of Tipperary on the N24
Green fees: Moderate
Telephone: (062) 33333   Fax: (062) 33711

CARRICK-ON-SUIR GOLF CLUB (parkland, par 73)
Location: About two miles from Carrick-on-Suir on the Dungarvan road
Green fees: Inexpensive
Telephone: (051) 640047   Fax: (051) 640558

CLONMEL GOLF CLUB (parkland, par 71)
Location: About three miles from Clonmel off the mountain road
Green fees: Inexpensive
Telephone: (052) 24050

COUNTY TIPPERARY GOLF & COUNTRY CLUB (parkland, par 72)
Location: About six miles northwest of Cashel off the N8 in Dundrum
Green fees: Moderate
Telephone: (062) 71717   Fax: (062) 71718
NOTE: Advance booking recommended for summer weekends

NENAGH GOLF CLUB (parkland, par 69)
Location: Northeast of Nenagh off the R491, the Old Birr Road
Green fees: Inexpensive
Telephone: (067) 31476

ROSCREA GOLF CLUB (parkland, par 71)
Location: Immediately outside the town of Roscrea off the N7

Green fees: Inexpensive
Telephone: (0505) 21130

THURLES GOLF CLUB (parkland, par 72)
Location: South of Thurles off the N62
Green fees: Inexpensive
Telephone: (0504) 21983   Fax: (0504) 24647

TIPPERARY GOLF CLUB (parkland, par 71)
Location: Not quite a mile from Tipperary town on the Glen of Aherlow road
Green fees: Inexpensive
Telephone: (062) 51119

County Waterford

DUNGARVAN GOLF CLUB (parkland, par 72)
Location: A little more than two miles east of Dungarvan, off the N25
Green fees: Moderate
Telephone: (058) 43310 or 41605   Fax: (058) 44113
E-mail: dungarvangolf@cablesurf.com

DUNMORE EAST GOLF CLUB (parkland, par 72)
Location: On the outskirts of Dunmore village
Green fees: Inexpensive
Telephone: (051) 383151

FAITHLEGG GOLF CLUB (parkland, par 72)
Location: About five and a half miles east of Waterford city off the
    Dunmore East Road
Green fees: Moderate
Telephone: (051) 382241   Fax: (051) 382664

GOLD COAST GOLF CLUB (parkland, par 72)
Location: About two miles from Dungarvan in Ballinacourty
Green fees: Inexpensive
Telephone: (058) 44055   Fax: (058) 43378
E-mail: cionea@indigo.ie

TRAMORE GOLF CLUB (parkland, par 72)
Location: Just outside the town of Tramore, south of Waterford city
Green fees: Moderate
Telephone: (051) 386170   Fax: (051) 390961
NOTE: Few or no visitors Sundays

WATERFORD CASTLE GOLF CLUB (parkland, par 72)
Location: About two miles from Waterford city on Waterford Castle's island
Green fees: Moderate
Telephone: (051) 871633   Fax: (051) 871634

WATERFORD GOLF CLUB (parkland, par 71)
Location: In Newrath, about a mile north of Waterford city
Green fees: Moderate
Telephone: (051) 876748   Fax: (051) 853405

WEST WATERFORD GOLF CLUB (parkland, par 72)
Location: About three miles west of Dungarvan off the N25 bypass
Green fees: Moderate
Telephone: (058) 43216   Fax: (058) 44343

County Westmeath

DELVIN CASTLE GOLF CLUB (parkland, par 70)
Location: Between Mullingar and Navan in Delvin on the grounds of Clonyn Castle
Green fees: Inexpensive
Telephone: (044) 64315   Fax: (044) 64671

MOUNT TEMPLE GOLF CLUB (parkland, par 72)
Location: In the village of Mount Temple, off the N6 between Athlone and Moate
Green fees: Inexpensive
Telephone: (0902) 81841 or 81545   Fax: (0902) 81957
E-mail: mttemple@iol.ie

MULLINGAR GOLF CLUB (parkland, par 72)
Location: About three miles south of Mullingar off the Kilbeggan Road
Green fees: Moderate
Telephone: (044) 48366   Fax: (044) 41499

County Wexford

COURTOWN GOLF CLUB (parkland, par 71)
Location: About four miles east of Gorey from the N11 and about a mile from Courtown
Green fees: Moderate
Telephone: (055) 25166   Fax: (055) 25553

ENNISCORTHY GOLF CLUB (parkland, par 72)
Location: Just southwest of Enniscorthy off the New Ross Road
Green fees: Inexpensive
Telephone: (054) 33191   Fax: (054) 37637

NEW ROSS GOLF CLUB (parkland, par 71)
Location: Just outside of New Ross town in the area known as Tinneranny
Green fees: Inexpensive
Telephone: (051) 421433

ROSSLARE GOLF CLUB (old course, links, par 72; new course, links, par 35)
Location: In the town of Rosslare, about six miles from the harbor and
    about ten miles south of Wexford town
Green fees: Moderate
Telephone: (053) 32203
NOTE: Advance booking is essential on summer weekends

ST. HELEN'S BAY GOLF & COUNTRY CLUB (parkland/links, par 72)
Location: About a mile from Rosslare Ferryport off the N25 in the village
    of Kilrane
Green fees: Moderate
Telephone: (053) 33234 or 33669   Fax: (053) 33803
NOTE: Advance booking is essential, especially on summer weekends

WEXFORD GOLF CLUB (parkland, par 70)
Location: Just outside Wexford town off the Mulgannon Road
Green fees: Inexpensive
Telephone: (053) 42238

County Wicklow

ARKLOW GOLF CLUB (links, par 68)
Location: Immediately outside the town of Arklow
Green fees: Inexpensive
Telephone: (0402) 32492
NOTE: Phone in advance on weekends

BLAINROE GOLF CLUB (parkland, par 72)
Location: About three miles south of Wicklow town on the coast road
Green fees: Moderate
Telephone: (0404) 68168   Fax: (0404) 69369
NOTE: Few or no visitors Sundays

CHARLESLAND GOLF AND COUNTRY CLUB (parkland, par 72)
Location: Just south of Greystones
Green fees: Moderate
Telephone: (01) 287-4350   Fax: (01) 287-4360
E-mail: charlesland@tinet.ie

COOLLATTIN (parkland, par 70)
Location: In the village of Shillelagh in the Wicklow Mountains, about
    halfway between Arklow and Tullow
Green fees: Moderate
Telephone: (055) 29125

DELGANY GOLF CLUB (parkland, par 69)
Location: In the village of Delgany
Green fees: Moderate
Telephone: (01) 287-4536   Fax: (01) 287-3977
NOTE: Few or no visitors on weekends

DRUIDS GLEN GOLF CLUB (parkland, par 72)
Location: Just outside Newtownmountkennedy, about halfway between
    Bray and Wicklow town just off the N11
Green fees: Very Expensive
Telephone: (01) 287-3600   Fax: (01) 287-3699
E-mail: druids@indigo.ie
NOTE: Book well in advance for summer and all year on weekends

THE EUROPEAN CLUB (links, par 71)
Location: Between Wicklow town and Arklow on the coast road at Brittas Bay
Green fees: Very Expensive
Telephone: (0404) 47415   Fax: (0404) 47449

GLENMALURE GOLF CLUB (parkland, par 71)
Location: Just outside Rathdrum
Green fees: Inexpensive
Telephone: (0404) 46679   Fax: (0404) 46783
E-mail: golf@glenmalure-golf.ie

GLEN OF THE DOWNS GOLF CLUB (parkland, par 71)
Location: About four miles south of Bray off the N11 opposite the
    Glenview Hotel
Green fees: Expensive
Telephone: (01) 287-6240   Fax: (01) 287-0063

GREYSTONES GOLF CLUB (parkland, par 69)
Location: Just outside the town of Greystones
Green fees: Moderate
Telephone: (01) 287-4136   Fax: (01) 287-3749
NOTE: Few or no visitors on weekends

KILTERNAN GOLF & COUNTRY CLUB (parkland, par 68)
Location: Just off the Dublin-Enniskerry Road in the village of Kilternan
Green fees: Inexpensive
Telephone: (01) 295-5559

OLD CONNA GOLF CLUB (parkland, par 72)
Location: About two miles from Bray off Ferdale Road
Green fees: Expensive
Telephone: (01) 282-6055   Fax: (01) 282-5611

POWERSCOURT GOLF CLUB (parkland, par 72)
Location: Off the N11 in the village of Enniskerry
Green fees: Very Expensive
Telephone: (01) 204-6033   Fax: (01) 276-1303

RATHSALLAGH GOLF CLUB (parkland, par 72)
Location: Between Naas and Carlow in the village of Dunlavin
Green fees: Expensive
Telephone: (045) 403316   Fax: (045) 403295
NOTE: Few or no visitors on weekends

ROUNDWOOD GOLF CLUB (parkland, par 72)
Location: Off the N11 in the village of Newtownmountkennedy
Green fees: Moderate
Telephone: (01) 281-8488   Fax: (01) 284-3642
E-mail: rwood@indigo.ie

TULFARRIS GOLF CLUB (parkland, par 72)
Location: Off the N18 in Blessington Lakes, on the Wicklow/Kildare county
    line
Green fees: Expensive
Telephone: (045) 867555   Fax: (045) 867561

WICKLOW GOLF CLUB (parkland/links, par 71)
Location: About a quarter-mile south of Wicklow town

Green fees: Inexpensive
Telephone: (0404) 67379   Fax: (0404) 66122
NOTE: Few or no visitors Sundays because of member competitions

WOODBROOK GOLF CLUB (parkland, par 72)
Location: About a mile from Bray on the coast road
Green fees: Very Expensive
Telephone: (01) 282-4799   Fax: (01) 282-1950
NOTE: Visitors must book in advance on weekends

WOODENBRIDGE GOLF CLUB (parkland, par 71)
Location: About four miles northwest of Arklow, follow signs to
    Woodenbridge and the Vale of Avoca
Green fees: Expensive
Telephone: (0402) 35202

Northern Ireland

Some golf clubs provided only their Standard Scratch Score (sss), as opposed to par, and are so noted.

County Antrim

ALLEN PARK GOLF CLUB (parkland, par 72)
Location: On the outskirts of Antrim town at 45 Castle Rd.
Green fees: Inexpensive
Telephone: (0801) 849-429001
NOTE: Few or no visitors Saturdays

BALLYCASTLE GOLF CLUB (links, par 71)
Location: About a half-mile southeast of Ballycastle off Cushendall Road
Green fees: Inexpensive
Telephone: (0801) 2657-62563
NOTE: Few or no visitors on weekends

BALLYCLARE GOLF CLUB (parkland, par 71)
Location: About two miles north of Ballyclare off Springvale Road
Green fees: Moderate
Telephone: (0801) 960-322696

BALLYMENA GOLF CLUB (heathland, par 68)
Location: About two miles east of Ballymena off the A42

Green fees: Inexpensive
Telephone: (0801) 266-86148
NOTE: Few or no visitors Saturdays

CAIRNDHU GOLF CLUB (parkland, par 70)
Location: About four miles north of Larne off the Coast Road
Green fees: Moderate
Telephone: (0801) 574-583324   Fax: (0801) 574-583324
NOTE: Few or no visitors Saturdays

CARRICKFERGUS GOLF CLUB (parkland, par 68)
Location: North of Carrickfergus off the Albert Road
Green fees: Inexpensive
Telephone: (0801) 960-363713
NOTE: Few or no visitors on weekends; no women Saturdays

GALGORM CASTLE (parkland, par 72)
Location: About one mile southwest of Ballymena in the village of Galgorm
Green fees: Moderate
Telephone: (0801) 266-46161
NOTE: Also has a nine-hole executive course

LISBURN GOLF CLUB (parkland, par 72)
Location: South of Lisburn off Eglantine Road
Green fees: Moderate
Telephone: (0801) 846-677216   Fax: (0801) 846-603608
NOTE: Few or no visitors Sundays unless with a member

MASSEREENE GOLF CLUB (parkland, sss 72)
Location: Between Antrim town and Belfast International Airport off the
   Lough Road
Green fees: Moderate
Telephone: (0801) 849-428096

ROYAL PORTRUSH GOLF CLUB (Dunluce Links, links, par 72; Valley
   Course, links, par 70)
Location: Immediately west of Portrush on the road to Bushmills and the
   Giant's Causeway
Green fees: Very Expensive
Telephone: (0801) 265-822311   Fax: (0801) 265-823139
NOTE: Book well in advance, especially for summer weekends

WHITEHEAD GOLF CLUB (parkland, sss 71)
Location: Immediately north of Whitehead village
Green fees: Inexpensive
Telephone: (0801) 960-353631
NOTE: No visitors Saturdays; Sundays with member only

County Armagh

ASHFIELD GOLF CLUB (parkland, par 69)
Location: About four miles north of the village of Crossmaglen off the B30
Green fees: Inexpensive
Telephone: (0801) 693-868180   Fax: (0801) 693-868611

COUNTY ARMAGH GOLF CLUB (parkland, sss 69)
Location: Off Newry Road in Armagh town
Green fees: Moderate
Telephone: (0801) 861-525861

CRAIGAVON GOLF CENTRE (eighteen-hole parkland, sss 72; nine-hole
  parkland, par 27)
Location: About two miles north of Lurgan off Turmoya Lane
Green fees: Inexpensive
Telephone: (0801) 762-326606   Fax: (0801) 762-347272

FORTWILLIAM GOLF CLUB (parkland, sss 69)
Location: About three miles north of Belfast city center off the A8 on
  Downview Avenue
Green fees: Moderate
Telephone: (0801) 232-370770   Fax: (0801) 232-770980

LURGAN GOLF CLUB (parkland, sss 70)
Location: The Demesne in Lurgan town
Green fees: Moderate
Telephone: (0801) 762-322087

PORTADOWN GOLF CLUB (parkland, sss 70)
Location: Off Gilford Road about three miles southeast of Portadown
Green fees: Moderate
Telephone: (0801)-762 355356

SILVERWOOD GOLF HOTEL & COUNTRY CLUB (parkland, par 72)
Location: 40 Kiln Rd., Lurgan

Green fees: Moderate
Telephone: (0801) 762-327722   Fax: (0801) 762-325290
NOTE: Golf packages available for hotel guests

TANDRAGEE GOLF CLUB (parkand, sss 69)
Location: Off Markethill Road in Tandragee
Green fees: Inexpensive
Telephone: (0801) 762-841272
NOTE: No visitors Saturdays

County Derry

CASTLEROCK GOLF CLUB (Mussenden Course, links, par 73; Bann
    Course, links, par 35)
Location: In the village of Castlerock about six miles north of Coleraine
Green fees: Moderate
Telephone: (0801) 265-848314

CITY OF DERRY GOLF CLUB (Prehen Course, parkland, sss 71; Dunhugh
    Course, parkland, par 33)
Location: South of Derry in Prehen, off Victoria Road
Green fees: Moderate
Telephone: (0801) 504-46369

FOYLE GOLF COURSE (parkland, par 72)
Location: North of Derry city center off Adler Road
Green fees: Inexpensive
Telephone: (0801) 504-352222   Fax: (0801) 504-353967
NOTE: Also has a short par-3 course

MOYOLA PARK GOLF COURSE (parkland, sss 71)
Location: In Castledawson village
Green fees: Moderate
Telephone: (0801) 648-468468

PORTSTEWART GOLF CLUB (Strand Course, links, par 72; Town Course,
    links, par 64; Riverside Course, links, par 32)
Location: Off the Strand Road on the western edge of Portstewart
Green fees: Expensive
Telephone: (0801) 265-832015   Fax: (0801) 265-834097
NOTE: Book well in advance, especially in summer

ROE PARK GOLF CLUB (parkland, par 70)
Location: Just outside Limavady in Roe Park
Green fees: Moderate
Telephone: (0801) 5047-60105
NOTE: Sometimes listed as Radisson Roe Park Golf Resort

County Down

ARDGLASS GOLF CLUB (links, par 70)
Location: In the village of Ardglass, about ten miles east-northeast of Newcastle
Green fees: Moderate
Telephone: (0801) 396-841219   Fax: (0801) 396-841841
E-mail: ardglassgolfclub@hotmail.com
NOTE: Few or no visitors on weekends

BALMORAL GOLF CLUB (parkland, sss 70)
Location: Off Lisburn Road about three miles southwest of Belfast city center
Green fees: Expensive
Telephone: (0801) 232-381514
NOTE: Few or no visitors on weekends

BANBRIDGE GOLF CLUB (parkland, sss 67)
Location: About a mile from Banbridge off Huntly Road
Green fees: Moderate
Telephone: (0801) 8206-62211
NOTE: No women Saturdays

BANGOR GOLF CLUB (parkland, par 71)
Location: In Bangor town
Green fees: Moderate
Telephone: (0801) 247-270922
NOTE: No visitors Saturdays

BELVOIR PARK GOLF CLUB (parkland, sss 70)
Location: At 73 Church Rd., about three miles south of Belfast city center
Green fees: Expensive
Telephone: (0801) 232-491693   Fax: (0801) 232-646113
NOTE: It's pronounced "Beaver"; no visitors Saturdays

BRIGHT CASTLE GOLF CLUB (parkland, sss 74)
Location: About four miles south of Downpatrick

Green fees: Inexpensive
Telephone: (0801) 396-841319

CARNALEA GOLF CLUB (parkland, sss 67)
Location: Not quite two miles west of Bangor off Station Street
Green fees: Inexpensive
Telephone: (0801) 247-270368   Fax: (0801) 247-273989

CLANDEBOYE GOLF CLUB (Dufferin Course, heathland, sss 72; Ava
    Course, heathland, sss 67)
Location: About one mile south of Bangor at 51 Tower Rd.
Green fees: Expensive
Telephone: (0801) 247-271767   Fax: (0801) 247-473711
NOTE: Visitors weekends with member only

DONAGHADEE GOLF CLUB (links, sss 69)
Location: Immediately north of Donaghadee
Green fees: Moderate
Telephone: (0801) 247-883624

DOWNPATRICK GOLF CLUB (parkland, sss 68)
Location: At 43 Saul Rd., about a mile northeast of Downpatrick
Green fees: Inexpensive
Telephone: (0801) 396-615947   Fax: (0801) 396-617502

DOWN ROYAL PARK GOLF CLUB (parkland, par 72)
Location: Southwest of Lisburn on the grounds of the Down Royal
    Racecourse in Maze
Green fees: Moderate
Telephone: (0801) 846-621339

DUNMURRY GOLF CLUB (parkland, sss 68)
Location: About four miles southwest of Belfast city center off Dunmurry
    Lane
Green fees: Moderate
Telephone: (0801) 232-610834

HOLYWOOD GOLF CLUB (parkland, par 68)
Location: South of Holywood off Nun's Walk
Green fees: Moderate
Telephone: (0801) 232-423135   Fax: (0801) 232-425040

KILKEEL GOLF CLUB (parkland, par 72)
Location: Southeast of Newry in Ballyardle's Mourne Park, about three
    miles west Kilkeel
Green fees: Inexpensive
Telephone: (0801) 6937-65095

KIRKSTOWN CASTLE GOLF CLUB (links, par 69)
Location: About fifteen miles south of Newtownards at 142 Main Rd. in Cloughey
Green fees: Moderate
Telephone: (0801) 247-771233   Fax: (0801) 247-771699
NOTE: Few or no visitors Sundays

KNOCK GOLF CLUB (parkland, sss 71)
Location: About four miles east of Belfast city center in Dundonald
Green fees: Moderate
Telephone: (0801) 232-483251

MALONE GOLF CLUB (Main Course, parkland, par 71; Edenderry
    Course, parkland, par 36)
Location: About five miles south of Belfast city center at 240 Upper
    Malone Rd. in Dunmurry
Green fees: Expensive
Telephone: (0801) 232-612758   Fax: (0801) 232-431394
NOTE: Few or no visitors Saturdays; book well in advance

MOUNT OBER GOLF & COUNTRY CLUB (parkland, sss 68)
Location: About four miles southeast of Belfast city center, off
    Ballymaconaghy Road in Knockbracken
Green fees: Moderate
Telephone: (0801) 232-795666
NOTE: Used to be called Knockbracken Golf Club

NEWRY GOLF CLUB (parkland, par 54)
Location: Immediately south of Newry
Green fees: Inexpensive
Telephone: (0801) 693-63871
NOTE: This is an executive-length golf course

ROYAL BELFAST GOLF CLUB (parkland, par 70)
Location: About eight miles northeast of Belfast off the Bangor Road in
    Holywood

Green fees: Very Expensive
Telephone: (0801) 232-428165   Fax: (0801) 232-421404
NOTE: Visitors require a letter of introduction

ROYAL COUNTY DOWN GOLF CLUB (Championship Course, links, par
    71; Mourne Course, links, par 65)
Location: In the Irish Sea resort town of Newcastle
Green fees: Very Expensive
Telephone: (0801) 3967 23314   Fax: (0801) 3967 26281
NOTE: Advance booking is essential for summer and all year on weekends

SCRABO GOLF CLUB (parkland, sss 71)
Location: About three miles southwest of Newtownards off Scrabo Road,
    follow signs to Scrabo Monument
Green fees: Moderate
Telephone: (0801) 247-812355   Fax: (0801) 247-822919

SHANDON PARK GOLF CLUB (parkland, par 70)
Location: About four miles east of Belfast city center at Shandon Park
Green fees: Moderate
Telephone: (0801) 232-401856   Fax: (0801) 232-402773
NOTE: No visitors Saturdays

SPA GOLF CLUB (parkland, sss 72)
Location: Immediately south of the village of Ballynahinch
Green fees: Moderate
Telephone: (0801) 238-562365

WARRENPOINT GOLF CLUB (parkland, sss 70)
Location: Just west of Warrenpoint, southeast of Newry
Green fees: Moderate
Telephone: (0801) 6937-53695   Fax: (0801) 6937-52918
NOTE: Book in advance, especially for summer weekends

County Fermanagh

CASTLE HUME GOLF CLUB (parkland, par 72)
Location: About four miles north of Enniskillen off the A46
Green fees: Moderate
Telephone: (0801) 365-327077   Fax: (0801) 365-327076
NOTE: Few or no visitors Wednesdays (ladies' day)

ENNISKILLEN GOLF CLUB (parkland, sss 69)
Location: Immediately east of Enniskillen in Castle Coole
Green fees: Inexpensive
Telephone: (0801) 365-325250

County Tyrone

DUNGANNON GOLF CLUB (parkland, sss 68)
Location: Immediately west of Dungannon off Springfield Lane
Green fees: Inexpensive
Telephone: (0801) 8687-27338

KILLYMOON GOLF CLUB (parkland, sss 69)
Location: South of Cookstown off Killymoon Road
Green fees: Moderate
Telephone: (0801) 6487-63762

NEWTOWNSTEWART GOLF CLUB (parkland, par 70)
Location: About a mile and a half southwest of Newtownstewart off the
    Drumquin road
Green fees: Moderate
Telephone: (0801) 6626-61466   Fax: (0801) 6626-62506

OMAGH GOLF CLUB (White Course, parkland, par 71; Green Course,
    parkland, par 72)
Location: Immediately south of Omagh off the Dublin Road
Green fees: Moderate
Telephone: (0801) 662-241442

STRABANE GOLF CLUB (parkland, sss 69)
Location: Off the Ballycolman Road south of Strabane
Green fees: Inexpensive
Telephone: (0801) 504-382007

Ireland's Nine-Hole Golf Courses

The Irish Republic

County Carlow

Borris Golf Club . . . .(0503) 73143

County Cavan

Belturbet Golf Club . . . .(049) 22287
Blacklion Golf Club . . . .(072) 53024
Cabra Castle Golf Club, Kingscourt .(046) 52372
Virginia Golf Club . . . .(042) 48066

County Clare

Clonlara . . . .(061) 354141
Spanish Point Golf Club . . . .(065) 84198

County Cork

Bantry Park Golf Club . . . .(027) 50579
Berehaven Golf Club . . . .(027) 70700
Castletownbere Golf Club . . . .(027) 70299
Coosheen . . . .(028) 28182
Cobh Golf Club . . . .(021) 812399

Doneraile Golf Club . . . .(022) 24137
Dunmore Golf Club, Clonakilty . . . .(023) 33352
Fitzpatrick Silver Springs . . . .(021) 507533
Frankfield Golf Club, Douglas . . . . .(021) 363124
Glengarriff Golf Club . . . .(027) 63150
Mitchelstown Golf Club . . . .(025) 24072
Raffeen Creek Golf Club,
     Ringaskiddy . . . .(021) 378430

County Donegal

Buncrana Municipal Golf Club . . . . .(077) 62279
Cruit Island Golf Club . . . .(075) 43296
Greencastle Golf Club . . . .(077) 81013
Gweedore Golf Club . . . .(075) 31666
Otway Golf Club . . . .(074) 58319
Redcastle Golf Club . . . .(077) 82073

County Dublin

Ballinascorney Golf Club . . . .(01) 451-2516
Carrickmines Golf Club . . . .(01) 295-5972
Dublin Mountain . . . .(01) 458-2622
Finnstown Golf Club . . . .(01) 628-0644
Foxrock Golf Club . . . .(01) 289-3992
Glencullen . . . .(01) 294-0898
Hazelgrove Golf Club . . . .(01) 452-0911
Killiney Golf Club . . . .(01) 285-2823
Rathfarnham Golf Club . . . .(01) 493-1201
Rush Golf Club . . . .(01) 843-7548
Stepaside Public Golf Course . . . . . .(01) 295-2859
Sutton Golf Club . . . .(01) 832-2965
Tyrellstown Golf Club . . . .(01) 821-3206
Westmanstown Golf Club . . . .(01) 820-5817
Woodbrook . . . .(01) 282-4799

County Galway

Ashford Castle . . . .(092) 46003
Connemara Isles Golf Club . . . .(091) 572498

Curra . . . .(0509) 45438
Dunmore Demesne Golf Club . . . . .(093) 38088
Glenlo Abbey . . . .(091) 26666
Loughrea Golf Club . . . .(091) 841049
Mountbellew Golf Club . . . .(0905) 79259

County Kerry

Ardfert Golf Club . . . .(066) 7134744
Ballybeggan . . . .(066) 7126188
Ballyheigue Castle . . . .(066) 7133195
Castlegregory Golf & Fishing Club . .(066) 7139444
Dunloe Golf Course . . . .(064) 44578
Kerries, The . . . .(066) 7122112
Listowel Golf Club . . . .(068) 21592
Ross Golf Club . . . .(064) 31125

County Kildare

Athy Golf Club . . . .(0507) 31729
Cill Dara Golf Club . . . .(045) 521433
Clane (Clongowes) Golf Club . . . . . .(045) 68202
Kilcock Golf Club . . . .(01) 628-7592
Lexlip . . . .(01) 624-4978
Woodlands . . . .(045) 860777

County Kilkenny

Castlecomer Golf Club . . . .(056) 41139

County Laois

Abbeyliex Golf Club . . . .(0502) 31450
Mountrath Golf Club . . . .(0502) 32558
Rathdowney Golf Club . . . .(0502) 46170

County Leitrim

Ballinamore Golf Club . . . .(078) 44346
Carrick-on-Shannon Golf Club . . . . .(078) 67015

County Limerick

Abbeyfeale . . . .(068) 32033

County Louth

Ballymascanlon Golf Club . . . .(042) 71124
Gormanston Golf Club . . . .(01) 841-2203

County Mayo

Achill Golf Club . . . .(098) 45172
Achill Island . . . .(098) 43456
Ashford Castle . . . .(092) 46003
Ballina Golf Club . . . .(096) 21050
Ballyhaunis Golf Club . . . .(0907) 30014
Belmullet . . . .(097) 82292
Mulrany Golf Club . . . .(098) 36262
Swinford Golf Club . . . .(094) 51378

County Meath

Black Bush . . . .(01) 825-0021
Gormanstown . . . .(01) 841-2203
Killock Golf Club . . . .(01) 628-4074
Trim Golf Club . . . .(046) 31463

County Monaghan

Castleblayney Golf Club . . . .(042) 40197
Clones Golf Club . . . .(047) 56017
Mannan Castle . . . .(042) 63308

County Roscommon

Ballaghaderreen Golf Club . . . .(0907) 60295
Boyle Golf Club . . . .(079) 62594
Castlerea Golf Club . . . .(0907) 20068
Roscommon Golf Club . . . .(0903) 26382
Strokestown . . . .(078) 33303

County Sligo

Ballymote Golf Club . . . .(071) 89059
Tubbercurry Golf Club . . . .(071) 85849

County Tipperary

Cahir Park Golf Club . . . .(052) 41474
Rockwell Golf Club . . . .(062) 61444
Templemore Golf Club . . . .(0504) 31400

County Waterford

Lismore Golf Club . . . .(058) 54026

County Westmeath

Moate Golf Club . . . .(0902) 81271

County Wexford

Ballymoney Golf Club . . . .(055) 21976
Tara Glen Golf & Country Club . . . .(055) 25413

County Wicklow

Ballinacarrig . . . .(0404) 47195
Baltinglass Golf Club . . . .(0508) 81350
Bray Golf Club . . . .(01) 286-2484
Djouce Golf Club . . . .(01) 281-8585
Glen O' The Downs . . . .(01) 286-4585
Glenmalure Golf Club . . . .(0404) 46679
Kilcoole (Glenroe) Golf Club . . . . . .(01) 287-2066
Vartry Lakes Golf Club . . . .(01) 281-7006

Northern Ireland

County Antrim

Aberdelghy Golf Course . . . .(0801) 846-662738
Ballyearl Golf & Leisure Center . . . .(0801) 232-848287

Bentra Golf Club . . . .(0801) 960-378996
Bushfoot Golf Club . . . .(0801) 2657-31317
City of Belfast Golf Course, Mallusk .(0801) 232-843799
Cushendall Golf Club . . . .(0801) 2667-71318
Greenisland Golf Club . . . .(0801) 232-862236
Larne Golf Club . . . .(0801) 960-382228

County Armagh

Edenmore Golf Course . . . .(0801) 846 611310
Silverwood . . . .(0801) 762 326606

County Derry

Ballyreagh Golf Course . . . .(0801) 265 822028
Benone Golf Course . . . .(0801) 5047 50555
Brown Trout Golf & Country Inn . . .(0801) 265 868209
Kilrea Golf Club . . . .(0801) 2665 40119
Manor Golf and Fishing Club . . . . . .(0801) 2665 40661

County Down

Blackwood Golf Course . . . .(0801) 247-852706
Cliftonville Golf Club . . . .(0801) 232-746595
Crossgar Golf Club . . . .(0801) 396-831319
Gilnahirk Golf Club . . . .(0801) 232-448477
Helen's Bay Golf Club . . . .(0801) 247-852815
Mahee Island Golf Club . . . .(0801) 238-541234
Mourne . . . .(0801) 3967-23889
Ormeau Golf Club . . . .(0801) 232-640700
Ringdufferin Golf Course . . . .(0801) 396-828812
Temple Golf Club . . . .(0801) 846-639213

County Fermanagh

Ashwoods Golf Center . . . .(0801) 365-325321

County Tyrone

Fintona Golf Club . . . .(0801) 662-841480

Index